THE SECRET HISTORY OF FOOD

THE SECRET HISTORY OF FOOD

Strange but True Stories
About the Origins of
Everything We Eat

MATT SIEGEL

ecco

An Imprint of HarperCollins*Publishers*

HarperCollins books may be purchased for educational, business, or sales promotional use. For information, please email the Special Markets Department at SPsales@harpercollins.com.

Ecco® and HarperCollins® are trademarks of HarperCollins Publishers.

A hardcover edition of this book was published in 2021 by Ecco, an imprint of HarperCollins Publishers.

FIRST ECCO PAPERBACK EDITION PUBLISHED 2022

Designed by Paula Russell Szafranski
Frontispiece © Shutterstock.com

Library of Congress Cataloging-in-Publication Data has been applied for.

ISBN 978-0-06-297320-7 (pbk.)

22 23 24 25 26 LSC 10 9 8 7 6 5 4 3 2 1

For my mother, and her cooking.

And my father, and his eating.

History celebrates the battlefields whereon we meet our death, but scorns to speak of the plowed fields whereby we thrive. It knows the names of the kings' bastards but cannot tell us the origin of wheat. This is the way of human folly.

—JEAN-HENRI FABRE

Of the many choices we make in our lives, what to eat is perhaps the most enduring and important. Whereas individual human beings can go through life without participating in political acts and without personal liberty and can survive without forming a family or having sex, none of us can go without food. It is the absolute biological necessity of food that makes it so central to cultural history and so inclusive of all peoples in all times.

—B. W. HIGMAN

CONTENTS

THE SECRET HISTORY OF FOOD

CHAPTER 1

A HISTORY OF SWALLOWING

. . . the pursuit of more and better food has helped to direct—sometimes decisively, more often subtly—the movement of history itself.

—REAY TANNAHILL

T ell me what you eat, and I shall tell you what you are."
    These are the words written by Jean Anthelme Brillat-
    Savarin, one of history's most enduring and influential
food writers—a guy who not only had a cheese named after
him (a triple-cream, semisoft cow's milk cheese with a "luxurious mouthfeel reminiscent of tangy, sour, and mushroomy softened butter") but whose book *Physiologie du goût* ("Physiology of
Taste") is still in print nearly two centuries after its 1825 debut.
    Granted, not all of Brillat's meditations have aged as well as
his cheese. For example, his belief that eating starches softens
a man's flesh and courage ("For proof one can cite the Indians,
who live almost exclusively on rice and who are the prey of almost anyone who wishes to conquer them."), his endorsement
of sugar water as a healthy and refreshing tonic, or his frequent
rants on obesity:

> Suggest to a charming fat lady that she mount a horse,
> and she will consent with great pleasure, but on three
> conditions: first, she must have a steed which is at one
> and the same time handsome, lively, and gentle; second,
> she must have a riding habit which is new and tailored

in the latest style; third, she must have to accompany her a groom who is agreeable and good-looking. It is rather rare to fill all three of these requirements, so she does not ride at all.

Or "I can remember only two really fat heroes."*

Others are open to debate, such as his opinion on serving a cheese course—and, simultaneously, on the material worth of disfigured cyclopean women: "A dinner which ends without cheese is like a beautiful woman with only one eye."

Yet he was clearly ahead of his time on other points, being one of the first to extol the benefits of a low-carbohydrate diet; to draw a connection between the consumption of refined carbohydrates and obesity; and to urge parents "to forbid coffee to their children with great severity, if they do not wish to produce dried-up little monsters, stunted and old before they are twenty," all notions that have since become common knowledge.

And he was also right in his premonition that what we eat defines us not just physically but psychologically, socially, symbolically, and spiritually—to a much greater degree, in fact, than he could have known in the 1800s.

Modern science, for example, has taught us that it's not only what *we* eat that defines us but what our *parents* ate.

Numerous studies suggest that our adult preferences for salt are predicted by our mothers' fluid loss during pregnancy—that heightened morning sickness and maternal vomiting (and thus

---

* Note that Brillat-Savarin wasn't exactly svelte himself; however, he reconciled his own weight struggles—according to *him*—by having nice legs: "although I carry around with me a fairly prominent stomach, I still have well-formed lower legs, and calves as sinewy as the muscles of an Arabian steed."

lowered electrolyte levels) trigger an increased yearning for salt in utero that can last into adulthood, prompting a lifetime of overcompensated salt consumption. Similarly, exposure to flavors in our mother's amniotic fluid and breast milk, which take on flavors from her diet, can result in acquired food preferences pre- and postnatally long before we take our first bite of food, given that the average fetus swallows somewhere between 500 milliliters and a full liter of amniotic fluid daily (the equivalent of about one and a half to three twelve-ounce soda cans). Researchers have detected flavors in amniotic fluid ranging from garlic to cumin and curry; meanwhile, breast milk has been shown to absorb an even broader range of flavors ranging from carrot, vanilla, and mint to alcohol, blue cheese, and cigarettes.*

In one study, infants whose mothers consumed carrot juice during pregnancy and lactation showed a greater preference for carrot-flavored cereal; in another, eight- and nine-year-olds whose pregnant mothers had consumed garlic had a greater preference for garlic-seasoned potatoes; and in another, adults who'd been fed vanilla-flavored formula as infants had a greater preference for vanilla-flavored ketchup. Children who were breastfed also tend to eat more fruits and vegetables and be more adventurous eaters than those who were given formula, owing to their exposure to a greater variety of flavors early on.

Of course, the notion that breast milk can influence human behavior is nothing new. For thousands of years, long before Brillat-Savarin, it was considered common knowledge that things like personality traits and intellect were passed on through

---

* Note that amniotic fluid is a lot more challenging to collect, for obvious reasons, so its diversity is, perhaps, underreported, meaning that it could taste like cigarettes, too.

breastfeeding, so mothers who were either unable to produce their own milk or too wealthy to bother would carefully screen their wet nurses for things like breast shape, emotional stability, and manners. An ancient Sanskrit text, for example, instructed that a wet nurse should belong to one's own caste; have healthy skin unmarked by any moles or stains; be free from such vices as gambling, day sleeping, and debauchery; be neither too old, too young, too thin, or too corpulent; and have breasts that are neither too pendulant* nor drawn up and nipples that are neither upturned nor unprominent. And as recently as 1544, the English *Boke of Chyldren* cautioned mothers, "ye must be well advysed in takyng of a nource not of yll complexion and of worse maners, but suche as shall be sobre, honest and chaste, well fourmed, amyable and chearefull . . . no dronkarde, vycyous nor sluttysshe, for suche corrupteth the nature of the chylde." Imagine those wanted ads.

Meanwhile, it was thought that drinking animal milk made you act like an animal.

And it's not just *what* our parents ate that defines us but *how much* they ate. A parent's diet and caloric intake can affect whether the genes handed down to us are switched on or off, a process called epigenetic inheritance that can impact everything from metabolism and body weight to disease resistance. For example, fruit flies that were fed a high-sugar diet for just two days before mating parented offspring with an increased likelihood of developing obesity, while mice that were fed a high-fat diet for six weeks before breeding parented offspring with an increased

---

* The concern regarding too pendulant breasts wasn't so much that they would produce bad milk but that "extremely pendulous (large and flabby) breasts may suffocate the child by covering its mouth and nostrils." (The parenthetical here comes from the source.)

likelihood of diabetes and a more than 20 percent increase in weight and body fat.

And these patterns seem to hold true for humans, too. A review of more than thirty studies from the Netherlands, the United States, France, India, Norway, Sweden, the United Kingdom, Germany, New Zealand, and Australia concluded that fetal exposure to poor nutrition in the womb increased the risk of obesity, heart disease, and type 2 diabetes through adulthood; while another study found that the foods parents and grandparents had eaten between the ages of eight and twelve impacted their children and grandchildren's risk of heart disease and diabetes.

Other inherited influences go back even further; you might take pride in your sophisticated palate for black truffles, sour ale, charred brussels sprouts, and single-origin coffee—but your preference for them is, to some degree, genetic. Similar to color blindness, roughly half of the population doesn't have the olfactory capacity to sense androstenone, the chemical responsible for a truffle's coveted earthiness, while a smaller portion of the population is overly sensitive and finds it revolting. People with a gene called OR6A2, which correlates to aldehyde receptors, tend to think cilantro (also known as coriander) tastes like soap or smells like "bug-infested bedclothes." In fact, there's evidence that the name *coriander* comes from the Greek *koris* ("bedbug"), and aldehydes similar or identical to those found in cilantro are found in soap and certain bug excretions, including those of bedbugs.

Similarly, our sensitivity to bitter foods is largely associated with a gene called TAS2R38, and you can measure yours at home by picking up some paper test strips saturated with a chemical called 6-n-propylthiouracil (PROP), which are widely available online. About half the population finds these strips moderately bitter ("tasters"), while a quarter finds them *unpalatably* bitter ("supertasters"), and another quarter describes them as having no taste at all ("nontasters"). Supertasters also tend to have a higher density of taste buds, and although this might sound like a coveted foodie superpower, supertasters are likely to be pickier eaters and avoid things like coffee, wine, spirits, dark chocolate, and various fruits and vegetables (e.g., grapefruit, broccoli, kale) because they find them too bitter.

In fact, it's plausible that *all* of our ancestors were effectively "supertasters" at one point, as it's no coincidence that a lot of things that are toxic in nature tend to be bitter or acidic, so the more our ancestors avoided them, the more likely they would have been to avoid death and sickness. Yet over time, those who consumed them out of desperation, palate fatigue, or bravado (and managed either to avoid those that were particularly deadly or reduce their toxicity through cooking or processing) would have passed on their tolerance genetically. Meanwhile, a lot of plants would have become less bitter and toxic over time as we developed agriculture and began selectively breeding crops for desirable traits. The wild ancestors of pumpkins, potatoes, and almonds, for example, were all bitter and toxic before human intervention, while ears of ancient corn were roughly the size of cigarettes with miniature kernels hard enough to break teeth.

This is basically the same story behind milk. Initially, humans were able to digest milk only as infants. Biologically, there are a lot of good reasons for this: particularly for mothers who are malnourished, breastfeeding can make it harder to get pregnant again, so a mother who stops breastfeeding earlier has more chances to add to the gene pool. Plus, you want the previous child to be finished nursing by the time the next child is born, as otherwise they'd have to compete for limited resources, and producing enough milk for one kid is already difficult.

So continuing to breastfeed beyond infancy wasn't good for the tribe. Like other mammals, people would naturally stop producing lactase, the enzyme needed to digest lactose, as they aged—and those who continued to drink milk, whether human or animal, would suffer gastrointestinal issues such as gas and bloating. But being gassy and bloated still beat starvation, so after thousands of years of evolution, our bodies developed an adaptive resilience to milk products, making us more tolerant of lactose in adulthood. (The discovery of yogurt and cheese making also helped, as both tend to reduce milk's lactose content, making them easier to digest; yet even so, roughly two-thirds of the adult population has trouble digesting milk products to varying degrees, so lactose intolerance is still the norm rather than the exception.)

Our genetic tolerance for alcohol consumption (e.g., level of inebriation, dizziness, facial flushing, and absorption rate) is a similar adaptation, likely arising from our ancestors' consumption of fermented fruit millions of years ago; in the same way, koalas developed a tolerance for eucalyptus leaves, which are highly toxic to other mammals and most other animals.

Yet far and away the biggest link between what we eat and who we are arose from the discovery of cooking—and we can trace a lot of the things we see in grocery stores (and modern society) back to our decision to start putting raw meats and vegetables into controlled fires (or waters heated by geothermal springs) somewhere between 2 million and 200,000 years ago, a pivotal milestone that transformed us just as much as it transformed our diet.

Cooking made it possible to eat a lot of foods that would otherwise have been toxic, inedible, or indigestible. Even modern staples such as wheat, corn, and potatoes aren't very palatable (or digestible) without exposure to heat or fire, let alone scavenged prehistoric roots and plant stems. Cooking potatoes, for example, not only makes them infinitely more pleasant going down but makes their starch content more than 90 percent more digestible, while properly cooking lima beans or cassava not only increases digestibility but also kills an enzyme that could otherwise cause potentially fatal cyanide poisoning. Meanwhile, cooking also increases the shelf life of foods, both in the short term by killing germs and bacteria and in the long term by removing moisture through smoking or drying, particularly in the case of meats. This, in turn, made foods more transportable, which also increased the odds of survival, as hanging around freshly killed animals tended to make one prey for other animals.

To be fair, cooking can also lessen the nutritional quality of food, depending on the food and the cooking method. As one look at your bright green cooking liquid after overly blanching your greens suggests, water-soluble nutrients tend to leach out during the cooking process; however, the result is still usually a net gain in terms of nutrients and calories. Basically, you lose some nutrients to cooking, but those that remain will be easier for the body to extract and utilize.

Much of this has to do with the fact that cooking makes foods softer (and thus easier to digest and chew) by denaturing proteins, rupturing cells, and gelatinizing things like starches and collagen. Chewing might not seem particularly arduous, but that's because we're used to soft, cooked foods and don't often bite into raw squash or potatoes; the fact is, before the advent of cooking, the simple act of chewing would have consumed much more of our ancestors' time and energy. Two of our closest relatives, for example, chimpanzees and mountain gorillas, spend approximately 37 percent and 55 percent of their days, respectively, swallowing and chewing, versus an average of just 5 percent for modern humans; in a sixteen-hour day, this translates to a potential *eight hours* less chewing time.

We're also saving a lot more energy per bite when we cook our food—about 14 percent less muscle use per chew for things like cooked yams, carrots, and beets versus those same foods in their raw states. Altogether, this might not seem like much, but it could very easily have meant the difference between living and dying thousands of years ago, when food sources were scarce and finding another bite to eat meant risking being eaten yourself.

So by cooking our food, we essentially outsourced some of our predigestive processes and made food not only more nutritiously available but also less costly to digest, two insurance policies against starvation that together became crucial to our survival. As a result, the early humans who came to prefer their food thoroughly cooked, versus raw or rare, would have had a better chance of surviving long enough to pass on their genes. We can still see the results of this in our modern diet; just as our sense of vision evolved to help us spot and identify safe and nutrient-rich food sources by giving us an edge in distinguishing certain colors in nature (e.g., the redness of ripe versus green fruit and freshly killed meat that had yet to spoil and turn gray), we developed a Darwinian taste for the nutritional safety signals of fire, e.g., foods that are energy dense and highly portable, preserved for an unnaturally long shelf life, and tender yet crisp around the edges with, perhaps, some visual charring—essentially, the

McDonald's menu.* Not to suggest that French fries are an ideal food source today, but they would have been a superfood a million years ago, when finding food required a massive expenditure of calories and ensuring the survival of the fittest meant finding as much food as possible to avoid starvation and live long enough to have children and perpetuate the species.

And all of this changed us. The more we ate soft, energy-efficient foods, the more our bodies adapted, resulting in smaller jaws and colons. In fact, one of our distant relatives who existed before the advent of cooking, *Paranthropus boisei*, is nicknamed "Nutcracker Man" because of his massive jaws and teeth—packing molars roughly four times the size of our own. Meanwhile, our modern stomachs and colons are less than one-third and two-thirds, proportionally, the size of those in other primates, owing to the efficiency of our cooked diet.

This evolution is still continuing. Explains science writer Nicola Temple, human jaw sizes have continued to shrink even within the last century, owing largely to the rise of processed foods (e.g., McDonald's). The adoption of forks and knives likely also contributed to this by offloading even more work from our jaws and teeth.

Some scholars, like primatologist Richard Wrangham, believe cooking also gave us larger brains. Wrangham argues that the added nutrition through cooking fueled the expansion of the

---

* In fact, just the name McDonald's itself has, rather ironically, become a modern safety signal; research has shown, for example, that children describe milk and carrots as tasting better when they're served from paper bags with McDonald's logos, which speaks not only to our materialistic nature but also to an instinctual suspicion of new and unfamiliar food sources.

human brain, a metabolically expensive body part that requires disproportionately more energy than the rest of our bodies, using roughly 20 percent of the body's basal energy despite accounting for only about 2.5 percent of our body weight. (Basically, the energy that would have gone to larger jaws and digestive systems instead went to our heads.) As a result, explains paleoanthropologist and evolutionary biologist Peter S. Ungar, "Our brains weigh nearly five times what you'd expect for a mammal of our size . . . the difference between an apple and a pineapple."

And cooking also gave us more to do with our brains. Charles Darwin called the discovery of fire ("by which hard and stringy roots can be rendered digestible, and poisonous roots or herbs innocuous") "probably the greatest ever made by man, excepting language." Yet we wouldn't have modern language without cooking—as heating our foods by fire not only reduced chewing times and the amount of time we spent searching for food but also gave off crucial light that extended our "daytime" hours, which vastly expanded our bandwidth for free time, socialization, and the shared development of things such as art and technology. At the same time, thanks to softer and more available foods, children could be weaned more quickly and surplus food shared with others, thus clearing the path for larger families and social circles. And cooking fires or hearths would have provided a warm and protected place to gather and socialize, while fueling and tending these fires (and breaking down animals to be transported, cooked, and shared around the fire versus eating them fresh immediately following a kill) would have required a level of complex collaboration and division of labor that would have been impossible without the development of language.

So cooking was really the perfect activity that brought all of the ingredients for modern language and society together: larger brains, larger gatherings, more free time, and more collaboration. This isn't to suggest that there was no language before cooking, but cooking certainly fed the development of complex language—just as the development of language fed the development of complex cooking.

By the same token, cooking also softened us psychologically by giving the advantage to those who could get along and work and live closely together without killing each other. This was essentially the same process used to domesticate wolves as, over time, natural and human selection favored wolves that were calm and mild-tempered enough to approach human fires and settlements and offer their protection, hunting skills, and companionship—a word that, poignantly, comes from the Latin *com* ("together") and *pānis* ("bread")—in exchange for human food scraps. And the same thing happened with other animals, such as domesticated goats and sheep, which submitted to human milking and shearing in exchange for grain or leftovers (or, in some cases, for the salt content in human urine, which our ancestors learned could be used to lure reindeer, similar to modern salt licks). So survival became less about one's brawn and capacity for killing and more about one's capacity for companionship and prehistoric table manners, and just as fire enabled man to tame nature (from wild wolves to poisonous vegetables), it also tamed us.

Granted, this was a gradual process that is still going on. It wasn't until seventeenth-century France, for example, that we started rounding the tips of our dinner knives to cut down on tableside stabbings (though much of Asia was a few thousand years ahead on this, having largely replaced bladed utensils with chopsticks for much the same reason); even today, some people still chew with their mouths open, eat their pizza with forks, and don't recycle, so we still have a ways to go.

Similarly, as we'll read in the following chapters, our relationship with food is not always one of sharing and companionship; certainly, it's had its low points—among them overfishing, the use of foods such as honey and hot peppers for ritual torture, vast divisions in the distribution and availability of food that leads some to starve while others grow fat, cannibalism, forced labor, British food . . .

But we wouldn't be where we are today—or be *who* we are—if food were just a passive source of energy and not a central part of our lives: simultaneously an obsession, hobby, competitive sport, and profession; a seasonal calendar and nostalgic time capsule; a social lubricant and peace offering; a family heirloom; a drug and spiritual rite.

Nor would food be where it is today, for better or worse, without our having planted the seeds, stoked the fire, and stirred the pot, both literally and figuratively.

CHAPTER 2

PIE, PROGRESS, AND PLYMOUTH ROCK

Take anything away, but leave pie. Americans can stand the prohibition of intoxicating drinks; but I believe the prohibition of pie would precipitate a revolution.

—DAVID MACRAE

And we must have a pie. Stress cannot exist in the presence of a pie.

—DAVID MAMET

Remember when we learned about the Boston Tea Party in middle school—how a secret society of armed radicals bled 342 casks of tea valued at roughly £9,650 into Boston Harbor? And how that single act of defiance was supposed to represent the sum of the American spirit at conflict with the insufferable evils of British tyranny, thus charting a course for revolution?

Well, it *was* pretty damn American, sure, especially the parts about Bostonians polluting their own harbor and painting their faces with coal dust to disguise themselves as Native Americans; however, it wasn't the only symbolic food fight to represent, and fuel, the fight for American independence—nor was it the most impactful.

In fact, some people, like nineteenth-century physician F. W. Searle, might argue that the American Revolution would never have happened had it not been for the influence of pie, a dish often served as breakfast, lunch, dinner, and midnight snack in the colonies.

A learned doctor, Searle wrote about pie as though it were the stuff of Arthurian legend, crediting it with the colonies' "indomitable perseverance, never failing strength, and don't-know-when-you'r beaten courage" and predicting that "when the history of New England shall be written in that spirit of careful investigation and research, and with that calm and dispassionate temper, which ought to animate every historian, then it will undoubtedly be found that the indigestible pie has exerted a mighty influence in the development and utilization of the resources of our country, and that pie and progress have always gone hand in hand."

Searle believed "that a certain amount of irritation within 'the inwards' of a man" made him tougher and more resilient, that American pie had a tendency to irritate a man's inwards "just sufficiently to make him wide awake, resourceful, and aggressive" and that calling pie "indigestible" was therefore a compliment.

"The brave men who made up the Boston Tea Party," he writes, "and who defied the whole English nation rather than pay an unjust tax, were pie-biters from Boston. The bands of untrained stragglers who defeated a disciplined army at Concord, at Lexington and Bunker Hill, sprung from the Puritan stock which introduced and made famous the American pie. The history of New England shows conclusively that the Yankee pie is a mighty stimulator of energy and that it is conducive to vigilance, aggressiveness and longevity."

This was all published as scientific fact in 1898's *Journal of Medicine and Science*.

And Searle wasn't wrong;* the history he describes has just been largely forgotten.

Indeed, pie—particularly apple pie—has an important place

---

* At least, not about pie's historical importance; he was probably wrong about pie and longevity, and we can only surmise that his ideas led a lot of people to an early death from diseases such as pie-stimulated diabetes, obesity, and cardiovascular disease.

in American history. It's as American as, well, apple pie: the ultimate symbol, and product, of American independence, innovation, experimentation, and excess.

And what makes it so American isn't its lineage—as the first recipe for a crude apple pie comes from 1381 England, while the apple itself originated from the mountainous regions of Central Asia known today as Kazakhstan and Kyrgyzstan—but rather the fact that we stole it from the British along with our independence, thus liberating it from the tyranny of British cooking, which at the time consisted primarily of pies stuffed with birds and nightmarish sea creatures. Consider the British eel pie, lamprey pie, pigeon pie, and swan pie, traditionally served cold.

Did you know that the secret to a nice lamprey pie, according to a recipe from 1737 London, is to "cleanse them well from the slime" *before* you mix their blood with cinnamon? If you plan on helping yourself to a slice afterward, it's probably also a good idea not to stare too long into their jawless parasitic sucker heads.

The trick with pigeon pie, in case you're curious, is to add lamb's stones, also known as lamb's testicles, or to top it with a "ragoo" of cocks-combs.

Of course, other recipes were simpler, say, for example, that for the English hare pie, comprising just six steps: "Get a hare, cut it in pieces, break the bones, and season it to your taste, and lay it in the pye with sliced lemon, and butter and close the same."

Because forks weren't common before industrialization[*] and

---

[*] When the English travel writer Thomas Coryat introduced forks to England in 1608 after observing their use in Italy, he was nicknamed "Furcifer" and mocked for being effeminate; ironically, he would later die of dysentery, which might have been prevented by the fork's widespread adoption. Several decades later, in 1633, John Winthrop, one of the founders of the Massachu-

most people ate with their hands or a pair of knives, a lot of early pie recipes called for keeping the bones inside, as this gave diners something to hold on to—and, as a bonus, imparted more flavor and gelatin (for thickening). Meanwhile, to "close" the pie meant closing the "coffyn," which was what the British appropriately called their inedible crusts. This wasn't an insult or a jab; rather, their crusts were *intentionally* inedible. Thick, hard, and meant to be tossed uneaten, they were viewed merely as disposable vessels for baking, handling, and storing their innards in the absence of modern bakeware or aluminum foil. This is why even today, British pie crusts are thicker and harder than American crusts, a relic of their heritage as the inedible Tupperware of the Dark Ages—which were, indeed, dark times for pie. So saying that British pies belong in coffyns would have been accurate on several levels.

Other recipes from the same cookbook—verbosely titled *The Whole Duty of a Woman: or, an Infallible Guide to the Fair Sex. Containing, Rules, Directions, and Observations, for their Conduct and Behaviour through All Ages and Circumstances of Life, as Virgins, Wives, or Widows. With Directions, How to Obtain All Useful and Fashionable Accomplishments Suitable to the Sex. In Which Are Comprised All Parts of Good Housewifry, Particularly Rules and Receipts in Every Kind of Cookery*—include those for pies made of lamb, veal, calves' foot, calf's head, squab, venison, goose, giblet, pigeon, rabbit, turkey, eel, trout, and oyster.

But not apple.

---

setts Bay Colony, is believed to have owned the only fork in America, but forks were slow to take off there as well, largely because clergymen demonized them as sinful, fearing both their resemblance to the devil's pitchfork and their implication that God's food was too unclean to touch with fingers.

And when the English did use apples, in their pies or elsewhere, they treated them largely as vegetables, adding them to various meat concoctions alongside onions or potatoes. Even English applesauce was savory rather than sweet. Called *apulmose*, it was traditionally made with beef broth or, during Lent, with cod's liver.

So pie, in precolonial England, was largely utilitarian: far from being a delicacy or dessert, it was merely a convenient way of congealing various bits of bird and beast into something portable and relatively stable. Its name comes from the magpie, a member of the crow family that was commonly colloquialized as *pie* in the Middle Ages, though it's unclear whether this namesake had to do with baking magpies in coffyns or the birds' reputation for stealing random objects to incorporate into their nests in much the same way British cooks tossed random animal parts into pies. (Nests and early pies would have also shared a rough resemblance owing to their rustic layers and golden-brown coloring.)

It would make sense if the phrase "eating humble pie" had been coined to describe these humble roots and practices, but the truth is, perhaps, less appetizing, as the word *humble* comes from the Middle English *umble*, which refers to the inner waste parts of animals. So umble pie was what servants made for themselves using the pig or deer guts left over from the fancier lord's or noble's pies described earlier.

Yet all of this changed with the colonization of America—an experiment not just in democracy and liberty but in survival, scale, excess, and New World cookery.

"When European colonists first landed in America they found not only Indians, virgin lands, and an alien style of life," writes historian Sally Smith Booth, "but the world's largest outdoor supermarket. Ducks, geese, and pigeons by the millions filled the skies.

Forests abounded with deer, hare, squirrels, and quail. In rivers
and on seashores thrived giant shad, eels, mussels, lobsters five feet
long, and crabs said to be big enough to feed four men each. Trees
hung heavy with wild fruits and berries. Vegetables, such as potatoes, squash, corn, and pumpkin, covered the rolling meadows."

This New World wasn't rich just in spices but in fish, game,
birds, berries, vegetables, and grain; the lands and waters were
teeming with new ingredients the colonists had never seen or
heard of, and the ingredients they had seen before tended to be
larger, sweeter, and more plentiful than their European counter-
parts.

Still, there's a reason these first few years were called the
"starving times"; however, the staggering number of early colonists who starved to death did so not because of a lack of food
but because of a lack of skill in acquiring it, an unwillingness
to heed the advice of the natives, whom they saw as uncivilized
savages, and a reluctance to try new foods. Surrounded by birds
they couldn't catch, fish they couldn't hook, deer they couldn't
shoot, and corn they were afraid to eat, they initially survived by
eating whatever they could scavenge, which often meant things
like acorns, ants, bats, cats, dogs, horses, and boiled shoe leather.

"Though there be fish in the sea, foules in the ayre, and beasts
in the woods," writes John Smith in 1608, "their bounds are so
large, they so wilde, and we so weake and ignorant, we cannot
much trouble them."

Smith recounts, for example, coming across waters so thick
with fish that their heads stuck out above the water, yet being
unable to catch any "for want of nets."

"We attempted to catch them with a frying pan," he writes,
"but we found it a bad instrument to catch fish with: neither better fish, more plenty, nor more variety for smal fish, had any of

us ever seene in any place so swimming in the water, but they are not to be caught with frying pans."

Yet within a generation, people were eating better in the New World than in the Old World they'd left behind, having acquired not just a taste for New World foods but the skill and equipment (e.g., fishing nets) by which to acquire them.

In 1614, just six years after his failed attempt to fish with frying pans, Smith describes hooking fish with such ease that even "a little boye" could do it.

"You shall scarce finde any baye, shallow shore, or cove of sand," he writes, "where you may not take many clampes, or lobsters, or both at your pleasure, and in many places lode your boat if you please; nor iles where you finde not fruits, birds, crabs, and muskles, or all of them, for taking, at a lowe water. And in the harbors we frequented, a little boye might take of cunners, and pinacks, and such delicate fish, at the ships sterne, more then sixe or tenne can eate in a daie."

And the amount of food the weakest boy could take home seems to have been a common measurement in the colonies. Francis Higginson, the first Puritan minister of Salem, writes in 1629 of lobsters so great, fat, and luscious, and the waters so full of them, that "the least boy in the plantation may both catch and eat what he will of them," while he complains of becoming "cloyed with them." Others describe lobsters six feet long, weighing up to twenty-five pounds and washing up on beaches in piles two feet high.

All this while most of Europe was living on bread and porridge.

The same abundance held true for crab, mussels, bass, salmon, flounder, and herring. John Lawson, who kept a journal of almost everything he ate in his eight years in Carolina (he once ate "fat barbacu'd Venison" on a Thursday),* describes a single cockle the size of five or six in England, stingrays at almost every door, and oysters or mussels, as many as you please, in every pond or creek.

And that was just the fish menu.

Others describe great migrations of birds so numerous they were forced to roost on top of one another, downing giant oaks from their weight and covering the forest in four inches of droppings. John James Audubon later described flocks so dense they eclipsed the sun and estimated seeing more than a billion pigeons in a three-hour span. To save on gunpowder and ammunition, colonists would often net and club birds to death, capturing some fifteen hundred at a time.

And perhaps more impressive than the number of birds was their size. Colonists describe mystery birds with heads "as big as a child's of a year old" and flocks of five hundred wild turkeys weighing forty to sixty pounds each. Lawson writes of half a turkey feeding eight hungry men two meals each, and Higginson, the same guy who complained of becoming cloyed on lobster, describes their meat as exceedingly "fat, sweet and fleshy."

And don't get the colonists started on the superiority of American bear meat.

"The Flesh of this Beast is very good, and nourishing, and not inferiour to the best Pork in Taste," writes Lawson. "It stands

---

* In addition to Lawson's detailed food menus, he recorded his close observations of Native American culture, select subtopics of which include "Naked Indians," "Civiliz'd Indians," "Fleas," "Indian Wives," "Indians buy their wives," "Selling Wives," "Indian Women handsome," "Night Rambles," "Indians not afraid to die," "Indians not afraid of spirits," "Drunkenness in Indians," "Indians make Maps," "Indian Robbery," "No hard Workers," "Indian Men not vigorous," "Indians learn of the Europeans," and "Indians Aversion to Christianity."

betwixt Beef and Pork, and the young Cubs are a Dish for the greatest *Epicure* living. I prefer their Flesh before any Beef, Veal, Pork, or Mutton; and they look as well as they eat, their fat being as white as Snow, and the sweetest of any Creature's in the World. . . . Those that are Strangers to it, may judge otherwise; But I who have eaten a great deal of Bears Flesh in my Life-time (since my being an Inhabitant in *America*) do think it equalizes, if not excels, any Meat I ever eat in *Europe*. The Bacon made thereof is extraordinary Meat."

And if this weren't reason enough to eat bear meat, it was also believed to give those who consumed it "great sexual prowess," while bear oil (meaning its melted caul fat) was good for drinking (Lawson describes drinking a quart of it without vomiting!) and for rubbing on your skin to ward off mosquitoes.

So there was plenty to eat in terms of both quality and quantity. In fact, in 1765, several years before the Boston Tea Party, a writer in London pompously argued that colonists would never survive without British tea, suggesting it was the only decent food staple the colonies had—which prompted Benjamin Franklin, of all people, to pen an open letter in response:

> Does he imagine we can get nothing else for breakfast?—
> Did he never hear that we have oatmeal in plenty, for water
> gruel or burgoo; as good wheat, rye and barley as the world
> affords, to make frumenty; or toast and ale; that there is
> every where plenty of milk, butter and cheese; that rice is
> one of our staple commodities; that for tea, we have sage
> and bawm* in our gardens, the young leaves of the sweet

---

* Burgoo was a sort of stew; frumenty, a porridge; and bawm, an antiquated name for lemon balm.

hickory or walnut, and above all, the buds of our pine, infinitely preferable to any tea from the Indies; while the islands yield us plenty of coffee and chocolate?—Let the gentleman do us the honour of a visit in America, and I will engage to breakfast him every day in the month with a fresh variety, without offering him either tea or Indian corn.

Many of the fruits and vegetables the colonists found, like corn, were native; others, such as figs, lemons, limes, and oranges, had been planted earlier by the Spanish; and others still—like the apple—they brought themselves. The first apple seeds arrived in the colonies on the *Mayflower* in 1620, where they would prosper more in a generation than they had in the entirety of apple history. And not because of Johnny Appleseed. Sure, there was a guy named John Chapman, born 1774, who traveled west from Massachusetts planting apple seeds, and his personal impact was significant. But everyone in the colonies was Johnny Appleseed—and they had more than a century's head start on the actual Johnny. If you were a landowner in the New World, you planted apple trees, and if you were a landowner in Virginia or some parts of Ohio, this was actually a legal requirement. (In chapter 10, we'll read how potatoes were similarly subsidized in Europe by threatening citizens with forty lashes or having their ears cut off for refusing to plant them.)

So by the late 1700s, the colonies were growing more apples, and apples of higher quality, than anywhere else in the world and shipping them overseas on a massive scale, providing much of the supply throughout Europe. And they weren't just better but more diverse. Like the colonists themselves, they'd been shaped and transformed by the New World: its soil, its climate, its untamed wilds, and its geographic diversity.

Before 1620, there were no apples in the New World, barring inedible crabapples, and only somewhere in the neighborhood of seventy varieties cataloged in England. And thirty-six of those varieties had likely been around since the first century, having been cataloged by Pliny the Elder in ancient Rome. So between the years 55 and 1620, there were roughly thirty-four new types of apples documented in Europe. But the colonies gave birth to some *seventeen thousand* new varieties, not including the countless experiments that weren't particularly appealing or worth cataloging.

Initially, this was due largely to the demand for hard apple cider, which served as not just the national beverage of the colonies but also as a currency for barter, the average colonial family generally consuming a few hundred gallons of it per year. However, apple pies quickly became a colonial staple, particularly in New England, where the growing season was so short and the winters so long that many fruits were sugared and preserved for winter rather than eaten fresh. The fibrous apple held up much better to this than other fruits; whereas softer fruits like raspberries and strawberries lent themselves more to soft jams and pastes, apples could easily be dried and reconstituted months later for pie filling.

So pies, long before Americans invented the McDonald's drive-through* and TV dinners, were the paramount of convenience—well suited to the get-up-and-go lifestyle in the colonies, where you didn't have servants to cook for you and do your dishes.

"The great beauty of an apple pie breakfast, aside from its power to generate indigestion," writes R. K. Munkittrick in 1891,

---

* Fittingly, apple pie was McDonald's first dessert, added to their menu in 1968.

"lies in the fact that it doesn't leave behind it a number of dishes thickly incrusted with ham grease to be cracked with a hammer or melted off over a candle."

Pies were everything that tea wasn't: hearty, available on demand, suited to travel, untamed, utilitarian, and unpretentious. They kept well, being sealed off from air and preserved with sugar; traveled well, being protected by a crust; and could easily be baked ahead and grabbed in the morning, so they met the demand for convenient, on-the-go meals Americans would become known for. During a time when the British were becoming increasingly proper, placing emphasis on decorum, etiquette, and social hierarchy (one of the reasons tea became popular in Great Britain was that coffeehouses were restricted to men), America's humble pie showed the world a new form of liberty and freedom, unencumbered by pomp and circumstance: a world without limits, wherein women could drink not only coffee for breakfast but hard cider or melted bear fat.

"The pie is an English tradition," writes Harriet Beecher Stowe in 1869, "which, planted on American soil, forthwith ran rampant and burst forth into an untold variety of genera and species. Not merely the old traditional mince pie, but a thousand strictly American seedlings from that main stock, evinced the power of American housewives to adapt old institutions to new uses."

Among those adaptations was the transformation of pie's crust; you see, despite there being an abundance of birds and berries, wheat was initially scarce in the colonies, particularly in New England, and this forced colonists to literally stretch their crust until it became flaky and thin—making American crusts not just more edible but also more appetizing.

In other words, colonists elevated and transformed pie to the point that it became not just "*a* great American institution" but "*the* great American institution."*

Writes Charles Dudley Warner in 1872, pie was so ubiquitous in the colonies that its absence would have been more noticeable than a scarcity of Bibles.

"This country was founded by men who had pie for breakfast, pie for dinner, pie for supper; in addition they usually had a slice or so before going to bed at night," reads a 1922 editorial in *The Nation*. "The only time they did not eat pie was when they were asleep, at work, or in church."

The author then goes on to blame the corruption of American youth on the invention of marshmallow nut sundaes and banana splits and to suggest Lincoln could never have freed the slaves if it weren't for his habitual indulgence in pie—this from a paper founded to "wage war upon the vices of violence, exaggeration and misrepresentation" in the media.

Meanwhile, the English continued to eat beans on toast for breakfast, stuff their pies with pigeon's blood, and in general treat pie like a second-class citizen; and while American doctors and journalists hailed pie as a cure-all and the elixir of life, the English condemned it as a social disease, declaring, "The present civil strife in America is to be looked upon as a hideous nightmare, produced by half a century's indulgence of an unhallowed appetite for pie." Again, this is from a medical journal.

In 1865, British journalist George Augustus Sala wrote in his diary of America that "the real social curse of the Atlantic States

---

* Note that colonists did the same thing with muffins, transforming the nooks and crannies of crumpetlike "English" muffins into the blueberry or cranberry muffins we know today, known as "gems" in the 1800s.

is Pie," "that an unholy appetite for Pie works untold woes," and that "the Pie fiend reigns supreme."

"The sallow faces, the shrunken forms, the sunken eyes, the morose looks, the tetchy temperament of the Northerners," he writes, "are attributable not half so much to iced water, candies, tough beefsteaks, tight lacing, and tobacco-chewing, as to un-bridled indulgence in Pie."

He went on like this for four pages, later accusing American girls of taking pies to bed with them. The bastard.

Meanwhile, Rudyard Kipling, the British author of *The Jungle Book* who moved to Vermont in the late 1800s, called New England "the Great Pie Belt" and questioned the "moral and physi-cal condition of a people which eats pie for breakfast, pie for dinner, pie for supper."

Americans, of course, fired back.

In 1884, the *New York Times* published a biting parody in re-sponse to British criticism of Ralph Waldo Emerson's habit of eating pie for breakfast:

An indiscreet and perhaps malevolent person who once breakfasted with the late Ralph Waldo Emerson has revealed the fact that Mr. Emerson was accustomed to eat pie at breakfast. This revelation has naturally caused a very painful sensation, and not a few persons who had hitherto admired what they conceived to be the philo-sophical ideas expressed in Mr. Emerson's writings have suddenly discovered that Mr. Emerson was not a phi-losopher and that his writings are filled with the vague-ness that characterizes a mind warped and weakened by pie.

After warning readers that eating pie might cause them to compose poetry, attend prestigious schools, and gaze silently at the moon, the authors went on to suggest that "no pie shall be eaten until it has been thoroughly disinfected by prolonged immersion in a bath composed of carbolic acid, Worcestershire sauce, and permanganate of Sulphur" to avoid any "danger of increasing the flood of poetry, philosophy, and generally misery which has hitherto devastated so large a part of our country."

And this back-and-forth continued for quite some time; eighteen years later, the *Times* was still declaring pie "the food of the heroic," boasting that "No pie-eating people can ever be permanently vanquished," and calling it "a significant historical fact that England's glory was greatest in the days when her gallant sons ate pie" and that such glory and greatness had long since crumbled.

During an 1889 debate on the national flower, a Milwaukee journalist even suggested that the United States abandon its search for a symbolic flower and look instead to apple pie—it being more substantial and indicative of American life than a flimsy plant:

What's the matter with the apple pie as a national emblem? The apple pie grows in every section of our beloved country, varying in thickness and toughness of crust, it is true, but always characteristically American. In the homes of New England, in the smack-houses of the South, on the lunch counters of the North, at the wayside stations of the towering Rockies—everywhere in this vast country the flaky or leathery crusts inclose the spiced fruit of the apple tree. Every true American eats apple pie. It is substantial, it is satisfying, it is hard to digest. And therefore it is no light and trifling symbol of the solid, satisfying and tenacious life of America.

That foreigners mocked America's apple pie was another key selling point:

Another thing in favor of the apple pie as a national emblem is that it is hated, reviled and feared by foreigners, just as our great Republic has been. Like our free institutions, the apple pie has held its own against all the world. The French pate, the German coffee-cake, the English tart, the Scotch oat-cake, have all been offered as substitutes, but on every loyal table the apple pie holds its place of honor.

The author then closes by suggesting:

We should go further than to make the apple pie the national flower; we should embody in the Constitution of the United States a requirement that no foreign immigrant should receive his final papers of naturalization until he should eat an apple pie in the presence of the Court.

And maybe they were right. The search for a national flower would last another ninety-seven years until the Reagan administration finally settled on the rose in 1986 and include many front-runners most Americans had never heard of, like goldenrod and arbutus. And what, really, has the rose done for America? The American colonies didn't survive on rose water. American soldiers weren't substantially taller than the British during the Revolution because they ate roses for breakfast.* American pioneers didn't ride west with roses in their bags. The majority of roses aren't even grown in America but in countries like Colombia or Ecuador, where they're often the product of child labor and banned pesticides.†

In fact, apple pie might have made a decent national bird, too. Benjamin Franklin would have been on board with this, having imported American apples by the barrel while living in London; introduced the English to the Newtown Pippin, a variety that would singlehandedly convince the queen to lift the tariff on American apples; and, in a 1784 letter, criticized the bald eagle for being lazy and immoral:

> For my own part I wish the bald eagle had not been chosen as the representative of our country; he is a bird of bad moral character; he does not get his living honestly; you may have seen him perched on some dead tree, where, too lazy to fish for himself, he watches the labor of the fishing-hawk; and, when that diligent bird has at length taken a fish, and is bearing it to his nest for the support of his mate and young ones, the bald eagle pursues him, and takes it from him. . . . Besides, he is a rank coward; the little *kingbird*, not bigger than a sparrow, attacks him boldly and drives him out of the district.

Franklin suggested the turkey as an alternative to the eagle but surely would have understood the repercussions of its being

---

* Pie, obviously, wasn't the only nutritional factor in this size difference, but it certainly played a role.
† According to *The Atlantic*, flower workers in both countries commonly suffer from health problems, including birth defects and miscarriages, owing to the use of pesticides restricted in the United States and Europe.

named after another country* and nearly wiped out by American colonists. (Try to recall the last time you saw a flock of five hundred turkeys running wild.)

Apples, meanwhile, are inherently diverse. They can be white or brown, pink or yellow, red or green; mixed or speckled, streaked or russeted; they can be fat, round, or pear-shaped; coarse or chalky; sweet, sour, or bitter; they can be English or Swiss, German or French; poisonous or forbidden. Add them to pie, and they become both sponge and catalyst.

"Do not suppose that we limit the apple-pie to the kinds and methods enumerated," writes Henry Ward Beecher in 1862. "Its capacity in variation is endless, and every diversity discovers some new charm or flavour. It will accept almost every flavour of every spice."

Perhaps most poignantly, the apple itself, like the colonists who planted it, refuses to be wrangled. "Sown by chance, or even sown intentionally," writes Maguelonne Toussaint-Samat, "apple trees almost always revert to the wild form instead of breeding true to the mother tree."

One could certainly say the same about early colonists—and the country they colonized.

Sure, pie is immoderate, overindulgent, unrefined, and potentially inflammatory, but so is America; so were Searle and Emerson and that guy who drank a quart of rendered bear fat without vomiting; so are free speech, New England winters, and Fourth of July cookouts; so was declaring independence, dumping shiploads of tea into Boston Harbor, and fishing uncharted waters with frying pans in pursuit of the sweet, if sometimes excessive, taste of liberty.

---

* In the 1400s, Europeans called it *galine de Turquie* ("chicken of Turkey") after Turkish traders.

CHAPTER 3

BREAKFAST OF CHAMPIONS

It tastes like all the naughty things, but has the advantage of being digestible and wholesome.

—NEW YORK LADY ON NUTTOSE

In this fast age, the less exciting the food, the better.

—ELLEN G. WHITE

Cold cereal is the "Breakfast of Champions," a morning staple enjoyed by 93 percent of Americans, and so prevalent on grocery lists that it not only gets its own aisle in the supermarket but plays a key role in the psychology of shelf allocation storewide. (One of the reasons supermarkets place their dairy cases in the back, far from a store's entrance, is that they know most shoppers are going to buy milk, for cereal, and want to funnel them past as many impulse buys as possible along the way.)*

Cereal transcends race, social class, age, gender—and even dietary guidelines; egg consumption has dropped by more than 40 percent in the United States since the demonization of cho-

---

* Similarly, once you make it to the cereal aisle, you'll find the children's cereals stocked on the lower shelves and adult cereals stocked on the upper shelves—which not only ensures that brands are seen by their target demographics but also influences consumer choice; studies have shown that customers are statistically more likely to choose Trix over Fruity Pebbles, for example, when the boxes are aligned so that the Trix rabbit ("Tricks") appears to make eye contact with them, as, instinctually, eye contact tends to foster trust and social connection. Similarly, brand-name cereals are usually on higher shelves than generics because people are lazy and willing to pay more if it means they don't have to bend down to grab something.

lesterol in the 1940s, yet decades of health warnings concerning milk and sugar (and millennia of heritable lactose intolerance) have failed to unseat cereal as the official champion of the breakfast table. For many people, it's the one food they still eat sitting down, at a table, or with family: their first and only taste of sweetness before venturing out into a bitter world of industrial coffee and eating in cars.

Cereal often serves as an excellent source of not just vitamins and minerals, as the labels claim, but nostalgia, free prizes, back-of-the-box activities, and aerated confectionary foams (better known as dried marshmallows or, in industry jargon, "marbits"). So it satisfies our hunger in ways that go beyond the merely caloric.

In fact, though it might lack pie's heartiness or indigestibility, cereal has several key traits that can trick us into feeling more satisfied by it than perhaps we should, given that it's made up mostly of sugars and simple carbohydrates. Research suggests, for example, that people tend to consume less food when consuming it from a spoon (as opposed to, say, their hands or a straw) without feeling any less full, owing to the additional time it takes to operate a spoon, which essentially tricks our bodies into thinking we ate more because it took longer. The fact that cereal is composed of many small pieces adds to this effect, triggering what psychologists call a "unit bias," wherein we assume that we ate more food because we ate more pieces.* (Similarly, if you lift your bowl while eating cereal to drink the cereal milk,

---

* This is similar to the "cheerleader effect" among people, so named because a person, say a cheerleader, tends to appear more attractive when part of a group than by herself, as our brains essentially average the sum of the faces (and presumably the other parts).

the weight of the bowl could lead you to believe you're ingesting more breakfast than you really are.) Finally, there's the Pavlovian response that conditions us to feel satisfied due to decades of television commercials painting cereal as a delicious part of a complete breakfast that's supposedly the most important meal of the day—so we feel satisfied, in part, because advertisers tell us to.

And here you thought you liked Frosted Flakes just because they're *gr-r-reat*.

Yet despite cereal's mass appeal and generally massive sugar content (in 2014, the average children's cereal was 34 percent sugar by weight and adult cereal, 18 percent),* it was never meant to be sweet; in fact, it was never even meant to be enjoyable.

Rather, cold breakfast cereal was created to be deliberately bland: the brainchild of religious health reformers who thought America needed a breakfast free from not just sugar and excess, à la the all-day-pie diet in the previous chapter, but from sin and gluttony—a way to "break fast" without breaking religious sanctity and becoming a godless pagan hedonist. No sooner had Americans emerged from the "starving times" and begun to enjoy their freedom and comfort, in fact, than a health craze swept the country, bringing with it a long list of dietary cautions. Unlike today's fad diets, however, which tend to target things like carbs or cellulite in the interest of living longer or looking good naked, this new wave of diets targeted "depraved desire and perverted appetite" in the interest of avoiding eternal fire and brimstone— and looking good in the eyes of God.

---

* In 2014, Kellogg's Honey Smacks contained more than 55 percent sugar by weight (15 grams in a 27-gram suggested serving size). The company has since updated the recipe and reduced the ratio to an even 50 percent—but also increased the serving size, so you now actually get even more sugar (18 grams in a 36-gram serving size).

Rich foods, alcohol, sugar, chocolate, caffeine, and even condiments, alleged health reformers, led not just to indigestion but to far more serious ailments such as crime, chronic illness, adultery, and ultimately eternal damnation.

One of the early leaders of this movement was Sylvester Graham (1794–1851), the guy graham crackers are named after—not that he would have eaten them.* A traveling preacher and staunch vegetarian, Graham yearned for simpler times without the artificial and material needs brought about by industry and civilization, what he calls "the rude state of nature," wherein the basic needs of hunger, thirst, and shelter were easily provided by nature and instinct rather than by factories and industrialization and a man could survive simply by plucking fruit from a tree, drinking water from a folded leaf, and wrapping "his body in the skins of beasts."

He was also, he believed, a messenger of God who believed that the secret to happiness was a routine of self-denial from such abominations as sexuality, masturbation, meat, and spices. Most commercial butchers and bakers, of course, disagreed with these notions, insisting that Graham was not only mortal but kind of an asshole—as he once provoked an armed riot in Boston after repeatedly accusing butchers of selling diseased meat and bakers of using spoiled flour, then barricaded himself inside his speaking venue and shoveled lime on them from above.

Note that Graham wasn't necessarily wrong in these accusations; in his 1820 book *A Treatise on Adulterations of Food, and*

---

* Though it is named after him, the modern "graham cracker" is more of an insult to Graham's legacy than a tribute; created decades after his death and first sold nationally by the National Biscuit Company (now Nabisco), it violates most of his life's work preaching against the dangers of sugar, refined flour, cinnamon, and commercial bakeries.

Culinary Poisons, Exhibiting the Fraudulent Sophistications of Bread, Beer, Wine, Spirituous Liquors, Tea, Coffee, Cream, Confectionery, Vinegar, Mustard, Pepper, Cheese, Olive Oil, Pickles, and Other Articles Employed in Domestic Economy; and Methods Of Detecting Them, chemist Fredrick Accum describes that it was common practice for bakers to make bread using damaged or spoiled flour masked with things like chalk or white clay powder. This, in addition to other nefarious practices of the period, such as flavoring wine with oak sawdust or adding molten lead to prevent it from turning; boiling various types of leaves with toxic pigments or sheep's dung to pass them off as tea leaves (or recycling used tea leaves taken from coffeehouses and dyeing them black again); selling "sham-coffee" made from burned peas and swept coffee grounds recovered from floors; and doctoring beer with powdered oyster shells and wood shavings to mask its sourness, fish skin or hartshorn shavings (shaved deer antler, particularly the inner "heart") to resolve cloudiness, and opium or nux vomica (also known as poison nut or strychnine) to make it more inebriating.

Still, Graham's philosophy was eerily similar to that of Unabomber Ted Kaczynski, whose manifesto begins:

The Industrial Revolution and its consequences have been a disaster for the human race. They have greatly increased the life-expectancy of those of us who live in "advanced" countries, but they have destabilized society, have made life unfulfilling, have subjected human beings to indignities, have led to widespread psychological suffering (in the Third World to physical suffering as well) and have inflicted severe damage on the natural world.

A key difference, however, was that Graham believed that life expectancy had rapidly decreased in advanced countries as a result of industrialization rather than increased—as evidenced by the fact that people in the Bible used to live hundreds of years before they became gluttons and stopped using the proper ingredients for bread.

Nevertheless, Graham developed a strong following as an expert on health and the science of human life, speaking across the country on such topics as the evils of feather beds and reasons to consign them to bonfires as well as the horrors of masturbation. Whether you side with Graham and his followers, called Grahamites, or the heathen butchers and bakers, it's undeniable that he was—and this is sincere—a phenomenally talented and historically underrated speaker and author. Consider, for example, his poetic and imaginative sketch of a chronic masturbation victim:

Sometimes this general mental decay continues with the continued abuses, till the wretched transgressor sinks into a miserable fatuity, and finally becomes a confirmed and degraded idiot, whose deeply sunken and vacant glossy eye, and livid, shriveled countenance, and ulcerous, toothless gums, and foetid breath, and feeble, broken voice, and emaciated and dwarfish and crooked body, and almost hairless head—covered, perhaps, with suppurating blisters and running sores—denote a premature old age—a blighted body—and a ruined soul!—and he drags out the remnant of his loathsome existence, in exclusive devotion to his horridly abominable sensuality. . . . More frequently, however, the mental powers maintain their existence, to inflict, if possible, a deeper and darker vengeance on the miserable offender. Beginning with occasional dejection of spirits, he goes on in his transgression, till an habitual depression, and then a deeper gloom, and then a cheerless melancholy, gathers in permanent darkness over his soul.

Or his warnings on the iron grip of pornography:

If he attempts to read or study, ever and anon his book will fade away, and a lascivious image will occupy his mental vision, and stir up the unclean fires of morbid lust. If he endeavors to give his thoughts to the most solemn and sacred subjects, still he is haunted with images of lewdness; and even when he attempts to pray to the omniscient and holy God, these filthy harpies of his imagination will often flit between his soul and Heaven, and shake pollution on him from their horrid wings! Almost every object that he sees, will, by a diseased association, suggest the debasing vice; and his eye can scarcely fall, by accident, on the sexual parts of any female animal, without awaking a train of obscene thoughts, and exciting a foul concupiscence.

Clearly, he could've made it as a horror writer.

Yet Graham's biggest impact was made with his guidance to eat coarsely ground whole wheat flour, which became known as Graham flour, in place of refined white flour. This, despite the fact that his reasoning was vastly misguided, as he believed white flour was too nutritious and that stripping away the outer bran made it too nutrient dense to absorb. (Today we know the opposite is true and that the bran and germ contain most of wheat's nutrients, phytochemicals, and essential minerals and that refined flour is, nutritionally speaking, relatively vacuous.)

And it was Graham flour—and Graham's groundwork in vilifying pleasurable foods—that helped inspire the first cold breakfast cereal, which was essentially just crumbled pieces of baked Graham flour and water. Called granula, it was developed in the 1860s by a follower of Graham named James C. Jackson, and while Jackson's granula never really took off, mostly because it was rock hard and had to be soaked overnight in milk to make it even remotely edible, Jackson's idea for a cereal that was pre-packaged and ready to eat, as opposed to time-intensive gruels and porridges (or sacrilegious pies), was novel enough to capture the interest of a man named John Harvey Kellogg.

Born in 1852, a year after Graham's death, Kellogg was raised by parents who believed Judgment Day and the end of the world were imminent and therefore saw little need for education in matters other than salvation; as a result, Kellogg spent most of his childhood reading Graham's works, preparing for Armageddon, and, in his own words, learning that "anything that was fun was regarded as wicked." He was also plagued by severe gastrointestinal issues during childhood and by the age of fifteen had dealt with bloody colitis, a scarred colon, chronic constipation, hemorrhoids, and an anal fissure—which, according to author and medical historian Howard Markel, resulted in a prolonged "cycle of bleeding, barbed wire–like pain, and nonstop burning, itching, and throbbing" in his nether regions.

Kellogg would eventually, thanks to the world not ending, go on to attend medical school and become a doctor; but it was his childhood obsession with salvation, ritual self-sacrifice, and colon health that would shape his life's work—and ultimately lead him to revolutionize the world of breakfast cereal.

In 1876, at the age of twenty-four, he became the medical director of a religious health spa in his hometown of Battle Creek, Michigan, and used his medical credentials to help scale the establishment from a humble two-story farmhouse with a dozen or so patients into the luxurious Battle Creek Sanitarium: a sprawling medical facility with steam-operated elevators; an eight-hundred-seat dining room with vaulted ceilings and its own orchestra; a one-thousand-seat lecture hall and concert venue; and ten thousand annual patients enjoying such amenities as vibrotherapy, medical gymnastics, mechanical camels (which patients rode like exercise bikes), a tropical garden with towering palms—in northern Michigan, mind you, more than fifty types of medicinal baths (at least one of which was radioactive), and an outdoor gymnasium where patients could "walk and trot around the running path, take swimming lessons, and engage in all kinds of exercises without other covering than simple trunks, so that the skin becomes hardened, toughened, and in many cases as brown as that of a North American Indian."

That last bit is taken verbatim from a sanitarium brochure.

It was sort of like—well, it was unlike anything else that's ever existed, really; if you've ever had that dream where you're chopping wood in a loincloth while recovering from a circumcision without any pain medication, all while surrounded by banana trees, and then all of a sudden you're ice-skating, it was exactly like that.

The san's official mission was "to combine with the special professional, technical, and institutional advantages of the modern hospital, the luxuries and comforts of the modern hotel, together with the genial atmosphere, security and freedom of the home." But it was more "acid trip" meets "high school detention" meets "indie horror film"—except you also had to eat twelve pounds of grapes.

Guests could have their bowel movements physically, chemically, and microscopically examined while relaxing in a garden of imported palms; take an aerobics class led by Dr. Kellogg himself; await their radiographic colon results while taking in a yogurt enema fresh from the creamery; or receive Kellogg's thoughts on such topics as hermaphrodites, nap taking and the dangers of imagination, round dances—especially the waltz— and their role in provoking unchaste desires, the exciting influence of pepper, mustard, ginger, spices, truffles, wine, and alcohol upon the genital organs, the reasons chocolate should be discarded, "wretches [who] ought to be punished in a purgatory by themselves, made seven times hotter than for ordinary criminals," reasons it might be better to cut the throats of children in cold blood than allow them to touch themselves, how to check for semen stains and vaginal discharges on children's pajamas, and people who shouldn't marry, Kellogg's complete list of whom spanned seventeen pages and included criminals, people suffering from syphilis or cancer, "cripples and defectives," "persons who are greatly disproportionate in size," paupers, "widely different races," tobacco users, jockeys, fops, loafers, and scheming dreamers, women who are giddy, gay, dressy, thoughtless, or fickle, and men who use profanity or whose "affections have been consumed in the fires of unhallowed lust." (Interestingly, however, he disputed the opinion that "the marriage of cousins results in the production of idiots, and other defectives," though he advised against it for other reasons.)

Today's feminists, in particular, would have had a field day with Kellogg, both because he wrote insulting books from the male perspective, e.g., *Ladies' Guide in Health and Disease: Girl-hood, Maidenhood, Wifehood, Motherhood*, wherein he mansplains such topics as "precocious puberty," "how to be beautiful," "secretion of milk in virgins," "why women as a class are dependent," "bad books," "the slavery of fashion," "sleeping of children with older people," "useful suggestions to young wives," "female weaknesses," and how to avoid becoming a prostitute—and because he was a strong advocate of female genital mutilation for nymphomaniacs, either by removing the clitoris altogether or by blistering it with carbolic acid, a chemical used in industrial paint strippers.

Though, to be fair, he also advocated punitive circumcision for immoral males in such cases where bandaging the genitals, tying the hands at night, or "covering the organs with a cage" failed to curb their enthusiasm for self-touching—further emphasizing that the procedure should be done without anesthesia or pain killers to ensure maximum punishment and remorse.

Draw your own conclusions, but some might say he was a real-world supervillain—and a creepy one at that.* He wrote at length about the bowel movements of schoolgirls† and, for some-

---

* Someone really ought to look into him as a candidate for Jack the Ripper, the infamous and still unidentified Victorian serial killer best remembered for mutilating London prostitutes in 1888, as there's reason to believe the killer was a surgeon (at least three of the victims had their organs removed) and, according to the only surviving witness, a foreigner. Kellogg, an American who would have been thirty-six at the time, would certainly have had the means and motive—and perhaps the opportunity—having traveled to London in the 1880s to study surgery.

† Writing, for example, that "school-girls are often very negligent" in "the necessity of attending promptly to the demands of nature for relief of the bowels and bladder" and that "ladies who desire a sweet breath—and what lady does not—should remember that retained feces are one of the most frequent causes of foul breath. The foul odors which ought to pass out through

one who hated intercourse, kept a separate bedroom from his wife, spent his honeymoon writing about the dangers of genitalia, and spent an awful lot of time administering thirty-minute massages of the womb and pelvic areas (both internal and external) to female patients twice a day, which he insisted on performing himself.*

Yet all of these remedies took a back seat to his obsession with food-based remedies, many of which were no less horrifying. Initially, the sanitarium's offerings consisted largely of zwieback, a sort of tasteless twice-baked German toast (made, ideally, using stale bread), and Kellogg's copycat version of granula, which he eventually renamed "Granola" in response to Jackson's lawyers; however, complaints of broken teeth soon inspired him to pursue softer alternatives. Among his lesser-known creations were Nuttose, a nut-based meat substitute meant to mimic the appearance and flavor of cold roast mutton (which for some reason never became a thing), and Nuttolene, a nut-based cream substitute that came in hermetically sealed cans, kept indefinitely, and could also replace butter or shortening—though it was his creation of a flaked corn cereal called Granose (the predecessor of Toasted Corn Flakes) that would make Kellogg a household name in the 1890s.

The first ready-to-eat breakfast cereal that didn't threaten to break people's teeth, Kellogg's corn flakes became so popular that they inspired what was essentially a cereal gold rush. Kellogg

---

the bowels find their way into the blood and escape at the lungs." He then quotes a Scottish physician: "Keep in the fear of the Lord, and your bowels open."

* "It is difficult for even the most intrepid medical historian to decipher just what exactly Dr. Kellogg was treating with pelvic massages," writes Howard Markel, an intrepid medical historian.

poured his first bowl in 1895, and by 1902 there were more than fifty cereal manufacturers in and around Battle Creek (a name that lent brands credibility by leading consumers to falsely believe they were associated with Kellogg's Battle Creek Sanitarium) followed by dozens more across the country: Boston Brown Flakes, Cerealine, Dr. Price's Corn Flakes, Famous Corn Flakes, Giant Flaked Corn, Jersey Bran Flakes, Mapl-Flake by Hygienic Food Company, Maple Flakes by Hosford Cereal and Grain Company, Oriole Breakfast Flakes, Purity Corn Flakes, Sanitarium, Squirrel Brand, University Brand Daintily-Crisped Flaked Corn, U.S. Honey Flakes, Watson Flaked Corn.

Many of these followed Kellogg's formula for outrageous health claims; for example, Grape-Nuts (created by a former patient of Kellogg's named C. W. Post, who allegedly stole the recipe from Kellogg's sanitarium safe) was billed as a "scientific health food" that cured malaria, heart disease, and appendicitis.* Others, like the makers of Korn-Kinks, sunk even lower by promoting their cereal with blackface and racial stereotypes. "It am suttenly wunnerful how w'ite folks kin mek jes' co'n tas' so good," read one 1907 advertisement.†

Yet Kellogg's biggest competition ultimately came from his own brother, Will "W.K." Kellogg, who, despite growing up in the same household, was less extreme than his older brother and

---

* In 1905, *Collier's* magazine refused to print these health claims in the interest of not killing off readers; Post fought back by publishing ads in competing papers accusing them of yellow journalism, blackmail, and journalistic prostitution, but *Collier's* successfully sued for libel and Post was forced to pay damages of $50,000 after a ten-day jury trial.

† Regrettably, this wouldn't be the last time racism was used to promote breakfast cereal; in the 1960s, Post advertised Sugar Rice Krinkles using a squinty-eyed mascot named "So-Hi the Chinese Boy," who carted the rice cereal around in a rickshaw.

disagreed with him on a number of key points. For example, he ate oysters, which his brother called the chemical equivalent of drinking urine and staged an intervention over; presumably slept with his own wife; and believed in making the lives of children happier rather than more painful.

These differences, combined with the fact that Will had played a crucial role in developing corn flakes behind the scenes and for years had helped his older brother run the sanitarium in exchange for little pay, little vacation time, and duties that included shining his brother's shoes, cleaning up after his horse, and taking dictation while he used the bathroom several times a day (during which he would often retrieve samples to prove his bowel movements smelled "as sweet as those of a nursing baby"), eventually inspired Will to begin manufacturing his own brand of breakfast cereal in 1906, calling it "Kellogg's Corn Flakes."

No surprise, Will's strategy for making cereal for everyone rather than just sick people—and sweetening his flakes with not just sugar but the industry's first free prizes, beginning with the *Funny Jungleland Moving Pictures Book* in 1909—turned out to be the better business plan; in fact, it's the reason Northwestern University has the Kellogg School of Management, endowed in 1979 by the John L. and Helen Kellogg Foundation, established by Will's grandson W.K. Kellogg II.

In 1920, following a decade of vicious court battles, Will won the legal right to the use of the family name (now known for such creations as Froot Loops, Frosted Flakes, Limited Edition Chocolate Frosted Flakes with Spoooky Marshmallows, Frosted Mini-Wheats, Corn Pops, Chocolate Peanut Butter Corn Pops, Rice Krispies, Cocoa Krispies, and Rice Krispies Treats), and the sanitarium eventually fell into bankruptcy.

And the rest of the industry followed suit (either by declaring bankruptcy, like the sanitarium, or adding sugar and marshmallows, like Will). In fact, more than a century after the creation of the original corn flakes, nearly 90 percent of American breakfast cereal is made by four brands, all founded during the original Kellogg era. These include Kellogg's; General Mills, which started out as a Minnesota flour mill in 1866 but went on to make such magically delicious cereals as Trix, Cocoa Puffs, Lucky Charms, and Cinnamon Toast Crunch; Quaker Oats, which began as an Ohio oat mill in 1881 but is now owned by PepsiCo and has gone on to make Cap'n Crunch, Cap'n Crunch's Oops! All Berries, Cap'n Crunch's Cotton Candy Crunch, Cap'n Crunch's Berrytastic Pancake Mix, and Cap'n Crunch's Ocean Blue Artificially Maple Flavored Syrup; and Post, founded in 1895 by the guy who allegedly stole the recipe for Grape-Nuts from the sanitarium safe and now responsible for Fruity Pebbles, Honeycomb, and Oreo O's.

So the industry as a whole pivoted completely, from Graham flour and granula to Cookie Crisp and Count Chocula.

And this wasn't the first time a food or ingredient has undergone such a dramatic shift; a lot of the foods in our pantries and refrigerators were, once upon a time, thought to be evil or dangerous. For example, potatoes, as we'll read in chapter 10, used to be associated with witchcraft and Devil worship; before they were America's most popular vegetable (owing largely to their use as French fries), people called them "the Devil's apples," blamed them for causing syphilis, and literally burned them at the stake. Tomatoes, similarly, were said to be poisonous and used to summon werewolves.

Almost anything we can put into our mouths or onto our skin has, at one time, been vilified—or praised—for stirring up "the unclean fires of morbid lust."

Explains Jeremy MacClancy:

A short list of aphrodisiacs might include anchovies, ant juice, artichokes, barbel,* bamboo shoots, basil, wild cabbage, calves' brains, camel bone, caper berries, stuffed capon, caraway, caviar, milk of chameleon, crab-apple jelly, crocodile tail, preserved dates, deer sperm, dill, doves' brains, eel soup, egg-yolk in a small glass of cognac, fennel, flea-wort sap, dried frog, gall of a jackal, game birds, garlic, ginger omelettes, goat's testicle boiled in milk and sugar, goose tongues, grapes, halibut, hare soup, haricot beans, herring, horse penis, horseradish, mackerel, lamprey, leeks, powdered lizard with sweet wine, marjoram, milk pudding, mugwort, musk, ninjin,† nutmeg, oysters, paprika, pâté of bone-marrow, Parmesan cheese, pepper, plaice,‡ quince jelly, ray, radishes, rhinoceros horn, rocket, rosemary, saffron, sage, salmon, candied sea holly, shallots, sheep's kidneys, spinach, swan's genitals, tarragon, terrapin soup, thyme, turmeric, viper broth, woodcock, and pineapple fritters.

Indeed, long before Graham questioned the wholesomeness of common bread, Athenian women were baking bread in the shape of penises and using olive oil as a lubricant to make economical sex toys called *olisbokollix* ("loaf-of-bread dildo"), and women in seventeenth-century England were baking loaves in the shape of their own sex organs (literally pressing the dough

---

* A relative of Carp, so named for the mustache-like barbs that hang from its mouth.
† Ginseng.
‡ A European flatfish.

against their skin as a mold) out of a magical belief that the men who ate them would fall in love with them.

Nor were Graham and Kellogg the first to suggest the moral superiority of a bland diet and implicate pleasure and flavor as barriers to happiness and spiritual fulfillment.

Writes Plato, circa 360 BC:

> Those, therefore, who have no experience of wisdom and goodness, and do nothing but have a good time . . . never rise higher to see or reach the true top, nor achieve any real fulfilment or sure and unadulterated pleasure. They bend over their tables, like sheep with heads bent over their pasture and eyes on the ground, they stuff themselves and copulate, and in their greed for more they kick and butt each other with hooves and horns of steel, and kill each other because they are not satisfied, as they cannot be while they fill with unrealities a part of themselves which is itself unreal and insatiable.

Similar ideals lay behind the Christian prohibition of meat during Lent; the Jewish tradition of eating bitter herbs on Passover; the Japanese philosophy of *wabi-sabi* that teaches "an acceptance and appreciation of the impermanent, imperfect, and incomplete nature of everything," often observed by the aesthetic of chipped or asymmetric tea bowls; and Brillat-Savarin's declaration that "Men who stuff themselves and grow tipsy know neither how to eat nor how to drink."

Meanwhile, the Greek philosopher Epicurus (341–270 BC), whose name has become falsely synonymous with sexual and culinary hedonism, was perhaps history's biggest fan of bland breakfasts, writing "To whom a little is not enough, nothing is enough. Give me a barley-cake and water, and I am ready to vie even with Zeus in happiness," "I am thrilled with pleasure in the body, when I live on bread and water, and I spit upon luxurious pleasures not for their own sake, but because of the inconveniences that follow them," and "We ought to be on our guard against any dishes which, though we are eagerly desirous of them beforehand, yet leave no sense of gratitude behind after we have enjoyed them."

His basic idea being that true pleasure was the absence of pain—and that bland foods tended to remove the pains of hunger, leading to sustainable pleasure, while luxurious foods tended to make the rest of the world seem bland by comparison, leading to short-lived pleasure and prolonged pain.

So Epicurus would have liked Kellogg's original corn flakes, not because they were hard or righteous, nor because sugar was evil, but rather because starting the day with frosting, free prizes, and marshmallows tends to make the rest of the day seem bitter.

CHAPTER 4

CHILDREN OF THE CORN

And thus it is that the maize plant was the bridge over which English civilization crept, tremblingly and uncertainly, at first, then boldly and surely . . .

—ARTHUR C. PARKER

Remarkably, the saga of corn flakes—from ready-to-eat torture device to the seed that spawned an industry of confectionery breakfasts that turn milk pink—might actually be the least interesting thing about corn. Certainly, it's one of the least impactful, just a blip in the annals of a grain that's responsible for not just the development of modern breakfast cereal but modern civilization as a whole.

In fact, corn is right up there with fire in terms of anthropological game changers. Yet while the domestication of fire turned out to be a lucky break, whether the domestication of corn has been a good thing is still up for debate, as it's a relatively modern invention. And to call corn an invention is entirely accurate, as it wouldn't exist without humans—nor would we, or most things we depend on, exist without corn.

You see, up until roughly ten or twelve thousand years ago corn wasn't a thing, and neither was farming. Up to that point, everyone who'd ever lived had survived by hunting and gathering: roaming around in nature and getting their groceries in the wild by foraging for things like roots, grains, acorns, snails, and seasonal berries.

It's tempting to picture these early foragers as savage and

uncivilized, because they were too ignorant to, say, live in over-crowded cities, fill oceans with single-use plastic containers, and breed animals in dark, crowded cages amid their own feces after cutting off their beaks, horns, and testicles without anesthetics. Certainly they weren't civilized in the sense that they weren't citizens of urban communities with immovable structures and civic laws and obligations, but that doesn't mean they were unintelligent—and in many ways they enjoyed a higher quality of life than the agrarians who replaced them.

Remember all that stuff in the last chapter about the Unabomber calling the Industrial Revolution "a disaster for the human race" and the Epicurean weariness of things that end up causing more problems than they're worth? Well, the shift from hunting and gathering to sedentary agriculture gives these arguments a lot of ammunition. Farming, for example, generally led to a decline in food quality and nutrition, as people started eating a smaller variety of foods due to their dependence on a small number of staple crops and consuming less protein, too, as they spent less time hunting, trapping, and scavenging for meat. And any plants and animals they did eat were generally less nutritious than their wild equivalents, having been either grown in depleted soils or fed crops from these soils. Breeding animals in close captivity also encouraged the spread of parasites and disease. Meanwhile, staying in one place wasn't good for humans, either, as it spread germs through contaminated food and water supplies and communal waste systems—or a lack thereof.

Plus, having land and resources meant people suddenly had to defend themselves from outsiders, so they had to erect fences and raise armies and create political structures and start paying taxes to fund all of this and put up with neighbors moving in across the street—all those buzzkills Epicurus warned us about.

Farmers also had to work harder than nomadic hunter-gatherers and generally had a lot less free time, as farming returned only about a third as many calories for one's labor as foraging once you account for things like land preparation, seeding, irrigation, and harvesting. Just think how much easier it would've been to teach a kid how to gather nuts and berries versus teaching a kid how to farm; would you eat better—and live better—if everyone in your family (including young children, pregnant women, and the elderly) were farming foods or gathering them?

In fact, in the 1960s a botanist named Jack Rodney Harlan asked himself that same question and decided to find out by using a primitive stone sickle to gather wild wheat in Turkey; in the end, he was able to collect "the equivalent of more than two pounds of clean wild einkorn grain per hour," suggesting that "in about a three-week period a family could gather more grain than it could possibly consume in a year." Conversely, three weeks of farming won't get you much other than blisters.

So in many ways, agriculture was sort of a misfire.

"Instead of being a universal diversion," writes British historian Felipe Fernández-Armesto, "hunting became an elite privilege and a varied diet became the reward of power. The ensuing refinements of civilization—towering monuments built at popular expense for elite satisfaction—meant, for most people, more toil and more tyranny. Women got shackled to the food-chain. Tillers of the soil became something like a caste, from which prowess could not raise them except in time of war."

So those uncivilized hunters and gatherers weren't so uncivilized after all.

There are a lot of theories as to why they started farming, but the general consensus is that our ancestors never consciously decided to "settle" and "stop playing the fields" but held out as long as they could and slowly surrendered to forces outside their control. For example, it's probably not a coincidence that the first instances of farming started to occur around the end of the last ice age, as warmer temperatures and melting glaciers began opening up these huge masses of previously uninhabitable (and unworkable) lands, which suddenly gave animals a lot more room to roam and evade hunters, making it more difficult to catch and eat them. As B. W. Higman puts it, "people were impelled to move on because they felt that they would starve if they stayed where they were and could only hope that where they went would be a better place. They were pushed rather than pulled."

At the same time, this also would have made the earth a lot greener and more fruitful, which would have made gathering food more lucrative and also made it possible to start amassing seeds and roots in excess and stockpiling them in subterranean pits, where they'd be cooler and out of the reach of most animals.

Eventually, some of these groceries would have gotten wet and started sprouting, and suddenly, people were farmers.

Or, at the very least, they had some incentive not to stray too far and to keep returning. It probably also didn't hurt that some of these wet ingredients, like wheat and barley, would have led to the discovery of fermentation and beermaking—which might have been the bigger incentive.

Then one thing led to another, and people had more free time, and no one had anywhere they needed to be in the morning, and there was alcohol involved, and they'd already dug pits for food and maybe even to bury their dead and to serve as foundations for houses, and they started having more kids, and then they needed more crops to feed those kids and more kids to work the crops, and before they knew it, they'd laid down literal and figurative roots and could no longer just pick up and leave. Pretty much the same thing that happened with fire.

And nothing captures this human-plant codependence better than our relationship with corn. This sort of domestication was happening all over the world at roughly the same time, as civilizations began cultivating the native grasses that would become their regional staples: things like rice in Asia, wheat in Europe, and an ancient ancestor of corn in North America called *teosinte* (though unlike indigenous rice and wheat, *teosinte* bears almost no resemblance to its modern form and was nearly inedible).

We're not even sure what the people who first ate *teosinte* actually did with it; for starters, an ear of it contained only five to twelve kernels compared to the five to twelve *hundred* on an ear of corn today, and each of them was only around one-tenth the weight of a modern kernel. So an entire ear of *teosinte* would have been about the size of a cigarette, though probably shorter.

And there wasn't a central cob, so you couldn't eat the whole thing as you can baby corn.* You could eat only the tiny kernels, which were individually wrapped in an almost impenetrable outer casing. Picture five or six grains of rice wrapped up like tamales and hot glued to a blade of grass, and that was pretty much what it looked like—and probably not far from what it tasted like. The best guess we can make is that the first farmers popped *teosinte* like popcorn, crushed it with their teeth and sucked on it, fermented it and drank the resulting liquid, or possibly ground it with stones and soaked it in water to remove the casing, then ground it again to make a dough for primitive tortillas.

---

* Baby corn, as the name suggests, is just ordinary corn that's been harvested early; however, it's actually harvested before being pollinated, so calling it "unfertilized corn ovaries" might be more accurate, if less appealing.

Yet for some reason our ancestors saw potential in this lowly grass and kept replanting it, choosing only the seeds with the most attractive traits—say, height, girth, tenderness, and disease resistance—until it grew into a tall and dependable grain they could live on. So it was a lot like dating in high school.

This was essentially the same process that gave us domesticated dogs from savage wolves, as we saw in chapter 1. The French bulldog, in particular, is a great illustration of this, as it was systemically bred (and inbred) to emphasize traits that humans liked as opposed to those that were actually advantageous or intended by nature, like facial folds that are prone to developing yeast infections and short noses that obstruct breathing and cause sleep apnea. Adorable, right? And this was done not just to the point that they could no longer survive in the wild but also to the point at which they could no longer survive without surgery; most French bulldogs, upward of 80 percent, have to be delivered by caesarean section because of their disproportionately wide heads—which, paradoxically, are often too small for their brains, causing neurological issues such as drooling and impaired movement, not to mention their predisposition to heart disease, reproductive issues, skin conditions, ulcers, pneumonia, and heatstroke.*

And we handicapped corn in much the same way. Remember

---

* Other notable examples of human interference with natural selection include black-and-white moth populations becoming predominantly black over time to better blend in with industrial soot; modern owls becoming increasingly brown instead of white in response to climate change and decreased snowfall; urban birds developing shorter wingspans to aid them in dodging traffic (after behaviorally adapting to build nests under bridges and highways in lieu of available trees); Atlantic cod becoming smaller and reproducing earlier in response to commercial fishery; and mice developing larger jaws in response to the local dominance and unnaturally large kernel size of corn.

that tough outer casing on *teosinte* (the one we gradually meta-morphosized into a soft, easy-to-peel husk)? Well, it turns out that it was put there for a reason: to protect the kernels from the elements and the digestive systems of animals so they could stay intact long enough to propagate and fulfill their ecological purpose as seeds.

The same goes for the small number of kernels and the lack of a central cob. You see, when ripe, individual kernels of *teosinte* would naturally separate and fall to the ground, where, protected by that tough outer covering, they'd essentially plant themselves. But corn's unprotected kernels stay attached to their cob, so if they do somehow manage to avoid rotting or being eaten in the wild, they still can't propagate because each cob deposits five hundred to twelve hundred of them in one spot, so any kernels that do germinate will fight the others for nutrients and essentially starve one another. And all this is compounded by the transformation of *teosinte* from a fat, wide bush that naturally spaced itself into these tall, thin stalks that can grow right next to one another, creating a condition in which you've got cobs basically committing mass suicide by dropping on top of cobs—making corn the only grass on the planet that can't re-seed itself.

And even once it is seeded, corn is still dependent on humans. A few hundred years ago, this relationship was more low maintenance. The Iroquois planted corn together with beans and squash in the same ground in a process called intercropping. The corn would deplete the soil of nitrogen but grow tall stalks for the beans to climb and wrap their vines around. Nodules on the roots of those beans would then provide a home for nitrogen-fixing rhizobia bacteria that would convert unusable nitrogen gas in the air into biologically available ammonia in the soil.

Finally, the squash would provide ground cover, inhibiting the growth of weeds while providing critical shade to keep the soil from drying out. No one knows how the Iroquois figured this out, by the way. Meanwhile, "civilized" colonists were attempting to fish with frying pans and eating their own dogs to keep from starving.

But that was before we committed to growing corn across a 350,000-square-mile belt of North America, a scale that required abandoning nature's symbiotic cycles for cold mechanical efficiency. Rather than waiting for nature to replenish itself seasonally by planting corn with mutualistic beans and squash, we now have to inject the soil with artificial chemicals and fertilizers, things like anhydrous ammonia and phosphorus, both of which have been designated "chemicals of interest" by the US Department of Homeland Security for their potential to be used in terrorist attacks (anhydrous ammonia also doubles as a key ingredient in the manufacture of methamphetamine, making it a common target of theft). And because this creates a giant sandbox for weeds and insects, we then have to treat the area with artificial pesticides and fungicides—and because the weeds and insects keep building a resistance to these poisons, we have to continually develop new formulas and come up with feasible alternatives, such as spreading lab-created STDs to make parasites sexually sterile or seeding croplands with sterile male insects to control the population, because that worked so well in *Jurassic Park*.

And think about what all this means in terms of fuel and irrigation; we're talking about more than 93 million acres of cropland in the United States alone, spread across states such as Texas, California, and Colorado, which aren't known for having a ton of expendable water. So in addition to consuming more fertilizer than all other US crops combined—about 19 billion pounds of it each year—corn requires roughly 400,000 gallons of water and 140 gallons of fuel per acre for transportation, processing, and equipment. Remember, we're talking about almost 100 million acres—and growing—in the United States alone. All that fertilizer also tends to pollute the groundwater, so we then have to spend billions of dollars sucking the same chemicals out of the ground that we put into it.

And the scary thing is, we can't pump the brakes on any of this because we depend on corn as much as it depends on us—practically to the point at which we can't reseed ourselves without it, either.

Sure, most developed countries could probably swear off foods such as corn on the cob and canned corn and maybe even corn flakes and tortillas*—but corn is a secret ingredient in almost everything we eat. So we'd have to swear off meat, fish, and poultry, too, as more than a third of our corn supply is used for animal feed, which means we'd also have to give up anything involving eggs or dairy products.

Thanks to the widespread use of corn-based sweeteners such as high-fructose corn syrup (the use of which peaked at 49.1 pounds per person annually in 1999 but has since dropped to a no less apocalyptic 31 pounds per person in 2019), we'd also have to cut out soft drinks, candy, condiments, breads, breakfast cereals (and marshmallows), chewing gum, snack foods, and baby food—or at least start buying better brands. Then there's cornstarch and corn flour, pervasively found in baking mixes, instant

---

* Note that a lot of developing countries couldn't do this, as corn is still the primary source of calories in areas of sub-Saharan Africa, South Asia, and Latin America.

foods, fried foods (in the breading and batter), frozen foods, and certain pan coatings.

We'd have to forget about Mexican food as a whole, as well as a lot of gluten-free products, which rely on corn to mimic the viscoelasticity of gluten, and a lot of beers, whiskeys, gins, and vodkas made from various fermented corn products. Not to mention any Chinese food that uses cornstarch as a thickener or nonfermented soy sauce made from hydrolyzed vegetable protein, corn syrup, and caramel color.

Oh, and anything that contains baking powder, caramel, cellulose, citric acid, dextrin, dextrose, inositol, malt, maltodextrin, monosodium glutamate (MSG), semolina, sodium erythorbate, sorbitol, starch, vanilla extract, xanthan gum, and xylitol. Note that corn isn't always present in this group, but it can be. Nor is this even close to an exhaustive list, so this doesn't constitute medical advice if you're allergic to corn—and if you are allergic, good freaking luck, as the legislation requiring food manufacturers to disclose the presence of potential food allergens like milk, eggs, fish, shellfish, tree nuts, peanuts, wheat, and soybeans doesn't apply to corn. And even if it did—well, we'll get to that in chapter 10. (Turn to page 186 to find out why food labeling is a meaningless sham.)

In fact, the average American consumes about three pounds of food containing corn or corn products every day, often unknowingly. Eat an apple, and you could be eating corn in the layer of food-grade wax that's applied to apples to make them look pretty and prevent them from drying out. Eat a cheeseburger, and there's a good chance you're eating corn feed in the beef and cheese; corn flour in the bun; corn syrup in the ketchup and pickles; corn-based ethylene gas in the tomatoes (used to make them ripen quicker); corn-based dextrose (as a stabilizer) in the salt; and, if the meat was frozen, cornstarch in the coating that protected it from freezer burn. Not to mention, probably, a slew of corn-based binders, emulsifiers, colorants, flavorings, sweeteners, preservatives, anticoagulants, and hair removal agents. (You might remember headlines from 2011, when Taco Bell admitted its beef was only 88 percent beef, with much of the remaining 12 percent coming from corn by-products like maltodextrin, citric acid, and modified cornstarch.)

And even if products containing these ingredients are labeled "grass fed," that doesn't mean the animals they came from weren't also corn fed. In 2018, consumers filed a lawsuit against the makers of Kerrygold butter for deceptively claiming it was produced from the milk of "grass-fed cows," when really they were also fed corn, soybeans, and other foods; however, a California federal district court dismissed the complaint, ruling that it was unreasonable for consumers to expect cows to eat only grass.

Still, human consumption accounts for only around 10 percent of the corn supply, as it's also an industrial ingredient in basically everything: adhesives, antibiotics, aspirin, ceiling tiles, chalk, cork, cosmetics, crayons, disinfectants, dry-cell batteries, engine fuel, fireworks, inks, plastics, rubber tires, soap, wallpaper, wallpaper glue; it's probably in the paper and the adhesive binding of this book.

So if you ordered that cheeseburger to go, corn was probably in the packaging, too, as well as in the paper and ink of your receipt; and if you cooked it at home on a grill, corn was in the charcoal briquettes and the match you used to ignite them.

And we haven't even covered ethanol, a corn-based biofuel that accounts for another few billion bushels, or roughly a third of the US crop yield. The Energy Independence and Security Act of 2007 mandated that transportation fuels in the United

States had to be blended with a certain amount of biofuel to reduce our dependence on foreign oil—phasing up from 9 billion gallons in 2008 to 36 billion gallons by 2022. Ethanol accounts for about 94 percent of this biofuel, and about 98 percent of that ethanol comes from corn, so approximately 10 percent of the fuel you buy from most gas stations is corn based.

Add all this up, and we're talking about trillions of dollars in investments we can't walk away from: a global economy of farmers, ranchers, exporters, refiners, food and beverage manufacturers, and . . . whatever you call workers in the fertilizer industry; 1.1 billion metric tons of raw material annually used by everything from food labs to furniture makers; and a primary food source for 230 million people and approximately 20 billion feed animals (not including the innumerable insects, worms, and rodents that feed on corn crops without permission).

And even if we could somehow walk away from corn without having to worry about things like foreign dependence, jobs, and logistics, policy makers would never let it happen thanks to the agricultural lobbyists who've spent more than $2.5 billion in the past two decades protecting the interests of farmers (interests that include the $5 billion in corn subsidies they receive annually) and farming by-products, not to mention food and beverage manufacturers, industrial manufacturers, pharmaceutical companies, ethanol producers, and so on.

Consumers wouldn't let it happen, either. When Coca-Cola infamously changed its formula in 1985 with the introduction of New Coke, consumers lost their shit, publicly emptying cans into sewer drains and overwhelming the company's switchboard with more than forty thousand complaints. Fans threatened class action lawsuits and founded support groups such as the Society for the Preservation of the Real Thing and Old Cola Drinkers of America, the latter of which reportedly received up to 4,200 calls a day from outraged sympathizers. When the company finally gave in and went back to its original formula after just seventy-nine days, it was such a big deal that television stations interrupted *General Hospital* to cover the announcement live. Senator David Pryor of Arkansas called it a "decision of historical significance . . . proof that certain American institutions can never change." (Meanwhile, the company had been secretly changing its formula all along for several years prior to this by gradually replacing cane sugar with corn syrup.)

And that was before the internet and social media.

How would people today react if virtually every soft drink and snack food they were familiar with instantly vanished from shelves? Or if suddenly they had to eat 100 percent beef instead of 88 percent?

What makes all of this more remarkable is that corn really isn't even that ideal a food source, as it's deficient in essential amino acids such as lysine and tryptophan, which the human body can't make on its own, and contains a biologically unavailable form of niacin, which the human body can make, but not without tryptophan.

This was another reason the Iroquois planted corn together with beans and squash: neither corn, beans, nor squash contains sufficient amounts of all nine amino acids essential for human life, but when eaten together, they provide a proper balance, similar to the way they balance the nutrients in soil. The Iroquois also cooked their corn in a mixture of water and ashes, which created an alkaline solution that chemically unlocked corn's protein-bound niacin to make it more digestible—a process called nixtamalization, from the Aztec *nextli* ("ashes") and *tamalli* ("masa"), also the source of the Spanish *tamale*.

Again, no one knows how they knew to do this—though the process also made corn kernels easier to grind; released pectin from the cell walls, which made it easier to create a pliable dough for tortillas; and gave corn an earthier flavor and aroma by catalyzing certain volatile compounds. So those may have been the intended outcomes, making balanced amino acids just a happy accident.

Regardless of their intent, the Iroquois were still way ahead of the rest of the world, as these processes enabled them to consume corn as a staple while still maintaining a balanced diet; meanwhile, the unfortunate world cultures that adopted corn without nixtamalization (including much of Europe, Africa, and the American South) faced deadly epidemics of niacin deficiency, causing pellagra, so named in 1771 after the Italian *pelle* ("skin") and *agra* ("rough")—as, in addition to symptoms such as death, diarrhea, dementia, insomnia, aggression, and sensitivity to light, the condition also causes hyperkeratosis, or rough, scaly skin. These outbreaks were endemic for hundreds of years before anyone made the connection to corn; in fact, medical knowledge was so far off that niacin deficiency symptoms might have been responsible for the mythology of vampires, reports of which started around the same time and in the same places as pellagra—according to some sources, within a year of each other.

As Jeffrey and William Hampl explain in the *Journal of the Royal Society of Medicine*, the symptoms of pellagra and vampire folklore were remarkably similar:

Just as vampires must avoid sunlight to maintain their strength and keep from decay, pellagrins are hypersensitive to sunlight, with the margins of their dermatitis sharply demarcated. Sun-exposed areas at first become red and thick with hyperkeratosis and scaling. This is followed by inflammation and oedema, which eventually leads to depigmented, shiny skin alternating with rough, brown, scaly areas. With repeated episodes of erythema, a pellagrin's skin becomes paper-thin and assumes a parchment-like texture.

Other pellagra symptoms include cracked red tongues and lips, easily mistaken for blood, and a rash or string of lesions on the neck (known as Casal's necklace after the physician Gaspar Casal, who first recorded the symptom in 1735 in Spain), which might explain the myth about vampires having visible neck bites. And the simultaneous symptoms of dementia, insomnia, and aggression would explain the correlation of pellagra epidemics and the reports of nighttime "vampire" attacks in eighteenth-century Europe, concentrated in areas such as Poland, Russia, and Macedonia (i.e., the general vicinity of Transylvania).

And this isn't that far-fetched. Look up photographs of pellagra sufferers, and ask yourself whether you'd try to run a stake through their hearts, too, if they stumbled into your house late at night.

In 2017, researchers also discovered a link between corn-induced niacin deficiency and cannibalism in hamsters, which developed black tongues and signs of dementia. Not coincidentally, the study specifically followed European hamsters, which are critically endangered largely due to the regional domination of corn and subsequent lack of alternative, niacin-rich food sources in their natural habitats; in other words, they're facing now what humans faced in the eighteenth century.

Ultimately, it took scientists roughly two hundred years to identify niacin deficiency as the real culprit behind pellagra when, in 1937, the American biochemist Conrad Elvehjem figured out that niacin supplementation cured the disease in dogs—and later in humans. Some twenty years earlier, another physician named Joseph Goldberger had come close when he narrowed down the cause to diet and was able to cure infected orphans and prisoners in the southern United States by feeding them fresh foods (as opposed to just cornmeal, molasses, and fatback). He wasn't able to identify corn or niacin in particular, however, and faced ridicule from the rest of the scientific community, which insisted pellagra was a disease spread by things like sewage systems or drinking water and attempted to treat it with arsenic and electric shocks. This, despite the fact that Goldberger had injected himself, his wife, and several friends with the blood of pellagra patients and held "filth parties" during which guests consumed pellagric blood, scales, fecal matter, urine, and nasal secretions to prove it wasn't infectious.*

All this for a plant that isn't even that good for us.

In fact, the history of corn reads a lot like Shakespeare's *The Taming of the Shrew*, wherein a man agrees to marry a woman no one else wants because she's too willful and independent—then proceeds to starve and torture her until she breaks and becomes obedient. (Or, some might argue, until she realizes it's better to placate her new husband and *feign* obedience.) Except it's not clear whether humanity or corn is the shrew here. Did we really

---

* If you're thinking this story belongs in a comic book, you're right; it was covered in *Real Life Comics* in July 1943: "Meanwhile—a slow death inched across America's southland!"

domesticate corn—or did corn domesticate us? Did we tame a wild weed and use it to spread our roots all over the world—or was it the other way around?

Then again, *Shrew* is more of a lighthearted comedy, so maybe corn's history is more like *Romeo and Juliet*, wherein two teenagers enter a tragic relationship because each imagines the other to be a perfect match, when really they don't know each other from Adam (or, in Romeo's case, from Rosaline, the other girl he falls madly in "love" with right before Juliet) and a lot of people end up dead or miserable because of it.

Or maybe it's more like the plot of *Invasion of the Body Snatchers*, the black-and-white version from 1956, wherein the world is quietly invaded by alien seedpods that take over people's bodies and assimilate with the population in order to colonize Earth and consume all of its resources, only nobody realizes until it's too late and the spores are everywhere—and the seeds are already inside us. . . .

CHAPTER 5

HONEY LAUNDERING

Instead of dirt and poison we have rather chosen to fill our hives with honey and wax; thus furnishing mankind with the two noblest of things, which are sweetness and light.

—JONATHAN SWIFT

Haceos miel, y paparos han moscas.
("Make yourself honey, and the flies will devour you.")

—MIGUEL DE CERVANTES SAAVEDRA

"He that would eat the fruit must first climb the tree and get it": but when that fruit is honey, he that wants it must first cut it down.

—ROBERT CARLTON (BAYNARD RUSH HALL)

The honey is sweet, but the bee has a sting.

—BENJAMIN FRANKLIN

For thousands of years, people have heralded honey not just as a sweetener and an important food source but as a metaphor for purity, love, compassion, even godliness. We tell our children that they'll attract more flies with honey than vinegar; call our loved ones things like "honey pie," "honey bun," or just "honey"; and celebrate the union of marriage with "honeymoons."

Ancient Babylonian and Sumerian priests used honey to exorcise evil spirits and poured it onto walls or foundations to consecrate temples; early Christians used it in baptisms; while medieval Jews smeared it on tablets so children would lick them and associate learning (and scripture) with sweetness; the Greeks, Romans, and Chinese placed it next to corpses to bid them a sweet afterlife; and in traditional Hindi weddings, honey was rubbed on, um, several of a bride's orifices to ensure a sweet marriage.

Hitler gave honey to wounded soldiers with a sweet note that read *"Ein Gruss des Führers an seine Verwundeten"* ("Greetings from the Führer to his wounded")—though, fittingly, it was really just cheap imitation honey made from beet syrup and yellow food coloring—while in ancient Germany, fathers were allowed to murder their own children, but only if they hadn't yet tasted honey, which magically protected them from infanticide.

Yet no one ever talks about the dark side of honey: how it kills babies and causes hallucinations—or how it's the one food that never goes bad* because it sucks the life out of everything it touches, making "honey" a much better nickname for toxic ex-lovers who shouldn't be left around children.

Look up the etymology of the term *honeymoon*, and you'll find that it wasn't coined to celebrate a couple's living happily ever after but sort of the opposite. The moon, here, isn't an allusion to enchantment, fairy-tale wishes, or all-night sex—but to fading, the point being that love, like the phasing moon, "is no sooner full than it begins to wane."

> *Honie-moone*: applied to those that love well at the first, and not so well afterwards, but will change as doth the moone.
>
> —John Minsheu, *Guide into Tongues*, 1617

> *Hony-moon*: applied to those married persons that love well at first and decline in affection afterwards: it is hony now, but it will change as the moon.
>
> —Thomas Blount, *Glossographia*, 1656

---

* Note that honey can crystallize or become cloudy over time, particularly if it's kept between 50° and 70°F or comes from floral sources that yield higher glucose ratios, such as alfalfa. However, crystallized honey is still perfectly good to eat—and is sometimes preferred, as in the case of creamed honey—and you can always return it to normal by gradually heating it in a water bath to between 140° and 149°F.

Look closer at the adage that honey attracts more flies than vinegar, and you'll find it's not that simple. The saying dates back to the seventeenth century, from the Italian *"Il mele catta più mosche, che non fà l'aceto"* ("Honey gets more flyes to it, than doth viniger"). Meanwhile, the practice goes back even further, to the Egyptian pharaoh Pepy II (2278–2184 BC), who allegedly slathered naked slaves in honey and made them stand around him like human flypaper, so flies would bother them instead of him.

But the actual science of attracting flies, explains Sean O'Donnell, professor of BEES (Biodiversity, Earth & Environmental Science) at Drexel University, is complicated. Adult flies don't tend to live very long, so they don't need a lot of nutrients; from the moment they're born, they're on an immediate decline during which they're just burning out their bodies, so they basically just need sugars to fuel their metabolically expensive flight apparatus and keep those fires burning—and from that perspective, honey is the more attractive food source.

However, female flies have the added burden of foraging for their offspring and finding places to lay their eggs, and their larvae require a completely different resource, namely rotting fruit, so they're attracted to vinegary chemicals not for themselves but for their larvae—and fertile males are sometimes drawn to these sources, too, because they're good places to pick up females. Then, to make things more complex, fruit that's overly decayed can have too much bacteria, which can be fatal to larvae, so flies tend to seek out Goldilocks concentrations of these vinegary chemicals and avoid sources that are either too vinegary or not vinegary enough.

So really, whether you'll attract more flies with honey or vinegar depends on the age, gender, sex drive, and mating status of each fly as well as the concentration of the vinegar—and possibly on the season, the thirst and stress levels of each fly, and the time of day, for reasons not worth getting into. If you're desperate to attract flies and don't know this information, you're probably best served by mixing honey and vinegar together, which has a cumulative effect, and maybe adding a packet of Truvia, which contains a low-calorie (corn-based) sweetener called erythritol that doesn't attract flies but does sterilize and kill them.*

Or you could try using beer or semen, which, evidence suggests, might work even better. There aren't a ton of studies on this, for obvious reasons, but beer outperformed decayed banana, fresh banana, sugar, vinegar, and sugar mixed with vinegar in a series of tests dating back to 1913—and Annalisa Durdle, a forensics expert who more recently tested the food preferences of flies for biological fluids commonly found at crime scenes (e.g., blood, semen, and saliva), calls semen "the crack cocaine of the fly world." (Coincidentally, beer and semen tend to be more popular than honey with humans, too, which is another reason to revise the adage.)

That history tends to euphemize honey isn't just due to its sweetness but also to its supposed simplicity. Even in ancient times, honey wasn't the only available sweetener. Before colonists introduced honeybees to North America (Native Americans called them "white man's flies"), indigenous cultures were cutting into maple trees with tomahawks to extract maple syrup; people in the Middle East were boiling raisins, grapes, and locust beans to make a sweet syrup called *dibs*; and the Romans

---

* Note that erythritol is generally recognized as safe for human consumption by the FDA, and O'Donnell is currently evaluating its use as a human- and pet-safe insecticide.

were boiling grapes to make a sweet reduction called *sapa* or *defructum* and using a sweetener they called *sugar of lead*, also known as lead acetate, which looked and tasted like rock candy but was also highly poisonous, sort of the Roman equivalent of eating lead paint chips. (Not to suggest *sapa* and *defructum* were any safer, as they were usually boiled in lead pots, resulting in a concentration about 170,000 times as high as today's legal limit for lead in bottled drinking water.*)

What stood out most about honey, then, wasn't just that it was sweet but that it was simple and ready to eat—no straining, skinning, boiling, fermenting, or killing required. If you think about it, eating, throughout most of recorded history, was a particularly bloody and noxious affair: you were either slaughtering and butchering animals or scavenging from those that were already dead, pulling your dinner directly from the dirt, or milking it from the glands of goats or cows (and maybe storing some of that milk in the dried stomach of another animal until it spoiled and turned into cheese). Even your bread would have pieces of dirt, insects, and stone in it from milling. So there was a lot of blood, sinew, and nature involved, and you also needed tools to clean things, make fire, and cut away the rot.

But then there's honey—this glistening, golden syrup that

---

* Some scholars believe that sugar of lead played a significant role in the fall of the Roman Empire by causing rampant lead intoxication among the Roman elite. Similarly, the use of lead acetate as a sweetener in Colonial bread making alongside lead equipment in the distillation of Colonial rum and cider may explain some of the strange behaviors described in the Salem witch trials—as behaviors such as violent contortions, hyperirritability, and aggression are all symptomatic of lead poisoning. (Another explanation is ergot, a precursor of LSD that comes from the fungal contamination of rye and can also cause muscle convulsions, hallucinations, and violent fits.)

just magically appears in the forest, prepackaged in cute little rows of tiny wax hexagons.

As food historian Bee Wilson writes, "Honey was so extraordinary, so ready to eat and utterly unlike the other basic foods—consider how much more edible and instantly nourishing a honeycomb is than a sheaf of wheat, a pig, a cow—that it seemed it could be fabricated only in the heavens."

And the fact that honey was made in the secrecy of a hive only reinforced this idea. By the way, we're not talking about the beliefs of Neanderthals or illiterate peasants but of great thinkers like Aristotle, who believed that "honey falls from the air, principally about the rising of the stars, and when the rainbow rests upon the earth." Pliny the Elder was slightly more specific, insisting that honey fell "mostly at the rising of the constellations, and more especially when Sirius is shining; never, however, before the rising of the Vergiliae, and then just before day-break," and that it was either "the sweat of the heavens," "a saliva emanating from the stars," or "a juice exuding from the air while purifying itself."*

This opacity over honey's origins also led to its biblical kosher status, even though it comes from "winged swarming things," which aren't kosher. The logic was that honey was the product

---

* Today, of course, we know that honey is mass-produced by enslaved insects who live in geometrically complex houses and break down the nectar of flowers by chewing it, vomiting it into each other's mouths, and fanning it with their wings—and that all of this is coordinated by dancing and enforced by guards who chew off the legs of troublemakers (bees who continually drink too much fermented nectar and show up to work drunk, for example), all of which probably sounds more like make-believe than Aristotle's idea that honey is a liquid that falls from the sky.

of flowers rather than bees and that bees merely transferred and transformed existing flower nectar rather than producing honey themselves. But that's sort of like saying cows transfer and transform grass into milk, cheese, and hamburgers. Also, honey in its natural state tends to have pieces of bees in it, which, being the flesh of an unclean insect, should have also precluded honey from kosher status—but scholars decided these pieces were theoretically part of a bee's exoskeleton and technically bones rather than flesh. So maybe they just really wanted it to be kosher.

Anyway, the point here is that honey is astoundingly complex and not as wholesome as one might think; it might be the one food that never goes bad, but it's still far from being *good*, as popular culture perceives it, and for every connotation of love or godliness in its sugarcoated history, there's an opposite connotation of death, pain, or the macabre.

The ancient Egyptians, for example, used honey to heal people—but also to bury them. More than half of early Egyptian medicines contained honey as an ingredient, and while there are a lot of bogus claims about the health benefits of honey and honey by-products like bee pollen and royal jelly, it does have medicinal value beyond just soothing sore throats. In 2007, the FDA approved medical-grade honey for the treatment of diabetic and arterial ulcers, first- and second-degree burns, and traumatic and surgical wounds—and there's further evidence it accelerates healing while decreasing pain, inflammation, and scar formation. A 2004 study even showed that honey healed genital and labial herpes faster and with less pain and crusting than prescription Acyclovir, a leading antiviral medication, while other studies suggest it outperforms leading cough medicines and kills antibiotic-resistant bacteria.

A lot of this is due to the same properties that give honey

its seemingly infinite shelf life; for example, honey is naturally acidic and hygroscopic, meaning it sucks moisture from its surroundings, not unlike salt, creating a harsh environment for bacteria and microorganisms to survive in by essentially burning and smothering them to death. This is why foods high in sugar like jams and jellies (or Colonial-era pies) tend to last longer, similar to foods that are salted, cured, or brined. Honey also contains a bee enzyme called glucose oxidase, which naturally produces small amounts of hydrogen peroxide, which your mother probably kept under the sink to sterilize cuts and scrapes.

So in a way, the Egyptians were way ahead of their time by using honey medicinally. Then again, they also believed in the medicinal value of beer, cooked dog vulva, statue dust, semen (primarily as a medical-grade flavoring agent, though, in a pinch, it could also be used to remove splinters), and penis water, meaning both urine and the actual water left over from washing penises. So their medicinal use of honey was probably accidental, and if we give them credit for treating burns with it, we should also take credit away for treating burns with crushed cake and cat hair.*

And we should take away credit, too, for their feeding honey to babies without realizing this can cause infant botulism—though, to be fair, no one else realized this until the 1970s. (Botulism spores thrive in the absence of oxygen, so honey's propensity for suffocating things paradoxically keeps them alive. For healthy adults, this isn't generally a problem, but it's potentially fatal to

---

* Other remedies of note include rubbing the head with the womb of a cat warmed in oil with the egg of the gabgu bird to revitalize gray hair; rubbing the teeth with honey and pebbles to strengthen them; and rubbing the skin with honey and bat's blood to prevent ingrown hairs, particularly ingrown eyelashes.

infants, as spores can colonize in their digestive tracts, which is why you shouldn't give honey to children younger than twelve months.)

Yet the Egyptians were right about honey being a preservative, even if they wrongly attributed it to magic and supernatural forces. Archeologists have uncovered three-thousand-year-old honey in Egyptian burial tombs that's still perfectly good to eat; however, you'd probably want to check it for hairs first. There's an old story about grave robbers who crack open an ancient jar of honey and start eating it with their hands—until, about halfway through, one of them finds a hair in his mouth, then a few more hairs . . . and finally grabs his torch and discovers they're coming from the head of a mummified child at the bottom of the container. No one knows if the story is true, but Egyptians did use honey to preserve the dead, so it's certainly plausible.

And the Egyptians weren't the only ones to do this; the Babylonians, the Greeks, and even the English used honey as embalming fluid, and traces of it have been found on bones in Bronze Age burial sites (alongside "astonishingly well preserved" 4,300-year-old berries) and leaking out of coffins from sixteenth-century England.

Many of the same cultures simultaneously used honey as an instrument of love—but also an instrument of war. For example, Cupid's arrows were dipped into honey, but also into gall (a bitter bile secreted from the liver of animals) to symbolize love's accompanying agony. Even Cupid's own mother, Venus, called him a tameless and deceitful brat with an evil heart and honeyed tongue for his habit of ruining marriages by sneaking into houses at night and shooting spouses with honey-tipped arrows to incite infidelity. There's also this great series of paintings done by Lucas Cranach the Elder in the 1520s called *Venus with Cupid the*

Honey Thief that depicts a naked Cupid being stung by bees while stealing honeycomb with an inscription that reads DVM PVER ALVEOLO FVRATVR MELLA CVPIDO,/FVRANTI DIGITVM SEDVLA PVNXIT APIS./SIC ETIAM NOBIS BREVIS ET MORITVRA VOLVPTAS/ QVAM PETIMVS TRISTI MIXTA DOLORE NOCET ("As Cupid was stealing honey from the hive/A bee stung the thief on the finger/ And so do we seek transitory and dangerous pleasures/That are mixed with sadness and bring us pain."). The inscription is based on a much older poem by the Greek poet Theocritus (c. 300–260 BC) that tells the story of Cupid stealing honey and complaining about his bee stings to his mother, who responds by telling him he deserves it for being—just like the bees—a small creature that brings both sweetness and profound suffering.

More tangibly, honey has also been used to inflict harm *in place of* arrows. In his book *Six-Legged Soldiers: Using Insects as Weapons of War*, entomologist Jeffrey A. Lockwood explains how beehives were used as wartime projectiles going all the way back to the Stone Age. Cavemen covered them with mud and threw them into enemy caves; Roman armies loaded them into catapults; medieval Englishmen tossed them over castle walls during sieges and even built permanent hives within their own walls, called "bee boles," for easy access; Mayans lobbed bee grenades at their enemies and constructed dummy warriors from hollow gourds that released swarms of bees when hit; and before cannonballs, ships' crews waged war at sea by hurling hives onto one another's decks. In fact, the word *bombard*, explains Lockwood, comes from the Greek *bombos*, meaning "bee."

Ancient Persians and Native Americans also used honey to inflict torture by smearing it on victims and marooning them on boats or anthills to attract stinging insects, with the Persians sometimes adding to this by force-feeding their victims honey to induce diarrhea, which would then attract flies to lay eggs in the victim's anus and festering bite and sting wounds.

And two thousand years ago, the Persians booby-trapped the path of the invading Romans by baiting it with enticing chunks of "mad honeycomb" that caused them to vomit and hallucinate—then killed them while they vomited.* (The honey had been collected from areas dense in rhododendron flowers, the toxic nectar of which makes the resulting honey poisonous and hallucinogenic—and today worth about $166 per pound on the black market, where it's sold as a psychedelic and natural remedy for everything from erectile dysfunction to cancer and hair loss.†)

Though the biblical reference to "the land of milk and honey" actually refers to date honey (a paste made from crushed dates) and goat or sheep's milk, actual honey still holds a place in a lot of religions: the Buddha ate honeycomb, delivered by a monkey, on his path to enlightenment; Jews dip apples in honey during Rosh Hashanah in hopes of a sweet New Year; and the Norse god Odin drank honey wine, or mead, that was served to him by virgins in the skulls of his enemies while his army of undead warriors sipped it from the teats of his celestial goat, Heidrun.

Meanwhile, beekeeping was closely tied to the Christian

---

* During the Vietnam War, the Viet Cong did something similar by rigging jungle beehives with firecrackers, allegedly prompting the US military to fire back with a top-secret program to target enemies with bee-attracting pheromones.

† Note that rhododendrons aren't the only source of hallucinogenic honey; some historians say the Mayans laced honey with peyote, morning glory, or magic mushrooms to calm victims prior to sacrifice, while others say that these sort of practices planted the seeds for ritual sacrifice by causing drug-induced mayhem and widespread hallucinogenic madness, not unlike the aforementioned theories of ergot and lead poisoning in Rome and Salem.

Church because it provided beeswax for candles. Explains food historian Bee Wilson, "Wherever Christianity spread in Europe, so did beekeeping and candlemaking. As candles were used more and more in church services, so Christians revered the bee and its works, with a kind of circular reasoning. The bee was a sacred being because it made sacred wax; and wax was holy because the bee was holy." Honey, then, became a churchly symbol of chasteness and virginity, both because it was pure and unadulterated (i.e., eaten in its natural state) and because bees were industrious virgins, which made honey a great allegory for abstinence and societal order—though most of that went out the window once people realized that all the power in the bee community was held by a single queen who kept a harem of male slaves to have sex with, several at a time, before ripping out their penises.*

Similarly, vegans who abstain from honey for ethical reasons, citing the exploitation of bees, face a similar predicament in the paradox that if honey isn't vegan, nothing is.

"There would be no almond crop—not to mention avocados, apples, cherries and alfalfa—without honeybees," writes *New York Times* columnist Stephanie Strom, adding that nearly three-quarters of the crops that account for 90 percent of the world's food supply require bees for pollination.

California almonds alone depend on pollination from nearly 1.5 million beehives annually; local insects just don't have the numbers to pollinate the state's 1.26 million acres of almond trees,

---

* Wilson also points out that the same beeswax venerated by the Church as a symbol of virginity was simultaneously "used by brothel-keepers to reseal the hymens of prostitutes wishing to offer their clients a virgin experience of an altogether different kind." Meanwhile, honey itself has been used as both a lubricant and an aphrodisiac.

so farmers rent commercial hives that are confined to trailers for months at a time and trucked across the country—feeding the bees, of course, on corn syrup.

This, in addition to the nearly eighteen hundred varieties of plants pollinated by bees, naturally or commercially, just in North America: agave, alfalfa, apricots, blueberries, cabbage, carrots, celery, corn, cranberries, cucumbers, grapes, hops, lettuce, lime, mint, mustard, okra, olives, onions, oranges, parsley, parsnips, peaches, pumpkins, radishes, raspberries, rosemary, sage, sorghum, squashes, strawberries, thyme, turnips, watermelons, yucca.

People tend to picture bees buzzing around wildflowers and ornamental gardens, but the truth is they're attracted to just about anything they can turn into honey, including the nectar of plants like poison oak and tobacco, and even industrial waste. Bees living near tourist attractions have been found to produce cola-flavored honey after sucking sugar from discarded soda cans, and those in the vicinity of chocolate makers, chocolate-flavored honey; meanwhile, urban beekeepers in New York have reported cases of green honey, traced back to bees drinking antifreeze, and red honey, traced back to red food coloring from maraschino cherry factories.

In 1969, a graduate student at Louisiana State University evaluated fifty-four commercial honey samples for her PhD dissertation in botany and found that nearly 80 percent contained traces of poison ivy nectar—noting that the beekeepers involved "seemed reluctant to admit . . . that poison ivy might be significant among the nectar-secreting flora," for obvious reasons.

Some artisan beekeepers, like Henry Storch of Old Blue Raw Honey in Philomath, Oregon, specialize in small-batch honeys from unconventional nectar sources, including pumpkin, coriander, and poison oak (reported to have mellow notes of butterscotch). Unlike "mad honey," these varieties are perfectly safe to eat; however, it's difficult to get past the stigma of the word *poison* on food labels.

Meanwhile, a lot of honey sellers aren't sure where their honey comes from. Vaughn Bryant—a legend in the honey industry who once helped the CIA search for Osama bin Laden by forensically analyzing pollen remnants recovered from terrorist weapons, cell phones, and shoelaces—has spent more than forty years analyzing honey samples and says that when it comes to honey, "consumers rarely get what is written on the label."

"Beekeepers and honey producers selling their products to commercial stores or at roadside stands," he adds, "are frequently amazed to discover they have been selling types of honey that are completely different from what labels they were putting on their jars."

Of course, this isn't really their fault. "The federal laws that govern labeling honey are minimal," explains Bryant, and testing requirements are basically nonexistent. And even if testing were enforced, the current methods are costly, time consuming, and not exactly foolproof. For example, DNA tests can tell you the sources of honey but not the amount that comes from each source, making it hard to tell whether your expensive Manuka honey is 99 percent Manuka and 1 percent lawn weed or the other way around.

That's not to say that fraudulent manufacturers don't exist; fraud is a massive problem in the honey industry, and although we've talked a lot about the symbolic and religious misrepresentations of honey, perhaps the bigger misrepresentation deals with the labeling of honey itself. Ever since the United States raised the tariffs on Chinese honey in 2001, there's been an epidemic of international honey counterfeiters conspiring to beat these tariffs by laundering shipments through places like India, Malaysia, Taiwan, and Indonesia to conceal their origins. To further cover their tracks and elude forensic experts like Bryant, who can use pollen fingerprints to trace honey's geographical source, they also take advantage of loose federal regulations that allow manufacturers to filter their honey excessively, removing all traces of pollen and essentially destroying the evidence.

Note that filtration in itself isn't necessarily nefarious, and a lot of manufacturers filter their honey in good faith to remove unwanted materials such as wax and dead bee parts. Removing pollen can also help inhibit crystallization, making honey more attractive to consumers. So filtered honey won't kill you, but it can have an economic impact, given that the United States gets about 75 percent of its honey (roughly 450 million pounds) from foreign imports, of which almost 100 million pounds are estimated to come into the country illegally.

Similarly, filtering is often used to conceal the origins of honey that comes from cheap manufacturing processes that expose it to heavy metals such as lead and potentially dangerous chemicals and pesticides. Chinese honey, for example, often contains traces of a banned and potentially fatal antibiotic called chloramphenicol, which was used in China to treat bacterial foulbrood epidemics in bee colonies. (In 2011, inspectors found lead and antibiotics in nearly a quarter of Indian honey exports.)

Meanwhile, some manufacturers take forgery even further by bypassing honey altogether and selling jars of counterfeit honey made of corn syrup and yellow food coloring.

Fortunately, various domestic industry and trade organizations have been working together to combat this. About 30 percent of the honey sold in North America is certified by True

Source Honey, a coalition of beekeepers, honey packers, and honey suppliers who conduct voluntary third-party testing to protect customers and encourage ethical sourcing. Some states, including California, Wisconsin, and Florida, have also passed state laws to enforce transparent labeling and prohibit the removal of pollen from honey; however, looser federal regulations tend to negate these—and the FDA is too overtasked and underfunded to enforce testing anyway, which means that we're basically on a honey honor system.

So to recap, honey is the one food that never goes bad—but it's also a terrorist informant, a paradoxically vegan and kosher antisiege weapon, a medical-grade antiseptic that doubles as embalming fluid, and an ancient torture device with ties to Hitler and human sacrifice; Cupid used it as a mythological sex drug to ruin marriages, even though the sweetness of marriages tend to wane after the honeymoon anyway; it's a product of forced insect labor and international counterfeit rings that's been known to contain hallucinogens, banned pesticides, heavy metals, and the body parts of both bees and mummified humans; and it's a natural attractant to flies and humans but less so than beer, semen, or vinegar.

That's not to say that honey is bad; certainly there are worse sweeteners (e.g., sugar of lead), and it's probably the only sweetener that can treat herpes and sweeten your tea at the same time; however, we should probably stop using it to refer to loved ones.

Or, if we insist on calling our loved ones "honey," we could at least acknowledge that it's not because they're sweet and pure but rather because our relationships are complicated—requiring, like honey, constant labor and equal amounts of pleasure and pain.

CHAPTER 6

THE VANILLA OF SOCIETY

I've spent my life developing scores of flavors, and yet most people still say, "I'll take vanilla."

—HOWARD JOHNSON

I f we really need a culinary term of endearment for our loved ones, in lieu of honey, we could always borrow from the French, who call their lovers *mon chou* ("my cabbage"), which is kind of cute but also confusing, especially if you're a Dutch cheesemonger, in which case *mon chou* refers to a soft cream cheese containing 73 percent fat and made from cow's milk.*

Or *ma fraise* ("my strawberry"), though strawberries are also a French euphemism for menstruation—e.g., *la femme fraise des bois* ("the strawberry woman") and *c'est la saison des fraises* ("it's strawberry season")—so calling a woman "strawberry" could also get confusing.

Or we could just go back to calling our loved ones "vanilla," which would make the most sense, as this was taken as a compliment up until at least the 1800s, meaning the recipient was rare and coveted, a flavor everyone loves:

"Ah, you flavour everything; you are the vanille of society."
—Reverend Sydney Smith, London, c. 1837

---

* Authorities differ on the etymology of *mon chou*. Some say it comes from *chou à la crème* ("cream puff"), while others trace it to the verb *choyer* ("to pamper").

Salt had a similar connotation back when it was a precious trading commodity and a necessity for food preservation prior to refrigeration; in fact, there's an old English fairy tale about a father who asks his daughter how much she loves him, to which she replies, "I love you as fresh meat loves salt." The father then gets angry and banishes her for comparing him to something so coarse and superfluous, until she arranges for a feast to be secretly prepared without any salt—wherein he realizes how bland life is without it and promptly forgives her. Nowadays, of course, salt is cheap and easy, and is also used as an adjective— "salty"—to describe crabby people, likely dating back to the stereotype of sailors being tough, foul-mouthed, and aggressive.

Whereas the semantics of vanilla shifted not because of any change in popularity, cost, or demand but, at least in part, because LGBTQ populations in the United States started using it as a metaphor to distinguish between conventional (straight) and gay or fetish clubs in the 1970s—as heterosexuality, much like vanilla ice cream, was ubiquitous and conventional, part of the fabric of so-called normality. Then the straight population appropriated the term to more generally mean plain or boring— though still largely in the context of sex and relationships—and "vanilla" became a synonym for "ordinary."

But you don't become the world's most popular ice cream flavor and second most expensive spice* by being ordinary—and actual vanilla is anything but.

---

* Vanilla is second in price only to saffron—the dried stigmas of saffron crocus flowers—a kilo of which can sell for as much as $30,000 because harvesting it requires handpicking the stigmas of 150,000 to 200,000 flowers (at three stigmas per flower).

For starters, vanilla is the only edible fruit (though we colloquially call it a bean or a pod) to grow on freaking orchids, despite their being the largest family of flowers, with more than 25,000 species. It can take years for one of these orchids, which grow only in select areas twenty-five degrees north or south of the equator, like Mexico and Madagascar, to bear flowers—and any flowers they do yield will bloom only for a few hours before they shrivel up and die, unless they're pollinated. To add to this inordinately tight window for pollination, their hermaphroditic sex parts are separated by a little flap called the *rostellum* that needs to be pushed aside for pollination and there's only one or two species that know how to pollinate them, at least so we think. Both of these species, the melipona and euglossine bees, are nearly extinct, which means that vanilla orchids in the wild have only around a 1 percent chance of producing fruit without intervention.

And speaking of sex parts, vanilla is one of the few ice cream flavors to be named after genitalia,[*] thanks to Spanish conquistadors who "discovered" it in the sixteenth century and called it *vainilla*, a Spanish diminutive of the Latin *vagina*, because of its resemblance when spread open to harvest its seeds (and probably because they hadn't seen their wives in a long time).[†] They then brought the plants back home to Europe and spent three hundred years trying in vain to pollinate them because they couldn't find the *rostellum*. (Insert clitoris joke here.)

---

[*] Avocado is another, from the Nahuatl *ahuacatl* ("testicle").
[†] Separately, the word *orchid* comes from the Greek *órχis* (also "testicle"), owing to the shape of the tubers in its root structure, so *vanilla* is sort of a double whammy in terms of sexual innuendo.

It wasn't until 1841 that a twelve-year-old slave named Edmond Albius figured out you could pollinate the flowers by hand using a stick or blade of grass to move the flap aside, which is how it's still done today. (Albius was freed seven years later when France outlawed slavery, then imprisoned for allegedly stealing jewelry, then freed again five years after that, after his former owner petitioned the French government to grant him clemency in honor of his contribution to the vanilla industry and for helping to position France as its largest producer, a title now held by Madagascar.)

Because its flowers tend to bloom only one at a time, it can take months to pollinate a single plant. Then, after pollination, it takes another six to nine months before the fruits are ready to harvest, also by hand. But at that point they don't have any flavor, so they need to be cured and conditioned through a process that involves hand massaging them, laying them in the sun to dry each morning, and wrapping them in blankets and tucking them in at night to sweat, which can take *another* nine months. So you could probably have a kid and put them through kindergarten in the same time, and for less aggravation, than it would take to seed and harvest your own vanilla crop.

Of course, if you did it right, your vanilla could be worth as much as six hundred dollars per kilo, more than the price of silver. But it'd also take around six hundred blossoms to produce said kilo, as there's a lot of shrinkage involved and the final cured beans contain only about 2 percent extractable flavor, so you're looking at about a dollar per blossom to plant, pollinate, harvest, massage, cure, and sell your own vanilla beans—if you're lucky.

And that's assuming you don't have any losses from fungus, pests, disease, or theft.

In Madagascar, a few kilos of vanilla beans can be worth more than the average per capita annual income, so theft can be a life-or-death problem. Some farmers harvest their beans months early to deter thieves, resulting in a lower-quality and less valuable fruit that's more prone to disease, while others seek vigilante justice with machetes or use pins or stamps to "tattoo" their beans with their names or identifying marks.

In fact, a lot of people who call vanilla ordinary have probably never tasted it, as up to 99 percent of the vanilla flavoring in foods is artificial, derived from things such as wood pulp, tree bark, rice bran, chloroform, or castoreum, a natural excretion extracted from the asses of North American beavers. In 2006, a Japanese scientist even proved that vanilla flavoring can be extracted from cow dung. In full transparency, it's not too likely that you'll ever consume anything flavored with castoreum or cow dung—but if you did, manufacturers wouldn't have to tell you about it, as the FDA's definition of "natural flavors" includes flavors isolated from natural plant and animal products such as fruit, bark, and beaver glands.

(Note that this caveat only applies to foods *intentionally* flavored with cow dung; the US Department of Agriculture has a "zero-tolerance" policy when it comes to fecal contamination of meat, but it applies only to visible contamination detectible with the naked eye. Accordingly, a 2015 study of 458 pounds of beef purchased from grocery stores in twenty-six US cities—using actual scientific equipment—found that all of it was contaminated with fecal bacteria. Meanwhile, the Food and Drug Administration has acceptable limits for mammalian excreta, rot, mold, insect fragments, rodent hairs, and maggots in food. These limits don't apply to meat, but it's worth knowing that you might be eating a gram of insect fragments per every gram of pasta—and one rodent hair, on average, in every 50 grams.)

As for the 1 percent of foods that do contain actual vanilla, odds are it's in the form of an extract diluted with alcohol, water, dextrose, stabilizers, and, you guessed it, corn syrup.

So vanilla isn't very vanilla. It was slandered as ordinary not because it was boring but because it was so well liked and ubiquitous (and probably because of its perceived whiteness, even though vanilla beans are black and vanilla ice cream, often yellowish with prominent black specks*—not as diverse, maybe, as rainbow sherbet, but not exactly sterile, either).

Yet what really makes vanilla an endearing name for loved ones is that, above all, it's comforting: churn it with a little cream and sugar at a temperature cold enough to create ice crystals (typically about 27°F), and it provides a pharmaceutical-grade level of comfort that's helped us cope with everything from bad breakups and oral surgery to Nazi fascism, as we'll see later.

That's not to say that vanilla is the only flavor of ice cream that's comforting. Flavored ices and frozen desserts have been coveted for thousands of years, across many cultures, by people who have gone to great lengths to procure them. The ancient

---

* "French vanilla" refers not to vanilla from French Polynesia (i.e., Tahiti) but rather to the French *style* of making ice cream with egg yolks, which is what gives authentic French vanilla ice cream its traditional yellow hue. (In lower-quality ice creams, this look is often imitated by adding coloring from caramel, annatto, or turmeric—and sometimes specks of ground uncured vanilla beans, which don't actually add any flavor but look as though they do and simultaneously allow manufacturers to claim that their ice cream is "made with real vanilla beans.")

Greeks and Romans used to climb mountains to harvest ice they'd mix with wine or honey to make sorbet, a word that comes from the Arabic *sharba* ("drink") and *sharbat*, a drink made by mixing snow with various spices and flower blossoms. The Chinese made sherbet by covering containers with snow and saltpeter (also used in making gunpowder) to lower the freezing point of milk mixed with rice, and the Mongols made ice cream by riding horses in subfreezing temperatures while carrying cream stored in animal intestines, which would then freeze and be churned smooth by the galloping of their horses.

Even as late as the eighteenth century, ice cream was often reserved for those patient enough to wait for snowstorms or wealthy and patient enough to harvest ice from mountains or frozen rivers and keep it from melting in underground pits insulated with layers of sawdust, straw, or animal fur.

Beethoven, for example, writes from Vienna in 1794, "the Viennese are afraid that it will soon be impossible for them to have any ice-creams; for as the winter was mild, ice is rare," while George Washington tried to avoid such a fate by harvesting snow and ice from the rivers surrounding Mount Vernon but was, he writes in a 1784 letter to colleague Robert Morris, "lurched"* when it melted prematurely:

> P.S. The house I filled with ice does not answer—it is gone already—if you will do me the favor to cause a description of yours to be taken—the size—manner of building, & mode of management, & forwarded to me—I shall be

---

* Defeated.

much obliged—My house was filled chiefly with Snow. have you ever tried Snow? do you think it is owing to this that I am lurched.

Despite Morris's instructions, Washington was lurched again a year later, writing in his diary on June 5, 1785, that "there was not the smallest particle remaining" when he checked on the ice he'd packed in his cellar months earlier. Fortunately, he was wealthy enough to throw money at the problem, later spending 51 pounds, 6 shillings, and 2 pence (equal to about two hundred dollars today) on ice cream during the summer of 1790 alone. And he still fared better in his experiments with freezing than Francis Bacon, who tragically lost his life in 1626 after catching a cold while attempting to freeze a chicken by stuffing it with snow.

And it wasn't just ice that was difficult to procure. Martha Washington once served guests a "stale and rancid" trifle in 1789 because she couldn't find fresh cream; this happened in New York City—to the *first* First Lady of the United States—so just imagine what things were like for the other 99 percent.

Even getting sugar was a pain in the ass. Explains Anne Cooper Funderburg (more politely) in *Chocolate, Strawberry, and Vanilla: A History of American Ice Cream*, "Refined sugar was sold in cones or loaves, which varied greatly in size but were always formidably hard." Cooks literally needed hatchets or mallets to break pieces off.

And even if you had all the ingredients, turning them into ice cream wasn't exactly a cakewalk. Thomas Jefferson's recipe for vanilla ice cream, acquired during his time in France, required specialty equipment and more than a dozen steps:

ICE CREAM.

2. bottles of good cream.

6. yolks of eggs.

1/2 lb. sugar

mix the yolks & sugar

put the cream on a fire in a casserole, first putting in a stick of
Vanilla.

when near boiling take it off & pour it gently into the mixture of
eggs & sugar.

stir it well.

put it on the fire again stirring it thoroughly with a spoon to
prevent it's sticking to the casserole.

when near boiling take it off and strain it thro' a towel.

put it in the Sabottiere*

then set it in ice an hour before it is to be served. put into the ice
a handful of salt.

put salt on the coverlid of the Sabotiere & cover the whole with ice.

leave it still half a quarter of an hour.

then turn the Sabottiere in the ice 10 minutes

open it to loosen with a spatula the ice from the inner sides of
the Sabotiere.

shut it & replace it in the ice

open it from time to time to detach the ice from the sides

when well taken (prise) stir it well with the Spatula.

put it in moulds, justling it well down on the knee.

then put the mould into the same bucket of ice.

leave it there to the moment of serving it.

to withdraw it, immerse the mould in warm water, turning it well
till it will come out & turn it into a plate.

---

* An inner canister that was kept on ice and hand turned inside a wooden
bucket.

So part of the reason ice cream was so coveted is that, like vanilla, it was scarce and impractical. Writes Funderburg, "the average family was too busy surviving to indulge in a luxury that melted, consumed scarce ingredients, and required substantial preparation time."

And yet, even as its availability and practicality increased, so, too, did its associations with comfort.

When the Eighteenth Amendment outlawed the sale, manufacture, and transportation of alcohol in the 1920s, many early American breweries such as Anheuser-Busch and Yuengling* turned to making ice cream and soda to stay afloat, capitalizing both on shared manufacturing processes, like bottling and refrigeration, and the fact that ice cream's ingredients (fat, sugar, and vanilla) made a decent substitute for alcohol for the drowning of one's emotions.

"The prohibition of the sale of liquor has had one important and easily visible effect," writes one reporter at the dawn of Prohibition:

> It has turned hundreds of thousands from beer and whisky to ice-cream and soda water. In one eastern city until recently there were three breweries. That city had been drinking about 300,000 barrels of beer yearly, which sold at retail for about $4,200,000. To-day the city is eating 3,000,000 gallons of ice-cream. It formerly drank about a barrel per capita each year. Now its annual consumption of ice-cream is about eight gallons per head. One of the breweries was making 65,000 barrels of beer every year, and is now making 800,000 gallons of

---

* Others, such as Pabst Blue Ribbon, turned instead to cheese.

ice-cream annually, with an increase in the value of its production of 150 per cent.

In fact, ice cream stood in for alcohol as a source of national comfort and diversion to such a degree that by 1929, ice cream consumption had grown by more than 100 million gallons annually, peaking at more than a million gallons per day. Its consumption dipped with the crash of the stock market later that same year, when the Great Depression ushered in a decade of depressing foods like mustard sandwiches and mock apple pies, which substituted crackers for apple slices.* Yet even then ice cream endured—not just in spite of rocky times but because of them.

There are disputing claims as to who created the flavor Rocky Road, but we do know that it was popularized by William Dreyer and Joseph Edy, two California ice cream makers who began marketing it as a culinary metaphor in 1929 to help people cope with the Great Depression. Toppings at the time were primarily relegated to the point of sale and sprinkled on top, so the idea of mixing in broken chunks of marshmallows and nuts (originally walnuts but later almonds, which, the story goes, Dreyer cut up with sewing scissors borrowed from his wife) was pretty much unheard of. The name "Rocky Road" has since blended into the vernacular in the same way we've appropriated "Popsicle" to mean "frozen ice pop," when really it's a protected trademark owned by Unilever, the only brand that can legally sell "Popsicles"; but it used to be symbolic of comfort

---

* Pies such as these date back at least to the 1800s and were made mostly when apples were out of season; however, they surged in popularity during the Great Depression, due in large part to the debut of Ritz Crackers in 1934 and the recipe for Ritz Mock Apple Pie printed on the back of the box.

and perseverance—a reminder that life could still be sweet amid broken, rocky pieces.

Yet probably the most critical contribution to the comfort of ice cream and vanilla came during World War II, when the same scarcity that had once made them so elusive paradoxically helped make them more ubiquitous, as the wartime shortage of sugar, milk, and eggs around the globe essentially triggered an arms race for ice cream and dairy production that would ultimately bring ice cream to the masses and cement its place as a democratized comfort food for everyone.

The role of food in war, of course, was nothing new. John O'Bryan, in his book *A History of Weapons: Crossbows, Caltrops, Catapults & Lots of Other Things That Can Seriously Mess You Up*, explains how "the sick fucking Romans" weaponized bacon by setting pigs on fire and releasing hordes of flaming "war pigs" to break up enemy formations. The English not only threw beehives over castle walls or dropped them through specialized slits, called *meurtrières* or "murder holes," to defend against sieges but also fended off attackers by dousing them with hot cooking oil and melted animal fat; and around the same time in feudal Japan, the Japanese were throwing sand cooked with chili peppers into people's eyes to blind them.

During World War I, the United States converted fruit pits and nut shells into carbon for gas masks, which apparently worked better than any other raw material or ingredient except for coconut shells. And during World War II, the United States created a Fat Salvage Committee to convert bacon grease into bombs. The latter effort, supported by a Walt Disney cartoon featuring Pluto, Minnie Mouse, and a patriotic narrator urging housewives of America to salvage their used cooking fats to be turned into explosives:

Don't throw away that bacon grease! Housewives of America, one of the most important things you can do is to save your waste kitchen fats: bacon grease, meat drippings, frying fats. We and our allies need millions of pounds of fats to help win the war, for fats make glycerin, and glycerin makes explosives! Every year, two billion pounds of waste kitchen fats are thrown away—enough glycerin for ten billion rapid-fire cannon shells, a belt one hundred and fifty thousand miles long, six times around the earth! A skillet of bacon grease is a little munitions factory, meat drippings sink Axis war ships, waste frying fats speed depth charges on their way to crush Axis submarines. Your pound of waste fat will give some boy at the front an extra clip of cartridges. Pour your waste kitchen fats in a clean, wide-mouth can. That's right, not a glass jar or paper bag. Please strain the fats through a kitchen sieve. Keep in a cool, dark place so it won't become rancid. When you have a pound or more, take it to your neighborhood meat dealer, who is patriotically cooperating.

Of course, the more savage—and effective—use of food in war wasn't to hurl it at your enemies but to take it from them, a strategy that goes all the way back to the fourth-century Roman strategist Publius Flavius Vegetius Renatus, who called food the single most effective weapon in combat, "For armies are more often destroyed by starvation than battle, and hunger is more savage than the sword."

What worked so well about starvation, explains Vegetius, is that unlike bacon bombs or incendiary pigs, it "fights from within, and often conquers without a blow." So while hot oil and honeybees made a decent defense against sieges, the winning strategy was often to conserve your food and simply wait for your invaders to get hungry and go away.

And Vegetius wasn't alone here. His strategy of hoarding food has been followed by everyone from George Washington, who allegedly carried an annotated copy of Vegetius into battle, to Napoleon, who, in perfect French stereotype, once boasted that all he needed to conquer Europe was fresh bread and in 1795 offered a twelve-thousand-franc reward for anyone who could improve the transport and preservation of military food supplies. It took fourteen years, but the prize was eventually claimed by a French confectioner named Nicolas Appert, who became the father of canned food and went on to write a cookbook, *L'Art de conserver, pendant plusieurs années, toutes les substances animales et végétales* ("The Art of Preserving All Kinds of Animal and Vegetable Substances for Several Years").

By the same token, invading armies could do the same by staying out of range and cutting off the defending army's food supply. And if you didn't want to wait for your enemies to run out of food organically, you could always speed things along by sabotage, like when the French destroyed their own ovens and mills in 1636 to delay the advancing Spanish or when the United States (in perfect *American* stereotype) used flamethrowers and tactical herbicides to destroy crops and ground cover in Vietnam. (The most well known of these herbicides was Agent Orange, so named for the orange band used to identify it on fifty-five-gallon drums; however, we actually employed a rainbow of cancer-causing poisons, including Agent Pink, Agent Green, Agent Purple, Agent White, and Agent Blue.)

Water for drinking and irrigation was another common target. "The crude contamination of water sources, including wells and reservoirs, meant for armies and civilian populations, with filth, cadavers, animal carcasses, and contagious materials, dates back to antiquity and continues even today," write the authors of a 2008 chemical weapons report. The Assyrians poisoned enemies' wells with rye fungus, the Athenians spiked drinking water with toxic flowers, the Germans dumped sewage into enemy reservoirs, and Confederate and Union soldiers sabotaged each other's water supplies with dead animals. (The United States was also accused of intentionally bombing dikes and irrigation systems in Vietnam, though the State Department refuted such claims, admitting, "A few dikes have been hit by stray bombs directed at military associated targets nearby" but insisting the damage was minor and the bomb craters could "be repaired easily" by "a crew of less than 50 men with wheelbarrows and hand tools").

So for thousands of years and across cultures, the military focus on food was primarily caloric: maximize the food intake of your own soldiers (and that of their horses and wives and children, who remained at home while much of the workforce was off fighting) and minimize that of your enemies. But that changed during World War I, when Herbert Hoover rallied Americans on the importance of food not just for *calories* during wartime but for *comfort*, officially classifying ice cream as "essential foodstuffs" during the war and making it an inseparable part of the American war machine from that point forward.

You see, before Hoover became the United States' thirty-first president in 1929 (and before the United States entered World War I in 1917), he was a philanthropist who organized food relief in Belgium, which was caught in the middle of a conflict between Germany and Great Britain. Essentially, the entire nation of Belgium was on the brink of starvation in 1914 because the

Germans had invaded on their way to France and were eating all the food—and the British navy was blocking shipments of food because they didn't want it to go to the Germans and didn't trust the Germans not to take it from the Belgians.

Fortunately, Hoover, who at the time was living in London, intervened and convinced both sides to let him organize food relief as a private citizen, essentially creating his own pirate nation with its own flag, naval fleet, and railroads. Between 1914 and 1919, Hoover's Commission for Relief in Belgium fed about 10 million civilian refugees in occupied France and Belgium, delivering, in total, about 4,998,059 tons of flour, grain, rice, beans, peas, pork, milk, sugar, and miscellaneous staples and food items valued at $861,340,244.21 (roughly the equivalent of $13,436,907,809.70 today).

But Hoover's neutrality ended when the United States entered the war in 1917; his pirate organization continued to provide food relief as a neutral entity, but Hoover himself volunteered to head the newly established US Food Administration, hoping to do for his own country what he'd done for Belgium—and even offering to take the position without pay.

He basically became czar of the US food supply, exerting totalitarian control over prices, distribution, and purchasing. But Hoover didn't want control; part of the reason he'd insisted on taking the job without salary was to demonstrate sacrifice to the American people. So while nations on either side of the conflict imposed mandatory rationing to conserve food supplies—as they'd always done in wartime—Hoover saw this as un-American ("of the nature of dictatorship") and appealed instead to the American "spirit of self-denial and self-sacrifice."

Not only did he promise Americans that "food will win the war," but he promised a win without losing the very freedoms and values they were fighting for—including simple pleasures like good old American ice cream and the freedom to purchase ingredients at will.

And Americans were eager to help. Within months he'd built a force of nearly half a million volunteers and convinced more than 10 million households to sign pledge cards vowing to "Hooverize" their meals by cutting down on staples such as wheat, fat, and sugar.

Corporate America also contributed. Restaurants and public eateries saved more than 250 million pounds of wheat, 300 million pounds of meat, and 56 million pounds of sugar (enough to feed 8 million soldiers for a month) by observing days such as Meatless Mondays and Wheatless Wednesdays; food manufacturers spent their own advertising budgets patriotically urging consumers to consume less of their commodities; and newspapers, retailers, and ad agencies volunteered their expertise and ad space—culminating in an estimated $19,417,600 in donated services and displays. Even the White House pitched in by grazing sheep on the front lawn.

The result was a tripling of US food exports almost instantaneously, producing 18 million tons of food exports in our first full year of war alone.

Yet the ice cream industry demanded more. An editorial in the May 1918 issue of *The Ice Cream Review* (an offshoot of Milwaukee's *Butter, Cheese & Egg Journal*) spooned out sharp criticism for the scant availability of ice cream overseas ("If English medical men knew what ours do every hospital would keep ice cream on hand for patients") and cried for Washington to intervene by subsidizing Allied ice cream factories across Europe: "Reports from nearly all the camps show that the per capita consumption of ice cream is nearly twice the figure for the average of the entire country. Are these boys going to miss something out of their lives when they go across? Yes, they are, and it is a shame that no one has thought to provide this home comfort . . ."

And it wasn't just comfort the ice cream industry sought to provide for soldiers but good health and morale:

> In this country every medical hospital uses ice cream as a food and doctors would not know how to do without it. But what of our wounded and sick boys in France? Are they to lie in bed wishing for a dish of good old American ice cream? They are up to the present, for ice cream and ices is taboo in France. It clearly is the duty of the Surgeon General or some other officer to demand that a supply be forthcoming.

Unfortunately, it wasn't that simple. The ice cream industry was still in its infancy. Flavors were still largely limited to chocolate, strawberry, and vanilla, and ice cream on a stick wasn't even invented yet; it wouldn't be patented until 1923. Refrigeration was also in its infancy, and a lot of the cooling technologies that did exist depended on toxic gases like ammonia, methyl chloride, and sulfur dioxide (as opposed to Freon, which was introduced in the 1930s and merely killed the environment). So refrigeration was not only expensive and inadequate but potentially deadly.

Meanwhile, sugar was in shorter supply than Hoover had let on. Despite conservation efforts, the United States was still consuming far more of it per capita than her allies overseas—and before the war had imported the bulk of its sugar supply from Germany, which obviously wasn't going to happen anymore; plus, not only had Germany stopped exporting sugar to the United States, but it had started taking it from their neighbors, too, making the market even more competitive.

So rather than building ice cream factories overseas, Hoover was eventually forced to ask manufacturers to reduce their use of sugar domestically—ruling in the summer of 1918: "Ice cream is no longer considered so essential as to justify free use of sugar in its manufacture."

Still, the ice cream industry fared better than others, having to cut just 25 percent of its sugar use as opposed to a 50 percent cut for manufacturers of "less essential" commodities such as chocolate, soda, and chewing gum. And Hoover's support for ice cream, coupled with the industrial boom of the postwar economy and a returning workforce who fondly recalled eating it in wartime camps and hospitals, helped the industry soar soon after the war ended.

In fact, we owe a lot of ice cream's postwar popularity not just to Hoover, Yuengling, and Rocky Road but to a World War I veteran named Howard Johnson who, after returning from service in France, purchased a dilapidated drugstore with a soda fountain and brought it back to life with an ice cream recipe he purchased from a German street vendor. The recipe, which called for twice the typical butterfat, resulting in a creamier texture, quickly accounted for the bulk of his business, inspiring Johnson to develop a trademark twenty-eight flavors[*] and introduce premium ice cream to the masses with an eponymous chain of roadside restaurants strategically located along the nation's expanding turnpike system. Howard Johnson's (truncated as "HoJo's") might not be a household name anymore, as his concept

---

[*] Still, Johnson confessed, most people preferred vanilla.

of a "landmark for hungry Americans" eventually eroded into a hotel chain now owned by Wyndham, but at one point it was the largest food chain in America, with more than a thousand locations and a new location opening every nine days.

The postwar twenties also saw the debut of the Eskimo Pie; the Popsicle (originally called the "Epsicle" by its creator, Frank W. Epperson, whose children took to calling it "Pop's Sicle"); and the ice cream bar, created in Youngstown, Ohio, by a candy maker named Harry Burt, who inserted lollipop sticks into bars of vanilla ice cream coated in chocolate and called it the Good Humor Sucker, later changed to the Good Humor Bar. Though it wasn't the chocolate coating and sticks that made his bars a hit (or even his idea to sell them from refrigerated trucks that patrolled neighborhoods, ringing bells initially borrowed from his son's bobsled) as much as his iconic branding.

In fact, a lot of ice cream's pure, wholesome image doesn't come from the supposed whiteness of vanilla but from that of the Good Humor man, who roamed American neighborhoods in immaculate white trucks and uniforms, tipping his hat and projecting Burt's vision of cleanliness and boy-next-door innocence.

"You are at all times while on duty to look your best," instructed one Good Humor training manual. "Always have a clean shave and neat haircut; wear a clean white shirt, black bow tie, black shoes neatly polished, clean white uniform, uniform cap and money changer. Your sales car must always be kept clean and in a neat condition."

A few years earlier, around 1916, a Polish immigrant named Nathan Handwerker had done something similar to dispel rumors that his five-cent Coney Island hot dogs contained dog and horse meat by paying college students to wear white jackets and stethoscopes and hang around his stand so people would think his "Nathan's Famous" hot dogs were endorsed by doctors. (Not to suggest that Nathan's hot dogs were anything less than advertised, but the history of sausages isn't exactly sterile; just a few decades earlier, in 1867, a book of recipes had cautioned readers, "Let me advise you never to use any sausages unless you know who made them, for of all things that are adulterated, the most offensive is the adulterated sausage. It is a fact that cannot be reasonably doubted that many sausages are composed in part of horse, hog and dog, together with diseased animals and many odds and ends by no means pleasant to think of . . .")

But Good Humor's chaste image wasn't just a publicity stunt; in 1929, the company even stuck up to the Chicago mob by refusing to pay them protection money—and had part of their fleet and factory blown up as retaliation. Allegedly.

By the summer of 1921, authorities on Ellis Island had even begun handing out ice cream to immigrants as part of their first American meal. "Ellis Island Authorities Gently Lead Immigrants to Appreciation of Good Points of America by Introducing Them to the Pleasures of Ice Cream Sandwiches," read one news lede. The article ("Ice Cream as Americanization Agent") went on to describe how immigrants would often spread their ice cream on bread as if it were butter and suggest that the practice (of giving ice cream to immigrants, not spreading it like butter) could help fight the spread of communism:

It augurs well for the future of the ice cream industry and its further expansion that the latest comers to the country are acquiring a taste for the characteristic American dish even before they set foot in the streets of New York. It has always been a cause of complaint by many that the recent immigrants do not adopt American standards of living, but the Ellis Island authorities are sponsors for the assurance that in this one respect at least the adoption of the American standard is as instantaneous as could reasonably be expected. Then, too, who could imagine a man who is genuinely fond of ice cream becoming a Bolshevik? Even strawberry ice cream would arouse no latent anarchistic tendencies, while vanilla or peach would be soothing to the very reddest of the Reds. There is as yet no record of a dangerous plot being hatched over a dish of ice cream; the temperature is too low to promote incubation.

So by the time World War II came around, ice cream (still largely vanilla, which accounted for roughly 80 percent of the market) had become inseparable from the American way of life, an emblem of American comfort, freedom, and democracy. Once again the rest of the world went back to banning ice cream as part of its rationing efforts (with Great Britain adding salt to the wound by endorsing carrots on sticks as the official wartime substitute for ice cream bars).* This time, however, the United States doubled down, building pop-up ice cream factories on the front lines; delivering individual ice cream cartons to foxholes; spending more than a million dollars on a floating ice cream barge that roamed the Pacific delivering ice cream to Allied ships incapable of making their own; and distributing 135 million pounds of dehydrated ice cream base in 1943 alone.

And you're goddamn right we won the war.

---

* Other wartime substitutes included mock fudge made from mashed potatoes.

In 1942, when Japanese torpedoes struck the USS *Lexington*, then the second-largest aircraft carrier in the navy's arsenal, the crew abandoned ship—but not before breaking into the freezer and raiding all the ice cream. Survivors describe scooping it into their helmets before lowering themselves into shark-infested waters. US bomber crews used to make ice cream while flying over enemy territory after figuring out that they could strap buckets of ice cream mix to the outside of their planes during missions; by the time they landed, the mix would have frozen in the cold temperature of high altitude and been churned smooth by engine vibrations and turbulence, if not machine-gun fire and midair explosions. And soldiers on the ground took to using their helmets as mixing bowls to improvise ice cream from snow and melted chocolate bars.

Ice cream became so tied to national morale, in fact, that when the most decorated member of the Marine Corps, General Lewis B. "Chesty" Puller, called it a "sissy food" in the 1950s and tried to convince his marines that they'd be tougher on a diet of beer and whiskey, he drew so much national backlash that the Pentagon had to intervene with an official statement promising ice cream would be served no less than three times a week.

Even Fidel Castro couldn't help but notice the transformative effect of ice cream on the American spirit. After a visit to New York in 1959, during which he was photographed licking an ice cream cone at the Bronx Zoo, he developed an obsession for American ice cream and dairy. In fact, while Americans were smuggling Cuban cigars into the United States, Castro was smuggling all twenty-eight flavors of Howard Johnson's into Cuba and building the world's largest ice cream parlor in Havana, a state-run "ice cream cathedral" named Coppelia (after the French ballet *Coppélia*) that occupied an entire city block and served state-subsidized ice cream to more than ten thousand daily customers who would wait in line for hours. Author Gabriel García Márquez even insists he once saw the dictator "[finish] off a good-sized lunch with 18 scoops of ice-cream."

That last bit might sound a bit like magical realism, but stranger things have happened—like when the CIA tried to assassinate Castro by spiking his daily milkshake with botulinum toxin, only to have the toxic capsule break when the would-be assassin tried to remove it from its hiding place in the kitchen of the hotel Havana Libre, where it had frozen to the inside wall of a freezer. Or when Castro got into a fight with the French dairy expert André Voisin (known for such works as *Rational Grazing* and *Soil, Grass and Cancer*) because Voisin wouldn't say Castro's cheese was superior to French cheese—and then Voisin suddenly died of a heart attack in his Cuban hotel two weeks later. Or when Castro spent decades funding the genetic manipulation of a dairy "supercow" to usurp US milk production and the program was marked by failure (including botched plans to develop a breed of miniature cows the size of dogs, intended to be kept at home as pets) until the birth of a single cow named Ubre Blanca ("white udder") who produced a record 241 pounds of milk in a single day, more than four times that of typical American cows. (Castro called Ubre "our great champion," assigned her a security detail in an air-conditioned stable—and after she passed in 1985 eulogized her with military honors and a life-size marble statue.)

But at least Castro recognized the contributions of dairy and ice cream; notice there's no national US monument to ice cream. (There's the Cotoni-Coast Dairies National Monument outside Santa Cruz, but that has more to do with the indigenous Cotoni and Swiss dairy farmers in the 1900s.)

None of this is to suggest that ice cream was the only food to provide comfort during the war—or that it was easily obtained. "No G.I. who passed through Europe in 1944 or 1945 could have failed to notice the plight of its inhabitants," writes historian Lee Kennett, who describes GIs going through chow lines two or three times to grab extra food for impoverished locals and guards turning their backs while food and fuel supplies mysteriously went missing.

Meanwhile, for American POWs being held captive overseas—where they were often forced to survive on things like maggot-infested rice, stale bread, rotten vegetables, and often far less or far worse—comfort food was, in the words of one POW, "as obtainable as a slice of the moon."

"Somebody listening in may have heard us talking about politics or sport, or anything else," recalls British World War II veteran Harold Goulding, who spent more than three years in Japanese POW camps, "but I think really those were just symbols and we were really talking about food all the time."

Other symbols, says Goulding, were less cryptic, like pictures of food they tore from old magazines and plastered to the walls of bunks in place of pinups.

Recalls 4th Marine Jorg Jergenson, "Perhaps it was just our rundown physical conditioning, but, after the first year and a half or so, in general, girls and femininity did not, any longer, enter into the POW's thought process."

"Belly empty think of food, belly full think of women," explains another POW.

Others passed the time by sharing recipes and filling scrap paper with menus for the elaborate Christmas dinners they'd cook if they made it back home.

"During the forty-three months that I was a POW I spent a

lot of time just writing out food and holiday menus to keep my-
self somewhat sane and focused," recalls Mess Sergeant Morris
Lewis:

> I don't know if I did this because I was craving food or
> to keep myself up to the task of being the Mess Ser-
> geant. . . . Imagine being asked by your soldiers to tell
> them what was going to be on the Christmas menu, all
> knowing that there would never be such a meal. But here
> we were with each soldier coming to me and asking if
> they could put their dish on the menu. It did give us all a
> sense of what we were remembering most and the will to
> go on another day. We were planning more than meals,
> we were providing a sense of hope for what should be or
> would be again someday.

And while these menus included far more than just vanilla ice
cream, they also highlight what it is that makes it so comforting.

Explains Sue Shephard, who cataloged many of these menus
in her paper "A Slice of the Moon," presented at the Oxford
Symposium on Food and Cookery, "Few tried to recall the el-
egant meals, in restaurants, of scallops and oyster, Dover soles,
pheasant or Chateaubriand steaks. That wasn't the food they
wanted to remember; it was home food of childhood which rep-
resented unconditional love, without cares or responsibilities."

And few foods represent that better than ice cream.

As food historian Margaret Visser so brilliantly describes in
her book *Much Depends on Dinner*:

> There are today two main kinds of nostalgia, and ice
> cream appeals to both of them. The first looks back to

past time. Ice cream is the delight of children and therefore evocative of childhood memories; eating it makes people feel young and at least temporarily secure and innocent. Ice-cream stalls are decked with striped awnings and gingham, merchants use clowns, stuffed toys, cartoon characters, and balloons, not only to please children but also to draw adults to indulge in childhood for a while.

The second, she writes, looks back not just to past time but to past ideals and a sense of bygone simplicity:

> Ice-cream sellers also like to pretend that they are very old-fashioned folks, and they give their premises not only a nursery air but a nineteenth-century look as well . . . black-and-white tiled floors (the tiles preferably hexagonal), bentwood chairs, "Tiffany" lamps, mirrors, cushioned booths, marble counters and so on.

Vanilla, in particular, takes us back to a time when life and ice cream felt simpler—even if the process of making ice cream might not have been: a time before the intrusion of artificial flavors, colors, stabilizers, emulsifiers, and preservatives.

Clinical research seems to confirm this. Researchers testing the neurological effects of ice cream, chocolate, and yogurt found that only ice cream inhibited the human startle response across genders with statistical significance, leading them to theorize that there's more at play than fat, sugar, and cold temperatures and that a large degree of ice cream's comfort is psychological: a result of learned associations from memories pairing ice cream with things like summer, vacations, and friendship.

Not to get too Freudian, but it's possible our comforting memories of ice cream and vanilla go back even further, all the way back to our very first comfort food, given what we learned in the first chapter about vanilla being a common flavor in human breast milk (and theoretically in amniotic fluid)—and the tendency of such flavors to impact lifelong food preferences. Indeed, human breast milk isn't really much different from vanilla ice cream base, minus the ice crystals, considering that human milk is significantly sweeter than cow's milk and also contains more fat.

Both breast milk and vanilla have also separately been shown to have calming and pain reduction effects in infants given heel pricks, while another study found that when nursing mothers ingested vanilla just prior to breastfeeding, their infants "spent significantly more time attached to their mother's nipple" and consumed 20 percent more milk; the study also found that when vanilla was added to bottled formula, infants tended to suck harder.

Perhaps that's why, at least in one POW camp, "ice cream" was the code for "news from home"—because, writes ex-POW Russell Braddon, that was "what all prisoners of war crave more than anything else."

CHAPTER 7

THE GHOSTS OF COCKAIGNE PAST

It has been an instinct in nearly all peoples, savage or civilized, to set aside certain days for special ceremonial observances, attended by outward rejoicing. This tendency to concentrate on special times answers to man's need to lift himself above the commonplace and the everyday, to escape from the leaden weight of monotony that oppresses him.

—CLEMENT A. MILES

A couple of flitches of bacon are worth fifty thousand Methodist sermons and religious tracts. The sight of them upon the rack tends more to keep a man from poaching and stealing than whole volumes of penal statutes, though assisted by the terrors of the hulks and the gibbet. They are great softeners of the temper, and promoters of domestic harmony.

—WILLIAM COBBETT

There's a lot more to comfort foods, of course, than just childhood innocence and nostalgia; while some comfort foods play to memories of childhood and home, others play to excess and indulgence, providing—like the alcohol replaced by ice cream during Prohibition—a ritual and illicit escape from the crushing constraints of reality and adulthood.

In fact, many of the guilty pleasures listed on prisoner-of-war Christmas menus in the previous chapter were exactly that—guilty pleasures—and the tradition of gathering to feast on them in late December isn't rooted in chaste morality or religious doctrine but hedonic harvest festivals (hedonic not in the balanced sense of Epicurus but more with a Mötley Crüe connotation, meaning gluttony, ritual sacrifice, political dissent, and sexual excess).

This isn't to suggest that the modern Christmas doesn't have wholesome and nostalgic comforts of its own; it's just that "Christmastime" was associated with presents, vacation days, and gluttonous feasts of carved meats, stuffed birds, and decorative pastries long before the advent of Christianity, Santa, or even Christ, for purposes that were both practical and primal. Ever since the onset of farming and stock raising, December has been peak comfort food season because it meant winter was coming, which meant livestock had to be slaughtered before snow covered the seasonal grasses that made up their food supply and fresh meat and vegetables had to be either eaten or preserved before the winter frost. Generally, November was the month for harvesting crops and fattening animals, while December was for baking the resultant grains and slaughtering animals at their fattest. In fact, the old German and Anglo-Saxon names for November were *Slagtmonat* ("slaughter month") and *Blodmonath* ("blood month").

Even though these traditions were secular, they still carried over to early churches, and you can sometimes find these "labours of the months" depicted in medieval cathedrals and illuminated manuscripts, either through illustrations, e.g., pigs being split with axes or having their blood drained, or Latin calendar descriptions: *"Semen humo jacto"* ("I sow the seed") for October, *"Mihi pasco sues"* ("I fatten my pigs") for November, and *"Mihi macto"* ("I slaughter my sacrificial victims") for December. Conveniently, wild birds such as geese—and eventually turkeys—were also at their best when slaughtered in December, having had time to fatten and mature since hatching the previous spring. And there was also lots of alcohol to go around, freshly fermented from the autumn grain.

So December, for most of recorded history, has been a month of ritual gathering and celebration, when people from various cultures would congregate to stuff themselves with massive amounts of food and drink—and maybe even dedicate some of their toasts and slaughters to various gods or spirits as a way of giving thanks for past prosperity or asking for goodwill in the year ahead. Light, by the way, was symbolically entwined with a lot of these gatherings, as this was also the time of the winter solstice, when days became shorter and darkness seemed to conquer light. And to ensure that light prevailed, various Roman, pagan, and Norse traditions called for rituals involving oil lamps, lanterns, and bonfires in tribute to the sun or gods of light. This is also where things like mistletoe, wreathes, and trees came in, each symbolic of life, luck, or fertility in a time when winter seemed to turn the world dark and lifeless.

Yet there was another common reason for these feasts: much like today's winter breaks and holiday office parties, they functioned as what food historian Ken Albala calls "a kind of safety valve—allowing people to blow off steam and then return to their proper stations the rest of the year." So they were essentially holiday bonuses from the elite, sanctioned orgies of excess and indulgence that allowed the poor to live like the rich for a change so they wouldn't revolt and kill their masters—again, just like today's office parties, only they would have been even more necessary, as life was more grueling back then (when people actually depended on gruel), and this was before things like unions and paid time off and maternity leave, making harvest festivals a rare, if not singular, chance for the common class to unwind.

One of these festivals was Saturnalia, from the Latin roots *sata* ("seed") and *serere* ("to sow"), which also gave us "season," "semen," "Saturday," and "sabbath"; this was a weeklong tribute to Saturn, the Roman god of sowing, observed around the time of the winter solstice, from December 17 to 23. Essentially, Saturnalia sought to re-create the mythical Golden Age of Saturn's reign, when he introduced the Romans to a utopian period of peace and prosperity by giving them the gift of agriculture, sort of the Roman equivalent of Eden. So it was a time of the year when people were nicer to one another, schools and businesses closed, presents were exchanged, pigs were sacrificed, and slaves were temporarily freed and allowed to borrow their master's clothing. Again, this was largely the burden of the wealthy, who were expected to hold banquets for their servants and open their doors to the poor, and just as we stress out about money around the holidays, so did they.

Another series of festivals, the Greek Dionysia and Roman Bacchanalia, were held in honor of Dionysus and Bacchus, their respective gods of the grape harvest, wine, intoxication, ritual madness, ecstasy, and fertility. The food at these festivals may have been a bit more primal than most of our holiday comfort foods, though it was also, perhaps, fresher, rumored by some to consist of raw flesh torn from live animals or, some say, sacrificial humans. But the good news is that people would have been too drunk to taste or remember it, as it was considered bad manners—sometimes even a crime—to be sober during these festivals, which would have shown a lack of gratitude to the sacred giver of wine.

These comforts might seem the most removed from subsequent Christian feasts (also because they involved drunken orgies, goat-skin loincloths, cross-dressing, and statues of penises), but if you think about it, the consumption of raw meat and wine isn't really that different from the modern Christian sacraments of wine and communion wafers to symbolize the blood and body of Christ; in fact, some scholars have suggested that Dionysian or Bacchanalian worshippers similarly believed that they were consuming the flesh and substance of God.

And because these rituals were often carried out at night and in secret, some scholars believe that their sights and sounds (e.g., the echoes of primal screams and glimpses of torchlit rituals held by people wearing animal masks) may have led to a mythology of mischievous gremlins wreaking havoc during the twelve nights of Christmas by stealing food, breaking furniture, and terrorizing children—and the subsequent Christian practices of lighting yule logs to keep them from climbing down chimneys and leaving food out as a peace offering on Christmas Eve (a precursor, perhaps, to leaving cookies out for Santa).

Note that the exact origins of yule are unknown; some say it was a Teutonic or Norse festival that involved fires, feasting, and presents; others that it was a Saxon rite of sacrifice, eating, and drinking in honor of Thor; others still that it came from the words *hwéol, iol*, or *iul* ("wheel") to mark the rotation of the sun and seasons. Regardless of its beginnings, it was eventually adopted by the Church to mark the twelve days of Christmas and later the Christmas season* in general. There is also a theory that yule comes from the Old Norse *jól*, which became the Old French *jolif*, giving us the modern "jolly." If only more people wrote things down . . .

Anyway, the rest of the winter feasts essentially suffered the same fate as Yule. Explains historian Madeline Shanahan, "No singular one of these festivals, which stretched from November through to January, is the direct ancestor of Christmas." But together, they laid the groundwork.

As Christianity spread across Europe, the Church basically adopted these various pagan, Norse, Roman, and Celtic traditions as their own, choosing to celebrate the birth of Christ on December 25, for example, because it was already associated with feasting, sacrament, and rebirth. So torches became Christmas trees and yule logs; the rebirth of the sun became the rebirth

---

* Isn't it poignant that we still call Christmas a *season*, by the way?

of the *son*; and heathen spirits and ghosts became *holy* spirits and ghosts. "Christian symbolism," writes Clement A. Miles in *Christmas in Ritual and Tradition Christian and Pagan*, "was merely a gloss upon pagan practices."

In fact, all of this was outlined in a 601 letter from Pope Gregory I, who essentially gave the blueprint for converting sacrificial feasts into Christian festivals:

> Because they are wont to slay many oxen in sacrifices to demons, some solemnity should be put in the place of this, so that on the day of the dedication of the churches, or the nativities of the holy martyrs whose relics are placed there, they may make for themselves tabernacles of branches of trees around those churches which have been changed from heathen temples, and may celebrate the solemnity with religious feasting. Nor let them now sacrifice animals to the Devil, but to the praise of God kill animals for their own eating, and render thanks to the Giver of all for their abundance; so that while some outward joys are retained for them, they may more readily respond to inward joys. For from obdurate minds it is undoubtedly impossible to cut off everything at once, because he who strives to ascend to the highest place rises by degrees or steps and not by leaps.

Another conversion tactic not outlined in his letter was to balance these feasts with periods of religious fasting, ensuring that carnal joys and the sins of gluttony were officially checked by periods of modesty and restraint—and that law and social order ultimately and publicly prevailed.

Writes historian Bridget Ann Henisch:

The medieval year resembled a chessboard of black and white squares. It was patterned with periods of fast and feast, each distinct and limited in time, yet each dependent on the other for its significance and worth. To give true spiritual refreshment, feast and fast had to follow each other like the seasons. A Church feast was ushered in by a period of fasting; a fast was rewarded with not only a feast in this life but the hope of a celestial banquet in the next. To be of value, each had to be a deliberate, conscious offering by the individual or by society. Endless, thoughtless wining and dining by the prosperous was nothing but gross indulgence; the nagging, perpetual undernourishment of the poor, "in suche bare places where every day is Lent," was nothing but misery.

An added by-product, of course, is that this showed who was really in control. Feasts weren't necessarily acts of charity but demonstrations of power, a way for hosts (both sacred and secular) to display their wealth, worldliness, and privilege by flexing excess in ways that went beyond the caloric, i.e., displaying not just *quantity* to their guests but freshness, variety, novelty, and presentation.

Because keeping food fresh back then was an ordeal, most of the foods commoners enjoyed outside of these festivals—meats, vegetables, even cheeses—would have been heavily salted or dried for preservation. And this was particularly true during winter. "The end of the year," explains historian Reay Tannahill, "was a time of salting down beef, pork, game, and freshwater fish for the gray days to come, and of feasting on the last fresh meat for several months." Even something relatively simple and frugal, like bread, the ultimate medieval peasant food, would (by most people) have been baked just once a week, owing to the labor of milling grain, making fire, and waiting for dough to rise, and the overall economy of baking larger loaves less frequently. And remember that this was before modern preservatives, so six-day-old bread back then would have been much harder and staler (on average) than six-day-old bread today. In fact, there are accounts of peasant breads in France so hard that they had to be chopped with axes to slice them.

In contrast, the upper class not only had the means to enjoy fresh foods, such as bread, every day but were given the "upper crust" at meals, which is where the phrase comes from; in today's cheap, presliced breads, the crust is often nothing to write home about, which is sad, because in proper bread the upper crust often has the most flavor, given both its texture and the common practice of sprinkling it with spices.

Variety was another way to display privilege; even today, the idea of multiple courses is, for most, a luxury, but medieval courses went even further. As historian Madeleine Pelner Cosman writes, "The medieval 'course' was closer than the modern to the Latin origins of the word *currere*, to run, a running, passing, flowing ordering in time." So a medieval course meant simultaneously a swift motion, the order of said motion ("Follow the course"), and a succession of events ("Dinner has run its course"). A single course, then, might easily have involved a dozen or more dishes brought out in quick succession.

The coronation banquet for King Henry IV in 1399, for example, included just three meat courses but more than forty dishes, including meat in pepper sauce, boar's head with tusks, cygnet (baby swan), fat capon, pheasant, heron, sturgeon, venison, stuffed pig, peacock, crane, rabbit, pullet (baby hen), egret, curlew, partridge, pigeon, quail, snipe, and eagle. And the funeral collation for Nicholas Bubwith, bishop of Bath and Wells, in 1424 featured just two meat and two fish courses but included such offerings as *nomblys de roo* (an umble pie made from the entrails of deer), pork chops, capon, swan, swan neck pudding, heron, pheasant, woodcock, partridge, plover, snipe, lark, venison, *yrchoun* (a stuffed pig stomach spiked with almonds, meant to resemble a sea urchin or hedgehog), eel, herring, millwell and ling tail, salmon, pike, codling, haddock, hake, sole, bream, perch, fried minnows, and crab.

Spices were also used to flaunt wealth, simultaneously serving as "superb insignia of conspicuous wealth" and "indicators of ostentatious waste." Essentially, by indulging diners with unprocurable flavors from all over the world, hosts demonstrated their mercantile reach and access to lesser-known spice routes and distant or even mythical lands.

Black pepper and cinnamon were two of the most common—and costly—medieval spices; in fact, spice traders used to make up stories about their exotic origins so they could charge more for them. Pepper was said to grow in forests guarded by serpents that had to be scared away by setting the trees on fire, which was why black pepper pods were the color of ashes. One story claimed that cinnamon came from giant bird nests (belonging to either the phoenix or something called the *cinnamologus*) that were too high for any man to climb and that had to be knocked down by shooting them with weighted arrows. Another story was that it had to be transported using rafts without oars, sails, or rudders on a treacherous journey that took five years and was powered by courage alone; another still that it grew in lakes guarded by winged creatures that would tear a man's eyes out unless he covered his entire body in animal hide. (The flip side of this, by the way, is that historically, whenever spices became affordable, they became less desirable, so once people figured out that cinnamon literally grew on trees, it was relegated mostly to desserts, while pepper and salt became free table ornaments; meanwhile, other popular medieval spices, such as mace and long pepper, all but disappeared from the spice cabinet.)

It's common, of course, to quantify the cost of spices by comparing their value in weight to that of gold, but that point is sort of moot in regard to medieval cooking because cooks also used actual gold to spice up their dishes alongside other pretentious ingredients such as crushed pearls and rose water. Again, the idea wasn't really to make foods taste better so much as it was to flaunt wealth, so spices were generally added with no real regard for finesse or balance. Writes William Edward Mead in *The English Medieval Feast*, "This means, of course, that simplicity was as far as possible avoided and that the cook, like the physician and the apothecary in their prescriptions, aimed to combine as much irreconcilable material in one dish as he could without making it impossible to swallow." So ingredients like sugar would be added to oysters (fittingly, in a recipe called "oysters in gravy bastard"), not because this tasted good or made any culinary sense but because it was something only a rich person would do.

Like the festivals themselves, then, many of the foods served during medieval feasts also subverted order—or appeared to. The illusion of conquering nature was really the ultimate status symbol, so cooks essentially played God in the kitchen by performing edible magic tricks like fashioning artificial snow from egg whites, which was called "dyschefull of snowe" and was similar to meringue; having wine or rose water spew from naked statues; or changing the colors of foods using a palette of edible paints and dyes: blood for brown or black; mint or parsley for green; egg yolk, saffron, or dandelion for yellow. (A modern relic of this, according to some scholars, is the Easter egg, decorated to celebrate the return of eggs to the diet following Lent.)

Another popular presentation technique was to sew together different animals and stuff them back inside their skin after cooking, creating, in essence, edible taxidermy; for example, roasting and stuffing a cock or a hen, then crowning it with a helmet, tucking a silver- or gold-leaf lance under its wing, and posing it atop a roasted piglet so it looked like the bird was riding it into battle—a dish called *coqz heaumex* ("helmeted cocks"); or skinning and roasting a swan before redressing it in its skin and using skewers to hold it upright as if it were still alive: the classic *cignes revestuz* ("redressed swans"). The same thing was done with peacocks, with the added step of stuffing a ball of cloth soaked with alcohol into the beak and lighting it just before service so that they appeared to breathe fire—sort of a darker version of the onion volcanos in hibachi restaurants. And there was also the *cokagrys* (*cok* meaning "chicken," *grys* meaning "pig"), which called for sewing the head of a pig onto the lower half of a chicken and the head of a chicken onto the lower half of a pig:

> Take an olde cok and pull hym (*pluck him*) and wasshe hym, and flee hym all, safe the lygges (*legs*); and fyl hym full of the same farse (*stuffing*); and also take a pygge, and flee hym from the middes dounward, and fyl hym als full of the same farse, and sowe hym faste togedur, and sethe hom; and when thai have sothen a god while, take hom up, and do hom on a spette, and roste hom welle; and take zolkes of eggus, and do therto saffron,

and endore hom therwithe; and when thai arne rosted
dresse hom forthe, and lay on hom golde foyle and sylver.

Probably the best example of all of this coming together—
and another key milestone in the evolution of Christmas feasts—
was Carnival, from the Latin *carne levare* ("to remove meat").
Described by French historian Emmanuel Le Roy Ladurie as
"one last pagan fling" before the sacrificial fasting of Lent, when
Christians abstained from eating meat and animal products in
recognition of Christ's forty days of fasting in the wilderness, Carnival was a hodgepodge of pre-Christian harvest rituals repur-
posed for Christian penitence; it had all the bells and whistles
we've covered so far—a safety valve for social tension, a lavish
show of power, sexual and gustatory excess—but it added the artificial problem of having to consume foods before they became
taboo for six weeks, so people had even more of an excuse to
indulge than when they were merely eating against the natural
threat of winter. This also, by the way, led to the inventive use of
ingredients so they didn't go to waste; for example, some historians attribute the origin of *pain perdu* (French toast) to the need
to use up eggs before Lent.

Yet the most important aspect of Carnival was its ending,
when a mock swordfight was staged between the personification
of Lent, typically an emaciated woman who'd emerge from the
chaos armed with fish and vegetables, and Carnival, a fat man
armored in meats and phallic sausages. Sometimes Lent would
be armed with bread or a wooden baker's peel (the giant spatula used to remove bread from ovens) and armor made of leeks,
fish scales, or mussel shells and Carnival would wear a boar's-
head helmet while mounted upon a stag; regardless, Lent always
won, signifying a return to normality and reminding people that

mayhem and misrule weren't sustainable: that righteousness and order inevitably won and sin and gluttony inevitably lost,[*] that playtime was over and people had to go back to work until the same time next year. Similarly, other medieval celebrations staged reenactments of Adam and Eve and the fall of Eden, a fearful reminder that bad things happened to people who didn't follow the rules. And this sort of became the carrot and stick of Christmas, the whole idea that you had to be good all year long so you didn't end up on the naughty list.

A lot of the same ideas were mirrored in medieval literature and fables, extending these themes throughout the rest of the year. Many of the cultures that celebrated Carnival, for example, also had tales of mythical, upside-down dream worlds "designed to make the miserable circumstances of everyday life more bearable." And just like those of the POWs who wrote fantasy Christmas menus, these dream worlds revolved largely around food.

Probably the most famous was the Land of Cockaigne, pronounced similar to the modern "cocaine" but originating from the Middle Low German *kokenje* ("cake"), though the Dutch similarly had Luilekkerland, a combination of *leuzig* ("lazy") and *likken* ("lick"), and the Germans had Schlaraffenland, an adaptation of *schlaff* ("loose"). They were all sort of the adult equivalents of the story of Hansel and Gretel, where you still had candy houses, only they were also filled with beer and loose women: adult fantasylands constructed on the ideations of sloth, gluttony, and a complete absence of compromise, where debauchery ruled and there was no such thing as death, work, or taxes.

---

[*] Unless you were wealthy, of course.

Notes historian of Dutch literature Herman Pleij, "By the Middle Ages no one any longer believed in such a place, yet the stories about it continued to circulate around Europe for centuries. Apparently it was vitally important to be able to fantasize about a place where everyday worries did not exist and overcompensation was offered in the form of dreams of the ideal life."

The climate in these dream worlds was perfect year-round, though it might rain the occasional pie or custard, snow a dusting of powdered sugar, or hail sugared almonds. The streets were paved with ginger and nutmeg, the rivers flowed with wine, beer, or sweet milk, and the architecture was entirely edible. Houses were made of bacon, sausage, and cake held together with nails made of puddings or cloves; their beams were made of butter or pork; and their rooftops were tiled with warm pancakes or tarts.

Work was strictly forbidden, sometimes punishable by jail time; sloth, encouraged. So if you were hungry, all you had to do was open your mouth and a bird would fly into it, perfectly stewed and sprinkled with cloves and cinnamon; or a pig would run up to you, fully cooked with a knife and fork stuck into its back, crying "Eat me!"; or a grilled fish might jump into your hand from the river. Hot pastries slid from rooftops; plump cherries grew on the ground so you didn't have to reach for them, their centers made of sugar rather than hard pits; trees grew scones, pies, and doughnuts; and donkeys, dogs, cows, and horses, respectively, "shit nothing but sweet figs," nutmeg, pancakes, and poached eggs.

Meanwhile, sex was attained just as easily—and, crucially, enjoyed without shame, judgment, or "the encumbrance of having to wed."

"Loose women are highly thought of in that country," reads one description of Luilekkerland from 1546, "and the more wanton and frolicsome they are, the more they're loved. Even though it's said that lecherous whores are expensive to keep, this is certainly not the case in that land, where all sensual pleasures are readily available and at no cost whatever. One only has to say, or even just to think: Mouth, what do you want? Heart, what do you desire?"

In fact, Schlaraffenland was sometimes divided into districts where each vice was given its own territory; for example, there was the Republic of Venerea, home to such landmarks as Abortiva, Lustig, Bastarda, Concubina, and Lupanar ("wolf's den"), which was medieval slang for a brothel, derived from the practice of calling prostitutes *lupae* ("she-wolves") because they were "sexual and economic predator[s]" who "aggressively stripped their clients of wealth."

Also, there was a fountain of youth that kept one perpetually thirty years of age, and you were paid for sleeping and telling lies.

But just as with harvest festivals (and Hansel and Gretel, and Adam and Eve), there was a rub: though these utopias existed year-round, their locations were cleverly hidden, and even if you did find them, you had to swim through an ocean of pig shit for seven years to reach them or eat your way through mountains of porridge three miles thick—essentially suggesting that there was no such thing as a free lunch.

Some tales reinforced this point using reverse psychology; for example, the same text that praised the loose women of Luilekkerland ends by reiterating that it's a great place to live—as long as you're a debauched vagabond and champion rogue who wants to waste his life away:

There is nothing more disgraceful in that country than behaving virtuously, reasonably, honorably, and respectably and wanting to earn a living with one's hands. Anyone leading such a virtuous and upright life is hated by everyone and eventually banished from the country. . . . On the other hand, those who are gruff, coarse, and foolish—and, moreover, either cannot or will not learn—such people are held in high regard. Whoever is found to be the biggest good-for-nothing, the most untrustworthy, rudest, most dull-witted, and moreover the laziest, most debauched vagabond and champion rogue—such a person is proclaimed king. And whoever is merely coarse and stupid is made a prince. . . .

The biggest wine guzzlers or beer quaffers, who think of nothing but swigging and swilling and keeping their throats moist from dawn to dusk, will be elevated to the rank of count. And lazy daydreamers who like nothing better than to sleep the livelong day are treated in those parts as refined noblemen. If here in this country there are any prodigal children who intend to display such manners as those written of above—by abandoning all pretense to honor, virtue, honesty, and civility, not to mention wisdom and knowledge—then these uncouth louts should go to that land, where, upon their arrival, they will undoubtedly be esteemed and respected.

So, as with Carnival, the hero was eventually revealed to be not the person who sought adventure, riches, power, or personal freedom but the person who stayed at home and ate gruel—because someone had to be there to work the fields and plant the seeds for the next harvest, both literally and figuratively.

And this is really the only thing that's changed in the last two thousand years. People still celebrate the solstice by exchanging gifts, lighting fires, closing schools, feeding the poor, and gathering to feast—only instead of the jolly fat man having to die at the end to signify moderation and a return to balance, we now sit on his lap and leave him cookies.

CHAPTER 8

THE CHOICES OF A NEW GENERATION

Pour avoir assez, il faut avoir trop.
(To have enough, you must have too much.)

—FRENCH PROVERB

Pepsi. The choice of a new generation.

—1980S PEPSI-COLA SLOGAN

Choose life. Choose a job. Choose a career. Choose a family. Choose a fucking big television. Choose washing machines, cars, compact disc players, and electrical tin openers.

Choose good health, low cholesterol, and dental insurance. Choose fixed-interest mortgage repayments. Choose a starter home. Choose your friends. Choose leisure wear and matching luggage. Choose a three-piece suite on hire purchase in a range of fucking fabrics.

Choose DIY and wondering who the fuck you are on a Sunday morning. Choose sitting on that couch watching mind-numbing, spirit-crushing game shows stuffing fucking junk food into your mouth. Choose rotting away at the end of it all, pishing your last in a miserable home, nothing more than an embarrassment to the selfish, fucked-up brats you have spawned to replace yourself.

—TRAINSPOTTING

Today, of course, Cockaigne is no longer a fantasy, as advances in agriculture and food production have allowed us to indulge gluttony and excess year-round. By the seventeenth century, the mass cultivation of potatoes for animal feed had made it possible to delay the annual slaughter and keep pigs as late as January or February, and the industry has since progressed to the point at which seasonality has essentially evaporated, so we can now fatten and kill animals all year long and buy fruits and vegetables out of season, including things like year-round apples and shelf-stable orange juice.

So we're basically living in a modern-day Cockaigne, a utopian fantasyland where food has no limits and our choices defy natural order.

Instead of pies sliding from rooftops and roasted pigs running around with knives sticking out of them, we now have food delivery apps, grocery subscription services, drive-through windows, and disposable cutlery. We can indulge in all-day breakfast without leaving our cars; substitute hamburger buns with fried chicken breasts or glazed donuts; and buy pitted cherries, seedless watermelon, and presliced apple wedges in single-use plastic bags.

As Gregg Easterbrook writes:

Average Americans and Europeans not only live better than more than 99 percent of the human beings who have ever existed, they live better than most of the royalty of history. . . . As Robert Frank, a professor of economics at Cornell University, has noted, gas-station minimarts now sell cabernets and chardonnays "far superior in quality to the wines once drunk by the kings of France." Today supermarkets offer at low cost dozens of items almost everyone who has ever lived considered unattainable delicacies and died without tasting.

Granted, maybe fresh food hasn't made it to the masses, as food deserts still continue to haunt many low-income neighborhoods, making it difficult to find or afford things like fresh fruits and vegetables, but freshly *prepared* food has. More than 36 percent of Americans consume fast food daily, increasing to 80 percent monthly and 96 percent annually.

Writes Adam Chandler in *The Atlantic*, "No other institution, not libraries or gyms or the collective houses of worship, is that popular. Not even the internet comes close to garnering that much loyalty or participation as fast food. On a descending spectrum of American certainty, it goes something like death, premarital sex, fast food, and income taxes."

And all of this is getting faster, smarter, and more convenient. In addition to taking orders through mobile apps and text messages, chains such as McDonald's have started using artificial intelligence and machine learning to customize drive-through menus based on time of day, current weather conditions, and traffic patterns. And this is only the beginning; imagine drive-through sensors scanning your face and tailoring recommendations based on your estimated weight, pulse, and respiratory rate. Maybe you'd like extra fries to match your neck size? Maybe a chocolate shake if you're having a shitty day? Other fast-food chains are testing the use of license plate readers to remember customers' orders. (Who wants to bet that there's a correlation between expired registration stickers and irresponsible food choices—or vanity license plates and vanity espresso drinks?)

We face an avalanche of customizable food choices every time we open our mouths, which is ironic because the fast-food industry was built on systemic specialization and the idea that less is more. The initial success of McDonald's, for example, came from limiting their menu to focus primarily on making just three items—fifteen-cent hamburgers, twenty-cent shakes, and ten-cent fries—with speed, consistency, and economy. In fact, early on, you weren't allowed to customize your order at McDonald's because it slowed everything down, and part of what allowed them to sell their food so cheaply is that they sold it so quickly (reducing the wait time to just twenty seconds per customer) and they could sell more burgers, shakes, and fries per hour if they didn't have to worry about customization, wait staff, or turning over tables. Everything was streamlined and homogenized.

Writes social anthropologist Jeremy MacClancy:

A McDonald's outlet is not a "restaurant," but a smoothly functioning assembly line manufacturing a uniform and reliable product. There are no chefs, not even short order ones, and no real cooking. It is what businessmen call "a food management system." And this standardization is the key to McDonald's success. Everything is rational-ized: the product, the service, the cooking, the seating arrangements, the location of the outlets, and the technological hard- and software are all designed or planned according to the golden principle that there is only "one best way." . . . Every detail has been carefully thought out: the size of the counters, the number of tills, the space between each one, the standing room round the tills, the distances between tills and tables, the size of the tables, and the number of chairs and their position. This ensures the maximum use of production space, sufficient room to queue, and the right standing-to-sitting ratio. So that people do not linger in fast-food outlets, the hard, immovable chairs are deliberately designed not to provide prolonged comfort. That way, the clientele get fast food and the management get a fast turnover.

In fact, McDonald's cares so much about uniformity and efficiency that they add a silicon-based polymer to the fryer oil to reduce splatter, which cuts down on cleaning time; called dimethylpolysiloxane, the same chemical is also used in head lice treatments, condom lubricants, and breast implants. How neat is that?

Yet the industry has since shifted toward choice and customization. It's no longer enough to be served right away; we now demand to be served *our way*. The real watershed moment in this movement was the debut of Burger King's infamous "Have it your way" jingle in 1974, penned largely in response to 1960s and '70s counterculture, the quest for individuality amid corporate and governmental mistrust, the oppressions of patriarchal society, and the post–World War II military-industrial complex:

Hold the pickles, hold the lettuce
Special orders don't upset us
All we ask is that you let us serve it your way!
We can serve your broiled beef Whopper
Fresh with everything on topper
Any way you think is proper, have it your way!

So customizing your burger sort of became the fast-food equivalent of growing your hair long, symbolically burning your bra, or having sex in the back of a Volkswagen: a way to protest oppressive mainstream ideals, piss off your father, and show the world you weren't a corporate sheep.

And ever since, food brands have been increasingly pandering to customers to make them feel empowered and free by expanding their choices, making the offerings of Cockaigne and Schlaraffenland pale in comparison. In fact, a lot of fast-food advertising tends to emulate these fantasylands, most notably Burger King's 2005 "Fantasy Ranch" commercial featuring the vocals of Darius Rucker against a backdrop of scantily clad milkmaids, farmer's daughters, and cheerleaders, taking the concept of "Have it your way" a few steps farther:

When my belly starts a rumblin'
And I'm jonesin' for a treat,
I close my eyes for a big surprise,
The Tendercrisp Bacon Cheddar Ranch.

I love the Tendercrisp Bacon Cheddar Ranch,
The breasts, they grow on trees
And streams of bacon ranch dressing
Flow right up to your knees.

There's tumbleweeds of bacon
And cheddar paves the streets.
Folks don't front ya 'cause you've got the juice,
There's a train of ladies comin' with a nice caboose,
Never get in trouble, never need an excuse,
That's the Tendercrisp Bacon Cheddar Ranch.

I love the Tendercrisp Bacon Cheddar Ranch,
No one tells you to behave,
Your wildest fantasies come true,
Dallas cheerleaders give you shaves,
Red onions make you laugh instead,
And French fries grow like weeds.
You get to veg all day, all the lotto tickets pay,
There's a king who wants you to have it your way,
That's the Tendercrisp Bacon Cheddar Ranch.

As Carrie Packwood Freeman and Debra Merskin remark in their essay "Having It His Way: The Construction of Masculinity in Fast-Food TV Advertising," many of these ads also seem to imply a lifestyle free from "nagging wives, girlfriends, and mothers," either by not portraying such relationships at all or by portraying wives and girlfriends as barriers to male freedom. And let's not even get into the category of "breastaurants" such as Hooters and Twin Peaks.

So food brands are basically doing the same thing medieval hosts were doing when they offered nobles the choice cuts of meat and the "upper crust" of bread during banquets, except these honors are now given to everyone. Not only can we choose to hold the pickles and hold the lettuce, we can even get limited-edition toys thrown in if we order an aptly named "Happy Meal" (a relic, of course, of Kellogg's free cereal prizes).

Consider the language Burger King used in 2014 when, after forty years, they updated their slogan from "Have it your way" to "Be your way":

> It's ok to not be perfect. Self-expression is most important and it's our differences that make us individuals instead of robots.
>
> BURGER KING® restaurants are, and always have been, a place where you come as you are, eat what you want, how you want, with whom you want, and step out of this world of standardization that tells you if you do something different, people might look at you. The BURGER KING® brand says, "bring on the eyeballs."

So really, Burger King has pivoted from the burger business to the self-esteem business.

The same press release goes on to explain that you can order a Whopper customized "221,184 different ways, with grill marks, which is why no two are ever the same," which is interesting coming from a chain that also brags about the uniformity of cooking their burgers on conveyor belts—though at least the marks aren't painted on, a common industry ruse to make frozen, precooked burgers seem fresh and artisan.

And it's not just Burger King and McDonald's. This is the same motivation behind made-to-order, fast-casual restaurants like Chipotle. (It's also not a coincidence that McDonald's once owned 90 percent of Chipotle.) As consumers, we essentially get to play king (or ancient harvest god) by telling servers to do things "our way" and reveling in our wealth of disparate food choices.

Writes Australian essayist Elizabeth Farrelly:

It's as though our childhood yearnings to play kings and queens, to wear ermine and live forever in vast palaces, still haunt us; as though personal opulence is still the biggest and brightest outpost of our imagining. . . . We presume—call it the castle-premise—that democracy has made the rights of kings available to us all, and that some kind of fairy dust has costlessly converted the undreamable dream into sustainable reality.

Starbucks, for example, offers more than eighty-seven thousand possible drink combinations,* many with ingredients that seem straight out of Cockaigne. There's whipped cream, "vanilla" syrup (which, by the way, is made of sugar, water, natural flavors, potassium sorbate, and citric acid), toasted white chocolate mocha sauce, skinny mocha sauce, dark chocolate curls, sea salt topping (which actually means sugar, sea salt, and silicon dioxide), smoked butterscotch, steamed apple juice, vanilla crème, holiday sugar sparkles, caramel drizzle, chocolate cookie crumble, cold foam, honey, "cloud powder," matcha powder, freeze-dried dragon fruit, something called "pink drink," Equal, Splenda, stevia with monk fruit—and, oh, let's not forget, coffee. In fact, Starbucks' drink menu reads a lot like an Egyptian medicine book; all that's missing is the cat hair and penis water.

---

* That's not counting the ability to order many of these drinks heated to your own perfect temperature.

Instead of seasonality, we now have seasonal lattes, cycling among pumpkin spice, gingerbread, eggnog, and iced mocha. And each of these drinks comes in its own special cup size—tall, grande, or venti—with our name written on it because selling small and medium drinks would be way too corporate and normalizing. And if you order enough of them, you can collect virtual stars and badges.

In an age of industrial consumerism and mass manufacturing, this freedom and personalization make us feel less like a cog in a machine or a corporate drone. It's our way of manifesting destiny in a world that's long been conquered and homogenized.

Reflect Stanford University researchers Heejung Kim and Hazel Rose Markus, "If a person orders a decaffeinated cappuccino with nonfat milk in a café in San Francisco, he or she can feel good about having a preference that is not exactly regular."

This also explains the popularity of craft beer as an individualistic response to "big beer" and the $100 billion per year we spend on bottled water globally despite the obvious environmental impacts (more than 4 billion pounds of plastic in 2016 alone) and the ubiquity of public tap water—which is a fraction of the cost of bottled water; on average, no less safe or clean;* and in many cases bottled from the very same source.

---

* This is not to suggest that clean actually means clean; remember all those agricultural pesticides and fertilizers we said are being added to soil? Well, those chemicals tend to make their way into water systems. And although the EPA does limit the contamination levels in public drinking water to certain maximums, there are a lot of chemicals it doesn't or can't regulate, such as pharmaceuticals, and studies have found everything from antidepressants and antibiotics to caffeine and pseudoephedrine in treated tap water, coming largely from human waste and sweat as well as improper disposal methods, such as flushing drugs down toilets.

Writes Yale University psychologist Paul Bloom, bottled water "is an example of what the sociologist Thorstein Veblen called 'conspicuous consumption,' a way to advertise how much money you have or, more generally, to show off your positive traits as a person," such as taste, supposed purity, or athleticism. "If the water were free or had obvious health benefits," says Bloom, "it would be useless as such a signal, and . . . fewer people would drink it."

This hunger for personalization and conspicuous consumption is also reflected in modern grocery stores. Before the first self-service grocery store opened in 1916, customers had to wait at a counter and ask a clerk to get their groceries, much as we still have to do with razors and certain cold medications to keep us from shoplifting or using them to manufacture crystal meth. And they probably had to go to several stores: the bakery for bread, the butcher for meat, the pharmacy for soda or drugs. Then clerks disappeared* and shopping carts came along—and bar code scanners and express lanes and self-checkout. By the 1940s, the average supermarket was stocking about three thousand products, whereas today a lot of stores carry closer to ninety thousand.

We can now choose from more than fifty types of Oreos: thins, reduced fat, golden, lemon, root beer float, fruit punch, peanut butter, Reese's peanut butter cup, chocolate, chocolate strawberry, white fudge covered, coco chip, filled cupcake, red velvet, cinnamon bun, watermelon, banana split, back to school

---

* Getting rid of the storefront clerks not only empowered customers to make their own selections but also streamlined the shopping process—not unlike what McDonald's did—and made it easier for self-service grocery stores to lower their prices, putting mom-and-pop stores out of business.

(with four different back-to-school designs), gingerbread, peppermint, caramel apple, pumpkin spice, cotton candy, strawberry shortcake, Swedish fish, firework (with popping candy inside), s'mores, cookie dough, key lime pie, brownie batter, Mississippi mud pie, Dunkin' Donuts mocha, birthday cake (which comes in both chocolate and golden), Halloween (with orange creme[*] and spooky designs), rainbow sherbet ice cream.

This isn't counting international flavors such as hot chicken wing and wasabi in China. And these choices are then compounded with variations in personal filling preferences (original, double stuf, mega stuf, most stuf) and packaging (king size, family size, go packs, snak saks, spooky edition glow-in-the-dark packs for Halloween).

Just as with medieval banquets and fantasylands, a lot of these food choices seem to subvert nature by promising the impossible: fat-free ice cream, zero-calorie soda, sugar-free pancake syrup, nondairy creamer, instant rice, crust- and carbohydrate-free bread, and meatless bacon. Or they're camouflaged to look like something they're not, so instead of stuffing medieval pig stomachs to look like hedgehogs or making peacocks appear to breathe fire, we now have dinosaur-shaped chicken nuggets and macaroni and cheese pieces shaped like Yoda and Darth Vader—which sort of makes them not macaroni anymore. Instead of gilding foods in silver and gold, we now have rainbow sprinkles, edible glitter, Halloween Whoppers with black hamburger buns, and hot pink Fruity Pebbles designed to "magically" turn cereal

---

[*] The "stuf" inside Oreos doesn't actually contain any dairy products, so it can't legally be called "cream"; in fact, in 2016, two Oreo flavors were recalled because they were manufactured with equipment that was also used to process dairy, causing fears that they could pose a risk to customers with milk allergies.

milk blue. And instead of sewing different foods together, we just alter them genetically.*

Writes Sophie Egan, "It's no longer enough to merely invent new products. Now you have to provide shock value. Nutritional train wrecks that are this over-the-top used to exist mostly at state fairs—fried butter on a stick, for example. But now these types of unbelievable combinations are being sold at national fast-food chains where people dine on a regular basis."

Recent examples include Starbucks' Unicorn Frappuccino, a Day-Glo concoction of mango syrup, sour blue drizzle, "vanilla" whipped cream, and sweet pink and sour blue powders that starts out purple and tangy but becomes pink and tart as you drink it; KFC's Double Down and Chicken and Donut sandwiches, which respectively have "buns" of fried chicken and vanilla-glazed donuts in place of bread; Heinz's limited-edition Ed Sheeran ketchup bottles adorned with the singer's autograph and images of his tattoos; and crossovers like Burger King's Flamin' Hot Mac n' Cheetos and Taco Bell's Doritos Locos Taco, the latter of which sold more than a billion units in its first year and created so much traffic that Taco Bell reportedly had to hire fifteen thousand new workers to meet demand.

Now, conventional wisdom would suggest that all of these choices should make us happier and that we should be grateful to live in a world our ancestors (or maybe even our childhood selves) could only dream of, where innumerable choices surround us and

---

* Right now this is done primarily agriculturally, giving us foods such as higher-yield soybeans, bruise-resistant potatoes, apples that resist browning, and herbicide- and pest-resistant corn, but scientists have also edited the genetic structure of animals to create extra-large pigs, faster-growing salmon, hornless cattle, and cows that produce "human" breast milk—all of which could be heading to grocery stores soon.

no one has to be ordinary or settle for chunky tomato sauce when they really want extra chunky. In fact, Malcolm Gladwell gave a viral TED Talk on this very topic ("Choice, Happiness and Spaghetti Sauce"), explaining how a psychophysicist* named Howard Moskowitz made the world a happier place by convincing food brands to abandon their pursuit of a single perfect formula and instead give consumers more choices by offering multiple formulas. One of Gladwell's examples is Diet Pepsi, which was formulated to get its sweetness from aspartame rather than sugar (or corn syrup)—but before Pepsi could put it on shelves, they needed to figure out exactly how much aspartame was needed to achieve the perfect level of sweetness, so they hired Moskowitz to find the sweet spot. As Gladwell explains, "that sounds like an incredibly straightforward question to answer," but it wasn't. Instead, what Moskowitz found was that consumer preferences were all over the place. Rather than pointing to a perfect "sweet spot," the data was scattered, which suggested to him that Pepsi had been asking the wrong question—that they shouldn't have been looking for the perfect Pepsi but the perfect *Pepsis*.

Apparently, that wasn't very economical for Pepsi, so they settled somewhere in the middle, but Moskowitz applied his insight to other brands. So when Campbell's hired him in the early 1980s to help Prego, their then-struggling line of pasta sauces, compete against Ragù, he told them the same thing: that instead of trying to please everyone with the perfect *sauce*, they should try to please everyone with the perfect *sauces*. If you never had the pleasure of shopping for tomato sauce in the early 1980s, it was nothing like it is today, where you have entire aisles of

---

* A branch of psychology that deals with the study and measurement of sensations in response to physical stimuli, e.g., taste and texture.

choices. If you were lucky, you could choose between, well, Ragù and Prego. What Moskowitz helped identify was that there were preferences no one in the industry was catering to. It wasn't enough to have original and chunky—some people (roughly a third of Americans, in fact) wanted their sauce *extra chunky*. So, as Gladwell explains, Prego ended up launching a line of extra-chunky sauces and making more than half a billion dollars from them over the next ten years.

And this is why we now have an endless variety of tomato sauces, why Prego alone now offers traditional, lower-calorie traditional, no-sugar-added traditional, sensitive recipe traditional, roasted garlic and herb, fresh mushroom, sausage and garlic meat sauce, spicy sausage meat sauce, mini-meatball meat sauce, three cheese, chunky tomato with leafy greens, garden chunky zucchini, creamy vodka, tomato basil garlic, lower sodium mushroom, lower sodium roasted red pepper and garlic, Florentine spinach and cheese, spicy red pepper, pesto marinara, bacon and provolone. These, in addition to entire lines of alfredo (homestyle alfredo, light homestyle alfredo) and farmer's market sauces (chickpea and kale, white bean and roasted garlic). You get the point.

According to Gladwell, having so many choices makes consumers "deliriously happy," and by "embracing the diversity of human beings, we will find a surer way to true happiness."

But there's really only a very small area in which this holds true (at least in terms of food choices, as opposed to other forms of diversity). Certainly, having some choice in what we eat is better than having no choice, and we're biologically wired to crave abundance and variety for a lot of reasons we've covered earlier, like avoiding starvation if the one crop we rely on fails or it doesn't rain enough or winter comes early or preventing things like pellagra and scurvy by eating a varied diet. Writes Elizabeth Farrelly, "In evolutionary terms, of course, the 'reason' for desire is clear. The scarcity environment in which humanity evolved prioritised appetite: whoever got the most sex, or food, or stuff was likely to be a successful spreader of the seed."

So none of us would be here if it hadn't been for the pursuit of new and exciting food sources and our innate desire for variety packs and family-size packaging.

Yet there comes a point at which enough is enough—when the bell curve correlating choice and happiness starts to go back down again and our unquenchable thirst inevitably drowns us. If we gave everyone their own perfectly formulated Pepsi, would they really be happy? Or would they expect that level of diversity and perfection—an impossible standard—everywhere else in life? (Remember Epicurus's point that "To whom a little is not enough, nothing is enough"?) In fact, numerous studies suggest that adding food options makes us happier only to the point of four or six, after which they tend to make us *less* happy.

"The more choice you have, the greater the number of appealing options, no matter how discriminating your tastes," explains psychologist Sheena Iyengar:

At some point, you simply won't have enough space or money or time to enjoy all those options. So you'll have to make some sacrifices, and each of these carries a psychological cost. Your enjoyment of the chosen options will be diminished by your regret over what you had to give up. In fact, the sum total of the regret over all the "lost" options may end up being greater than your joy over your chosen options, leaving you less satisfied than you would have been if you had had less choice to begin with.

Psychologists call this "the paradox of choice." ("When people have no choice," explains psychologist Barry Schwartz, "life is almost unbearable. As the number of available choices increases, as it has in our consumer culture, the autonomy, control, and liberation this variety brings are powerful and positive. But as the number of choices keeps growing, negative aspects of having a multitude of options begin to appear. As the number of choices grows further, the negatives escalate until we become overloaded. At this point, choice no longer liberates, but debilitates. It might even be said to tyrannize.")

So basically, our fear of missing out is compounded by each additional product SKU; instead of being freed by choice, we become burdened by it.

And just like Moskowitz, Iyengar drew her conclusions directly from the grocery store, specifically, Draeger's Grocery store in Menlo Park, California, where she conducted a landmark study of consumer purchase behavior by handing out free samples of jam. She and her Stanford colleagues set up a tasting booth and changed the number of jams they were sampling every few hours, offering customers an option to choose from either a large assortment of twenty-four jams or a small assortment of just six jams. (The jams, by the way, were from Wilkin & Sons, "supplier of jams to the Queen of England.") As one might expect, more customers were drawn to the large offering than the small one (60 percent of customers compared to 40 percent). However, a much smaller percentage of those customers actually purchased jam afterward: just 3 percent of the customers who sampled from the large assortment made purchases compared to *30* percent of the customers who'd sampled from the smaller assortment, which is a statistically massive spread. So even though the larger booth attracted far more traffic, more than six times as many purchases were made by those in the smaller group who'd sampled fewer jams.

And not only did visitors to the larger table tend to walk away without buying any jam, they also seemed weighed down by the pressure, so afraid of choosing the wrong jam that they'd eventually give up—some after ten minutes of scrutinizing different jars and discussing "the relative merits" of each flavor.

Explains Iyengar:

> When the options are few, we can be happy with what we choose since we are confident that it is the best possible choice for us. When the options are practically infinite, though, we believe that the perfect choice for us must be out there somewhere and that it's our responsibility to find it. Choosing can then become a lose-lose situation: If we make a choice quickly without fully exploring the available options, we'll regret potentially missing out on something better; if we do exhaustively consider all the options, we'll expend more effort (which won't necessarily increase the quality of our final choice), and if we discover other good options, we may regret that we can't choose them all. This dilemma can occur for choices from the mundane, like picking a restaurant, to the highly significant, like whom to marry or what career to pursue.

It's no wonder our divorce rates are so high. How can we expect to spend our lives with someone if we can't commit to a jar of strawberry jam?

Meanwhile, all of this is made even worse by the impossible standards behind our food choices. How can we be happy with 15 percent body fat when our ice cream and mayonnaise are both fat free? How can we be happy with someone giving us 100 percent when we can get more than 100 percent of our recommended daily vitamins from a single bowl of fortified cereal? How can we expect to cope with our bitter reality when our morning coffee tastes like pumpkin spice or funfetti?

Many of the foods we see in commercials and on social media are given so much hair and makeup that they bear as much resemblance to real food as pornography does to real sex, so the term *food porn*—described by food columnist, chef, and cookbook author Molly O'Neill as "prose and recipes so removed from real life that they cannot be used except as vicarious experience"—is apropos.

Explains Anne E. McBride:

> Today, *food porn* generally evokes the unattainable: cooks will never achieve the results shown in certain cookbooks, magazines, or television shows, nor will they ever master the techniques. In fact, portrayals of food have been so transformed by food styling, lighting, and the actions of comely media stars that food does seem increasingly out of reach to the average cook or consumer. As with sex porn, we enjoy watching what we ourselves presumably cannot do.

Indeed, it's no coincidence that food stylists and adult film stylists tend to use a lot of the same tools behind camera to make objects look sexier. Granted, food styling has come a long way in the past few decades, trending, like media in general, toward authenticity, but it's not unusual to see food stylists using things like lipstick to redden berries, eyeliner to paint in grill marks, nail polish and personal lubricants like K-Y Jelly to keep foods looking moist and glossy, and white lotion in place of milk to prevent cereals from getting soggy on set. These, in addition to less sexy ingredients such as vegetable shortening as a heat-resistant stand-in for ice cream; shaving cream in place of whipped cream; Scotchgard to prevent pancakes from absorbing syrup, which might actually be motor oil instead of actual syrup; and lit cigarettes or wet, microwaved tampons hidden behind foods to make them appear steaming hot.

In fact, a lot of fruits and vegetables don't even make it to the grocery store because they're not pretty enough, so they're thrown away, left to rot on farms, or incorporated into things like soup or animal feed. In fact, up until recently, Quebec had an "ugly fruit" ban that prevented stores from selling produce with "abnormal physical characteristics," resulting in an esti-mated 10 percent of fresh fruits and vegetables going to waste, while American farmers report having anywhere from 20 to 70 percent of their yields rejected by commercial buyers because of unflattering curves or blemishes that make them commer-cially unattractive.

Even the foods that are pretty enough to make it to stores are often sprayed with edible coatings and antibrowning agents to help them stay attractive. You know that mist grocery stores spray over their produce section? Its purpose isn't to keep foods fresh so much as to make them *appear* fresh. In fact, spraying too much water can actually encourage spoiling and the spread of bacteria, and in the 1990s the Centers for Disease Control traced a fatal outbreak of Legionnaires' disease to a produce mis-ter in Louisiana. (Some, meanwhile, allege that the real purpose of these mists is to add water weight to produce that's sold by the pound.)

So the real irony is that even though our food choices have skyrocketed, our food has paradoxically become less diverse. The engineered efficiency that McDonald's applied to its burgers and fries now applies to pretty much everything.

Seventy percent of the French fries in the United States are made from one type of potato, the Russet Burbank (also known as the California Russet, English Russet, Golden Russet, Idaho Potato, and Idaho Baker), in part because McDonald's, the largest buyer of potatoes, wants their fries to be uniform in crispness, color, texture, oil absorption, strip length, and "retention of good fry quality after 8 months of storage."

Iceberg lettuce is on menus not because it tastes like packing material but because it *packs* like packing material. Explains food historian B. W. Higman:

Down to World War I most of the lettuces consumed in the United States were leaf or butter varieties, the most successful being the "Big Boston," but after the war the growing market dominance of California was followed by a shift to crisp head varieties, notably the iceberg or "New York" lettuce, with characteristic compact heads and resistance to damage in the near-freezing temperatures that made possible their journey across the continent, packed in crates and resting on layers of chipped ice. By the 1920s the iceberg lettuce had emerged as the first truly seasonless fresh vegetable.

Similarly, writes neuroscientist Rachel Herz:

Store-bought tomatoes look prettier and last longer than they used to, but most of the time they are mealy, slightly sour, and lacking in flavor. In fact, for the last seventy years or so, breeders have been selecting for tomatoes that are uniform in color, since consumers prefer these over the blotchy kind, but the genetic mutation that produces their consistent appearance has an unintended consequence: it disrupts the production of a protein responsible for the fruit's concentration of sugar, so they don't taste as good.

So natural character and diversity, writes Martin Teitel, "are bulldozed in favor of the genetic uniformity on which mass marketing thrives."

Sure, we might have endless choices of tomato sauce, but, really, we have *less* variety because they're made from tomatoes that have been bred for industrial consistency, bruise resistance, and the extent to which they can endure storage in warehouses and long-haul trucks—in part because McDonald's is also one of the largest buyers of tomatoes. We can choose from nonfat, 2 percent, heavy cream, and whole milk at Starbucks—yet 94 percent of the nation's milk comes from one type of cow bred for its industrial uniformity and production volume.

Writes Michael Symons in his book *A History of Cooks and Cooking*:

> To think that three million years of human development, all that experiment, all that risk, all those dreams, all that heartbreak, all that repetition, have led to this. We have nibbled. We have stirred the pudding. We have ended with McDonald's. To think that the sum total is Coke clutter—dispensers, billboards, television slots, athletic sponsorships, cities draped in neon. Profit-minded zeal-

ots, with a standardised "formula" and global reach, devalue the human enterprise. We end it smothered in cost-cutting corporate cooking, our mouths agape before a thin, anorexic screen. We have sold our birthright for a mess of globally marketed pottage. We have participated in the complete manufacture of choice. We have the power only to decide our baked potato topping.

Just like in the stories, our fantasies of Cockaigne were too good to be true.

"We always knew that having what you wanted didn't make you likeable," writes Elizabeth Farrelly in *Blubberland: The Dangers of Happiness*. "Now we know it doesn't make you happy or successful either."

CHAPTER 9

FORBIDDEN BERRIES (OR APPETITE FOR DISTRACTION)

Healthy, sane humans do not stab themselves in the thighs, or bathe their eyes in lemon juice. So why do we so love to assault one of the most sensitive organs in the human body, the tongue, with what amounts to chemical warfare?

—JASON G. GOLDMAN

Humans, as we've seen, like to eat a lot of strange things—pigeon pies, rendered bear fat, tiny ancestors of corn, sugar of lead, pigs sewed together with chickens, and fire-breathing peacocks—yet perhaps even stranger is our taste for chili peppers: a fruit* that, ecologically speaking, specifically evolved to repel us.

You see, whereas corn developed that tough outer casing to protect its seeds and other berries developed thorns, chilies developed a chemical defense mechanism in the form of capsaicin, the principal function of which is to cause predators pain.† The industry term for this is *directed deterrence*. Birds, which are natural seed dispersers and excrete seeds whole and intact, are

---

* Although chilies meet the grocery store definition of a spice or vegetable (both culinary terms), botanically they're fruits—berries, to be specific—named after the Sanskrit *pippali* ("berry"), which, confusingly, is also the origin of the names of the spices long pepper and black pepper, both of which are of no relation to the chili pepper, which, also confusingly, is interchangeably written as "chilli" or "chile" pepper.
† Chilies actually contain a number of chemical compounds for this purpose, called capsaicinoids, including dihydrocapsaicin, nordihydrocapsaicin, homocapsaicin, and homodihydrocapsaicin. However, capsaicin is by far the most abundant, making up roughly 70 percent of capsaicinoids.

immune to capsaicin, a biological reward for helping chilies spread and propagate. And this mutualistic relationship extends even further than just birds air-dropping seeds with piles of natural fertilizer in the form of their droppings. Explains culinary historian Maricel E. Presilla, the journey through a bird's intestinal tract not only camouflages seeds from seed-eating predators but also eliminates some seed-destroying funguses; as a result, seeds excreted by birds have nearly 400 percent better odds of surviving in the wild.

Meanwhile humans, whose mammalian teeth tend to crush and destroy seeds, making us an ecological threat to chilies, can sense capsaicin at less than one part per million. In contrast, the human threshold for sensing salt (sodium chloride) begins at about two thousand parts per million and sugar (sucrose) around five thousand. And it's not our sense of taste that's doing the work here, as is the case with things we perceive as salty, sweet, sour, bitter, or umami, but rather our trigeminal or chemical sense, which registers sensations of irritation, temperature, and touch to alert the body of potentially harmful chemicals and bacteria. In fact, the same pain sensor that alerts us to capsaicin, TRPV1, also responds to physical heat, specifically temperatures above 109°F. So eating a pepper isn't unlike, say, being stung by a bee, licking a nine-volt battery, or burning your tongue on scalding hot coffee—all sensations intended to warn the body of exposure to harm and if necessary trigger a series of protective reflexes to mitigate the effects and prevent further exposure.

Bite into a habañero or order your food "Thai hot," and your body essentially thinks it's being attacked by a chemical weapon. Beyond the burning pain, which is supposed to compel you to reject or eject spicy food, you'll probably begin to sweat as your body attempts to flush your system; your nose will run to protect your nasal passages; your eyes will water to protect your corneas; you'll produce excess saliva to purge your mouth; and you might cough or sneeze to protect your airways—a lot of the same defense mechanisms you'd expect if you were to eat something you were allergic to or choke on a pretzel.

In contrast, foods that nature actually intended us to eat tend to elicit positive reflexes, such as triggering the production of stomach acid or pancreatic hormones. Explains Gary K. Beauchamp, emeritus director and president of the Monell Chemical Senses Center in Philadelphia, "The traditional view of taste receptors is that they have to do with conscious perception and food selection," helping us differentiate between quality food sources and potentially hazardous poisons or bacteria. However, taste receptors also exist downstream in places like the gut and airways* to screen for criteria we're not completely conscious of (nutrients, calories, proteins) and help regulate satiation and digestion.

And this deterrence isn't limited to humans. Capsaicin is an effective threat deterrent almost unilaterally, from predatory insects and rodents to seed-destroying funguses. In lieu of electric fences (which are cost prohibitive and no match for elephants with nonconductive tusks), some farmers in Africa plant chilies along the barriers of their farms, mix chili powder with motor oil and smear it on fences, burn bricks of chilies and dried elephant

---

* Brillat-Savarin was ahead of his time here, too, proclaiming way back in 1825, "Anyone who has been born without a tongue, or whose tongue has been cut out, still has a moderately strong sense of taste. The first instance can often be found in literature; the second has been fairly well described to me by a poor devil whose tongue had been amputated by the Algerians, to punish him for having plotted with one of his fellow prisoners to break out and flee."

dung, or throw condoms filled with chilies and firecrackers to keep elephants away from their crops.*

Ranchers smear capsaicin on sheep to keep wolves away, manufacturers have put it in wallpaper adhesive to ward off rats, and some carmakers have started wrapping electrical wires with capsaicin-infused tape to keep rodents from chewing them (a problem that may have been exacerbated by the switch to soy-based wiring, which smells similar to vanilla when heated). Chili-flavored birdseed is also a thing and is used to prevent squirrels from pilfering bird food.

Capsaicin has even been used underwater to keep mussels from attaching to boat hulls, and natives of the San Blas Islands off the coast of Panama allegedly drag lines of chilies behind their canoes to repel sharks—though there's little evidence this is effective, as numerous attempts by the US Navy to develop chemical shark deterrents have found that even those that are strong enough to kill sharks generally fail to deter them from eating the bait before dying.†

And similar uses apply to humans. In the 1960s, two professors at the University of Georgia developed pepper spray as an

---

* Other methods used to repel elephants from crops include cutting off their tusks with power saws to improve the efficacy of electric fencing and covering fences with beehives to release swarms of agitated African honeybees when disturbed.

† At least one recipe for shark deterrents was developed with the help of Julia Child, who, before introducing mainstream America to French cuisine, worked for the Office of Strategic Services (the World War II equivalent of the CIA), where she was tasked with cooking up coatings to prevent sharks from accidentally bumping into and setting off underwater explosives. This is also where she met her eventual husband, intelligence officer Paul Child, who, in 1948, was transferred to the US Information Agency in France, fatefully exposing Julia (and thereby much of the world) to the joys of French cooking.

animal repellent, which was initially used by postal workers and meter readers to defend themselves against dogs but was quickly adopted by joggers and law enforcement for defense against other humans; mothers apply capsaicin to their breasts to initiate weaning or to children's thumbs to stop the habit of thumb-sucking; and in the 1980s, some New York City transit employees sprinkled chili powder on turnstile slots in hopes of keeping teenagers from sucking out used subway tokens,* a practice that could net the vandals up to one hundred dollars a day—at the time equivalent to about thirty hours of minimum wage.

Yet humans are the only animal stubborn enough to seek out this pain by putting hot sauce on our eggs—and it's not for a lack of trying to convert others.

Repeated attempts to induce a preference for chili peppers in rats, including gradually lacing their food with capsaicin, inducing sickness whenever they ate food without it, and provoking thiamine deficiency, then nursing them back to health with capsaicin in their recovery food, have failed, suggesting that rats have an innate aversion to capsaicin that disappears only upon destroying their senses. In all scenarios the rats showed a clear preference for foods that didn't burn them and an aversion to those that did, leading researchers to conclude, "One cannot fail to be impressed by the resistance shown by laboratory rats to the acquisition of a preference for chili pepper."

And neither can one fail to be impressed by the resistance

---

* One would think the presence of rampant germs alone would have been deterrent enough, but seasoning the token slots wasn't effective either, as enterprising teenagers began bringing buckets of water with them to wash off the coin slots before sucking on them—then dumping the remaining water on transit employees.

shown by humans to physical pain and our own biological distress signals.

Ironically, our stubborn pursuit of chilies has taken them further than birds ever could.* They're now the most commonly used spice in the world, where they're grown on every continent (if we count a greenhouse in Antarctica designed to test plant cultivation technologies developed for human space exploration) and eaten daily by roughly a third of the global population, making up such staple components of regional cuisines as North African harissa, Korean gochujang, Thai sriracha, Indonesian sambal, and American Flamin' Hot Cheetos. More than six thousand years after first cultivating them, we're still spreading them like wildfire—and selectively breeding them to be even more potent, creating entirely new varieties like the Carolina Reaper, reportedly up to four hundred times as hot as jalapeños.

So clearly, our attraction to chilies wasn't just a phase; the heart wants what the heart wants—which is, apparently, frequent heartburn.

The Aztecs probably captured the inanity of this best. They revered chilies and ate them with every meal, going without them only during periods of ritual fasting (sort of the Aztec equivalent of sacrificing meat during Lent), and used them medicinally to treat everything from eye infections to labor pains. Their cure for acne? Wash your face with chili powder and hot urine. And, yet, they also used them for ritual punishment, rubbing chilies on

---

* Note that we've also taken them higher, as you can now buy so-called space peppers grown from experimental seeds that have been launched into space to test the effects of zero gravity and cosmic radiation on genetic plant mutation, which would make a great opening for a zombie-pepper film.

the genitals of misbehaving children or holding their children over piles of burning chilies to choke and suffocate them with the fumes.*

Of course, our oral sadism isn't just limited to capsaicin. "The majority of adults in the world ingest, every day, at least one innately rejected substance," write Paul Rozin and Deborah Schiller.

Consider the bitterness of dark chocolate and coffee, the latter of which people often enjoy at temperatures high enough to cause tissue damage; the caustic burn of alcohol and wasabi (or cigarettes) in the throat and nasal passages; the pins and needles of soda or champagne carbonation, caused by carbonic acid; or the astringency of black tea and dry wine. Like chilies, these are all innately unpalatable to the uninitiated—and there's no scientific consensus as to why we consume them.

Probably the simplest explanation is to pin things on food preservation, as chilies also happen to kill bacteria and mask the taste and odor of foods that aren't the freshest. This would explain why spicy foods tend to be more prevalent in hotter climates, where higher temperatures make food preservation more challenging, places like Central America, southern Asia, and Indonesia. And the same idea extends to the use of spices in general. When researchers at Cornell University analyzed nearly five thousand recipes from thirty-six countries, they found that the number of spices per dish increased alongside the average annual temperature of the region—and that cultures in warmer climates tended to use not just more spices in their dishes but specifically those with the strongest antibacterial potency, the av-

---

* Other Aztec punishments involving pantry items included binding the hands and feet of naked children and stabbing them with the spines of agave leaves.

erage spice inhibiting around 67 percent of bacteria compared to 80 percent inhibited by chilies. (Surprisingly, sour acids such as lemon and lime juice inhibited a mere 24 percent.)

So chilies may have helped preserve food before the age of refrigeration and may also have functioned as a primitive form of air-conditioning, as the gustatory sweating meant to flush the body of capsaicin also has a cooling effect that helps regulate body temperature, which helps explain why people eat *vindaloo* in India and *pad prik king* in Thailand.

Meanwhile, people in arctic or subarctic regions tend to eat foods that are higher in fat content, such as whale meat or *akutuq*, an Alaskan dish of whipped caribou fat, seal oil, and berries, often referred to as Eskimo ice cream, as well as fermented foods such as sauerkraut, fermented seal oil, or decomposed Icelandic shark meat that's been buried underground for months and marinated in lactic acid (described by Anthony Bourdain as the single worst thing he had ever put in his mouth, which is significant coming from a man who had eaten Namibian warthog rectum). The fat, of course, provides energy, and the fermentation, similar to capsaicin, provides another low-tech way to inhibit pathogens, yielding a lot of the same benefits of cooking (e.g., softening foods and breaking down or predigesting fats and proteins) without sacrificing valuable fuel.*

It could also be that eating chilies helps us cope with other types of pain, both physical and emotional, similar to the mechanisms of watching sad movies, running marathons, or scratching

---

* Sort of opposite of chilies and their induced cooling effect through sweat, fermented foods might also make it easier to survive in colder climates by reducing the metabolic energy needed to chew and metabolize food, thus conserving more energy for bodily heat production.

insect bites to the point of tissue damage—forms of self-inflicted torture that not only provide tangible distractions from real-world pains (in essence, giving us something else to cry about) but also trigger the release of feel-good chemicals that help block and suppress pain, one of the reasons distance runners experience a "runner's high."

John Launer, a physician who has suffered from eczema his whole life, similarly describes how eczema sufferers will sometimes plunge their hands into near-boiling water to stop the itching. "Only hot water close to boiling point will crack it," he says. "Almost everyone with eczema knows this."

This helps explain why capsaicin is a common ingredient in over-the-counter topical pain treatments for things like arthritis, sore muscles, and joint pain—and why the Aztecs used chilies as an anesthetic during childbirth.

As with childbirth, we tend to forget the intensity of pain from chilies once the initial sensations have faded,[*] leading us to continually burn our mouths after vowing never to do so ever again—yet another relic of evolution designed to ensure the fate of the species by encouraging individual risk. "The evolutionary advantages of this convenient amnesia are obvious," explain Terry Burnham and Jay Phelan, "and all of us who are not the first-born in our families should be thankful."

Those of us popping prescription-strength antacids as a result of capsaicin, maybe not so much.

Another theory is that our habit of eating spicy food evolved as a method of peacocking, i.e., displaying bravado and masculinity in order to attract mates by showcasing an ability to protect

---

[*] As Seneca wrote in the first century, *"Quæ fuit durum pati meminisse dulce est"* ("What was grievous to endure is sweet to remember").

them. Indeed, research shows a correlation between a preference for spicy foods and testosterone levels as well as personality constructs associated with the pursuit of money, sex, and social status, particularly among college-age males.

Anyone who has ever been to high school, of course, knows that hypermasculine bravado and self-inflicted harm are hallmarks of teenage citizenship used to establish social hierarchies. Back in Aztec times, coming-of-age adolescents were given *pulque*, a beerlike beverage made from fermented agave sap, and held over fires to mark their transition from youth to adulthood, symbolizing their transformation from "raw" to "cooked." Meanwhile, some modern cultures practice similar coming-of-age rituals, such as walking over hot coals or enduring toxic insect bites, giving new meaning to "toxic masculinity." Writes Chip Brown in *National Geographic*, "Mardudjara aboriginal boys in Australia are expected to swallow their own foreskins," "Sambia mountain boys in Papua New Guinea push sharp sticks into their nostrils to make their noses bleed and have to swallow semen after oral sex with young men," and "Satere Mawe boys in the Brazilian Amazon insert their hands into gloves filled with bullet ants (*Paraponera clavata*) whose neurotoxic sting is said to be among the most agonizing in nature."

Here in the United States, of course, teens just pierce and tattoo themselves, assault one another's senses with AXE body spray, and challenge one another to eat spoonfuls of cinnamon or Tide pods on social media—which are really just modern versions of the intercollegiate goldfish-swallowing competitions of 1939, which started out at Harvard and quickly spread across the country.*

---

* Your author can attest that these were still going on in the 1990s.

It's also possible that humans turned to chilies out of boredom and a desire to escape their monotonous routine through "the seeking of varied, novel, complex, and intense sensations and experiences, and the willingness to take physical, social, legal, and financial risks for the sake of such experience." This, according to psychologists who place chilies in the same category as things like scuba diving, binge drinking, gambling, and sexual nonconformance.

This would explain why astronauts in orbit almost universally tend to crave spicy foods like hot sauce, cocktail sauce, and wasabi. Granted, microgravity plays a role here, too, by causing a swelling of the tongue and nasal passages that blocks a lot of the pathways to taste receptors, mimicking the effects of a head cold and leading astronauts to seek out stronger flavors—or, in the case of chilies, stronger chemical sensations. But boredom likely plays an equal or greater role, given the time astronauts spend performing repetitive tasks while floating in sterile, colorless environments deprived of the senses of home.

The military faces a similar struggle when it comes to feeding soldiers in the field. Granted, military rations have come a long way since the canned biscuits, unmeltable chocolate bars, instant coffee, and Spam* of World War II (even though, in some ways, we've gone backward since the days of the American Revolution, when rations included things like beer, cider, whiskey, and rum). Today's MREs ("meal, ready-to-eat") include foods like

---

* Many soldiers found Spam to be a better tool than food during World War II, using it, for example, to lubricate their guns or waterproof their boots, while others report having used its metal can as an emergency field patch for bullet holes in aircraft wings.

pepperoni pizza, smoked almonds, and instant cappuccinos with a choice of Irish cream, French vanilla, or mocha, but they're still a far cry from the comforts of home, which aren't typically formulated to be dropped out of helicopters, consumed from self-heating plastic pouches, or endure years of extreme weather. So, surviving on rations alone can be quite boring, which is why, depending on whom you speak to, MRE also stands for "Meals Rejected by Everyone." It's also why Tabasco sauce has become a preferred condiment of soldiers, with so many carrying it on them in the field to combat the monotony of long deployments that, beginning in Iraq in 1990, the US military started officially issuing miniature glass bottles of it with meals, later switching from glass to ketchup-style packets to cut down on weight, breakage, and manufacturing costs. More recently, they've also added menu items like jalapeño cashews, packets of crushed red pepper, and jalapeño ketchup.

Cultural psychologist Paul Rozin, a legend in the study of human food selection and avoidance who coined the term *benign masochism* to describe our attraction to chilies and other "initially negative experiences that the body (brain) falsely interprets as threatening," similarly likens the attraction of chilies to that of roller coasters and horror movies, the idea being that we crave not just varied and complex sensations but the thrill of simulating danger and the rush of pushing ourselves to our limit.

Notes Yale professor of psychology Paul Bloom, "Some teenage girls enjoy cutting themselves with razors; some men pay good money to be spanked by prostitutes."

"It's not that we like [these experiences] despite the pain," explains Bloom. "We like them, at least in part, *because* of the pain."

In fact, it's not just horror movies that chilies are similar to but movies in general—dramas, action movies. Think about all the kids' movies with plots involving dead parents, evil villains, and perilous quests: *Bambi, Peter Pan, Ratatouille, Harry Potter* . . .

As Terry Burnham and Jay Phelan observe in their book *Mean Genes*, "We watch movies about rebels without a cause, not about people buying insurance." This is because we're the *product* of rebels, "descended from the humans who left their caves, who took risks and won."

Even though our jaws have softened and we've since reached the top of the food chain, where we hardly have to chew our food, let alone hunt or gather it, that taste for adventure—to push past our comfort level and endure the pain—is still inside us; it's how we got to the top of the food chain.

Then again, maybe the explanation is simpler; maybe we just can't resist the temptation of forbidden fruit—or, in this case, forbidden berries.

CHAPTER 10

ATTACK OF THE KILLER TOMATOES

There are known knowns; there are things we know we know. We also know there are known unknowns; that is to say we know there are some things we do not know. But there are also unknown unknowns—the ones we don't know we don't know.

—DONALD RUMSFELD

It's easy to look back in disbelief at history's lost and dated food beliefs—the idea that cinnamon came from giant bird nests (and, if you mixed it with lamprey blood and inedible crust, made for a delectable pie); that honey fell from the sky (and, if you added it to breakfast cereal, became a gateway drug to chronic masturbation and, by proxy, baldness, habitual depression, morbid predispositions, fetid breath, and permanent darkness over one's wretched soul); that corporations like McDonald's and Starbucks actually care about consumers' health or happiness.

Yet despite our litany of progress—our discriminating palates, our trove of food blogs, and our supernatural pantries—things have hardly changed. Our grandchildren, and certainly *their* grandchildren, will no doubt look back at us with the same wonder and bewilderment we feel when looking back at Kellogg's Battle Creek Sanitarium or John Smith's colonial attempts to fish with frying pans.

In 1893, a solid three hundred years after tomatoes were first cultivated in Europe, it took the US Supreme Court to decide whether tomatoes were a fruit or a vegetable. At the time, imported vegetables were subject to a 10 percent tariff to protect

American farmers, owing to the Tariff Act of 1883, but in 1887 a tomato importer named John Nix sued the collector of the port of New York to get his money back, arguing that tomatoes were fruits and therefore exempt. And this argument was contested for *six years* in escalating court battles before making its way to the nation's highest court, where Supreme Court justices read from various dictionaries and heard testimony from expert witnesses before ultimately ruling that tomatoes were vegetables because they "are, like potatoes, carrots, parsnips, turnips, beets, cauliflower, cabbage, celery, and lettuce, usually served at dinner . . . and not, like fruits generally, as dessert."*

This happened not long after people finally decided tomatoes weren't poisonous, a belief that had lasted for hundreds of years, owing largely to their botanical relationship to mandrakes and deadly nightshade, which are in the same family and not only are poisonous but were also said to be used in "witches' brew" and to summon werewolves. In fact, the tomato's scientific name, *Solanum lycopersicum*, literally means "wolf's peach," from the Greek *lykos* ("wolf"), which also gave us *lycanthrope* ("werewolf") and *persicon* ("peach")—while its old German name is *Wolfspfirsich*. And as recently as the 1860s, widespread rumors warned of tomato crops infested with poisonous worms capable of spitting their fatal venom several feet, causing terrible agony and instant death—but fortunately, the worms turned out to be harmless caterpillars. Another, more credible complaint was that the tomato's innards were too acidic, causing them to leach toxic lead

---

* One wonders if savvier lawyers might have appealed the decision, citing Brillat-Savarin's insistence that a dessert course "without cheese is like a beautiful woman with only one eye" and presenting tomato dessert recipes from the era, such as tomato jellies and tomato tarts.

or copper from dishes and cookware. Meanwhile, others warned simply of their taste, calling them "sour trash" or "odious and repulsive smelling berries."

Potatoes, which come from the same family, suffered a similar reputation. In addition to their associations with witchcraft and devil worship, they were once thought to cause syphilis and leprosy, largely because of the way they looked, bearing a resemblance to the gnarled hands of lepers and, um, other afflicted body parts. Eighteenth-century Russians called them "the Devil's apples" and burned them at the stake, while others warned that eating potatoes at night caused mothers to bear children with abnormally large heads or that pinning someone's name to a potato cursed them to certain death. Meanwhile, wealthy people used them as decoration, growing potato plants in ornamental flower gardens and wearing potato flowers on their lapels or in their hair.

Ultimately, it wasn't until widespread famine and crop failures forced people's hands that Europeans begrudgingly offered the potato a place at their tables—even then, many resisted. Peasants in Austria "were threatened with forty lashes if they refused to embrace it," while Prussia's king Friedrich Wilhelm I threatened to cut off the ears and nose of dissidents who refused to plant them. In France, a scientist named Antoine-Augustin Parmentier took a softer approach; after struggling to convert skeptics by way of reason and science, he appealed to their sense of envy by serving potatoes to famous people and hiring armed guards to surround potato fields outside Paris, and *voilà*, now we have *pommes frites*.

Now, of course, tomatoes and potatoes are the most consumed vegetables in the United States by far, with per capita annual consumption weighing in at about thirty-one pounds of tomatoes and forty-nine pounds of potatoes in 2019, led largely by French fries and tomato sauce. In comparison, the consumption of onions, the third most popular vegetable, is only about nine pounds per capita.*

And these weren't the only ingredients people feared. As recently as the nineteenth century in England, there was a myth that raw fruits were poisonous, with "death by fruit" commonly listed as a cause of death on Victorian death certificates, a belief likely stemming from a 1569 ban on the sale of uncooked fruit to prevent the spread of the plague (which actually had merit, given that it was common practice at the time for butchers to throw leftover blood and entrails into rivers, where they'd often wash up on shores, and that this same polluted water was often used to wash fruits and vegetables).

And the fog has hardly cleared since.

People were afraid to eat Patagonian toothfish, a type of oily cod that was traditionally thrown back by fisherman, until they were rebranded with a sexier name in 1994: Chilean sea bass. This despite the fact that they're neither technically a bass nor, a lot of the time, Chilean; many come from waters off the coasts of Africa and Australia. Now, of course, they sell for $29.99 a pound at Whole Foods, owing both to their desirability and the fact that this desirability has led to overfishing, going from a global capture of just 579 metric tons in 1979, when they were

---

* The consumption of corn, of course, surpasses all of these, officially accounting for roughly sixty pounds per capita annually if we count products such as corn syrup, cornstarch, and corn flour (and somewhere in the neighborhood of one *thousand* pounds per capita if we count foods such as meat and dairy products from corn-fed animals). However, when eaten purely as a vegetable (e.g., fresh, frozen, or from a can), it accounts for only about six pounds per person.

known mostly to Antarctic scientists, to a peak of more than 44,000 tons in 1995.

The same thing happened with rock salmon (formerly "spiny dogfish"), blue cod (formerly "oilfish"), Torbay sole (formerly "witch"), and orange roughy (formerly "slimehead"). The uni (sea urchin) on your sushi platter used to be called "whore's eggs" by fisherman, owing to their tendency to accumulate unwanted, fouling their equipment; before that, in ancient Greece, sea urchins were metaphors for women's pubic hair. As David A. Fahrenthold writes in the *Washington Post*, "Today's seafood is often yesterday's trash fish and monsters."

And the same state of confusion extends to almost everything else we put into our mouths, from pasta to multivitamins.

Certainly consumers are more familiar with spaghetti than yesterday's trash fish, but that doesn't necessarily make them savvy or any less gullible. In 1957, for example, the BBC aired a news segment on "spaghetti plantations" as an April Fool's Day joke, showing footage of cooked spaghetti strands hanging from trees (to which they were affixed with tape) as farmers plucked them for harvest and placed them into baskets to dry—and people actually believed it. So much so, in fact, that the network was overrun with calls from viewers asking where they could buy their own spaghetti trees. Even members of the show's production crew, who'd been kept in the dark, fell for it. Again, this was in 1957, twelve years after the development of the atom bomb.

In the 1980s, A&W tried to one-up the McDonald's Quarter Pounder by releasing a third-pound hamburger that was also less expensive and rated higher in consumer taste tests. It failed, however, because Americans are bad at fractions and thought a third was smaller than a quarter.

And in 2016, lawmakers in West Virginia were sent to the

hospital after drinking raw milk in a celebratory toast for striking down a ban on raw milk that had clearly been put there for a reason. (Or *reasons*, among them E. coli, listeria, salmonella, and Guillain-Barré syndrome, which can result in paralysis, kidney failure, stroke, and death.) To be fair, Scott Cadle, the Republican delegate who'd distributed the milk, denied that the incident had anything to do with the milk, telling reporters, "It didn't have nothing to do with that milk" and "It ain't because of the raw milk." And it's impossible to know for sure, as he flushed the remainder of the milk down the toilet before samples could be tested, which is, apparently, something he normally does with perfectly good milk.

Meanwhile, our top nutritionists still can't decide whether or not eggs are good for us.

In 1980, the US Department of Agriculture's "Dietary Guidelines for Americans" consisted of a twenty-page pamphlet stapled in the center, offering such sage advice as "Maintain ideal weight," "Avoid too much fat, saturated fat, and cholesterol," "Avoid too much sugar," and "Avoid too much sodium."

By 2005, its guidelines had become slightly more specific, recommending that Americans consume less than 300 milligrams per day of cholesterol. Its 2015 guidelines, however, weighing in at a massive *122 pages*, removed that limitation, prompting the American Egg Board to boast, "The U.S. has joined many other countries and expert groups like the American Heart Association and the American College of Cardiology that do not have an upper limit for cholesterol intake in their dietary guidelines."

Except that's not really true, because the actual guidelines explain that the body "makes more than enough" cholesterol on its own and that "people do not need to obtain cholesterol through foods" before ultimately recommending that "individuals should *eat as little dietary cholesterol as possible* while consuming a healthy eating pattern." But that doesn't mean we should eat none, apparently, because their Healthy U.S.-Style Eating Pattern outlined in Appendix 3, Table A3-1 recommends 2 to 3 cup-equivalents of dairy per day and 13 to 43 ounce-equivalents of meat, poultry, eggs, and seafood per week depending on which of the twelve caloric subgroups you belong to, which you can find in Appendix 2, Table A2-1 by cross-referencing your age, sex, and physical activity level.* And their Healthy Mediterranean-Style Eating Pattern outlined in Appendix 4, Table A4-1 recommends 2 to 2½ cup-equivalents of dairy per day and 13 to 50 ounce-equivalents of meat, poultry, eggs, and seafood per week. (Note, by the way, that cup- and ounce-equivalents don't always correlate with actual cups and ounces. One large egg, for example, is equivalent to 1 ounce-equivalent of eggs, yet, per the USDA's own guidelines, an egg has to weigh a minimum of 2 ounces when averaged by the dozen, in order to be *called* large, so technically, 2 ounces of eggs is equal to 1 ounce-equivalent of eggs. Similarly, 4 ounces of pork is equal to 4 ounce-equivalents, but 4 ounces of walnuts is equivalent to 8 ounce-equivalents.) And if you get out your decoder glasses and scrap paper and do the math, the maximum cholesterol intake suggested with these healthy eating patterns is—surprise—still about 300 milligrams, so nothing has changed other than the level of obfuscation.

Mind you, this isn't the USDA's fault, as they're simultaneously charged with protecting the economic interests of Ameri-

---

* Unless you're pregnant or breastfeeding, in which case you should follow the guidelines set by the Institute of Medicine (now the National Academy of Medicine), the National Research Council, the Food and Drug Administration, and the Environmental Protection Agency, not included.

can farmers and meat and dairy producers and protecting the nutritional interest of Americans, a Sisyphean task. So on the one hand, they're supposed to encourage us to buy more meat and dairy products—and on the other, to eat less of them. As a result, their messaging is often inescapably convoluted and schizophrenic, reading a lot like fortune cookies or Bill Clinton's 1998 grand jury testimony: "It depends on what the meaning of 'is' is."

In addition, the USDA has to split food oversight with the US Food and Drug Administration (FDA) according to a matrix of blurred and invisible lines. The USDA is responsible for overseeing nutritional guidance, pepperoni pizza, meat sauces with more than 3 percent red meat, open-faced sandwiches, and catfish, for example, while the FDA is responsible for nutritional labeling, mushroom pizza, meat-flavored sauce with less than 3 percent red meat, closed-face sandwiches, and fish other than catfish. The division of eggs is even more confusing; the USDA is responsible for the grading of shell eggs, egg-breaking and pasteurizing operations, and products that meet the USDA's definition of "egg products," such as dried, frozen, or liquid eggs, while the FDA is responsible for the labeling of shell eggs, egg-washing and -sorting operations, and egg products that do not meet the USDA's definition of "egg products," such as freeze-dried egg products, imitation egg products, cake mixes, French toast, egg sandwiches (if they're closed and don't also contain a certain quantity of meat), and ethnic egg delicacies like balut.

Plus, in addition to overseeing what amounts to roughly 78 percent of the US food supply, the FDA oversees more than 20,000 prescription drug products, 6,500 separate categories of medical devices, 90,000 tobacco products, and consumer products ranging from perfume, pet food, and deodorant to temporary tattoos, tampons, and microwave ovens. Also laser pointers. So they simultaneously have people regulating the prevention of maggots in consumer foods and the use of medicinal maggots in wound therapy.

As a result of this confusion, they don't have even a fraction of the bandwidth in terms of tools, funding, manpower, or daylight to do what they're asked to—so the majority of food facilities under their jurisdiction (56 percent) go more than five years without inspection and a much larger percentage (about 99 percent) of the imported foods they're responsible for go uninspected completely. All this while, according to the CDC, "48 million people get sick, 128,000 are hospitalized, and 3,000 die from foodborne diseases each year in the United States."

So no agency is really in charge of nutrition, transparency, or labeling, and we're basically on the honor system. The inmates are running the asylum.

And even if we set aside the political wavering over nutrition and the issues with bandwidth, jurisdiction, and food labeling that journalist Barbara Presley Noble once called "so opaque or confusing that only consumers with the hermeneutic abilities of a Talmudic scholar can peel back the encoded layers of meaning," we just find more and more layers of discrepancy and ambiguity.

Most experts seem to agree that olive oil is healthy,[*] citing things like monounsaturated fats, antioxidants, and an ability to lower "bad" cholesterol, but that's only if your olive oil is actually olive oil—and experts say there's a good chance it isn't. As Larry

---

[*] Others claim that its low smoke point makes it susceptible to degradation and oxidative instability under high heat, resulting in potentially toxic or carcinogenic by-products, though more recent research tends to negate this.

Olmsted writes, analysts estimate that between two-thirds and 90 percent of olive oil sold in the United States isn't what it's claimed to be and that "virtually every investigation, whether by universities, journalists, law enforcement, or government agencies has found an industry rife with fakery." So not much has changed since 1820, when Fredrick Accum warned that commercial olive oil was often rancid or tainted with lead. In 1959, an estimated ten thousand Moroccans suffered partial paralysis after consuming olive oil merchants had mixed with surplus industrial lubricants intended for jet engines, and in 1981, more than twenty thousand people were poisoned and hundreds died after consuming Spanish "olive oil" that turned out to be machine oil.

The bright side, if there is one, is that, although olive oil counterfeiting remains rampant, a lot of today's counterfeitting has to do with faking its graded virginity; i.e., passing off virgin for extra virgin or diluting it with oils that are less expensive but still edible, like canola, sunflower, or soybean. But you should still consider yourself lucky if your organic extra-virgin olive oil is even made from olives, let alone those rated for human consumption and not for use as lamp oil.

Similarly, a lot of experts say that fish is healthy, owing to its omega-3 content, but just as there are a lot of fish in the sea (and rivers and lakes and commercial fish farms), there's a lot of methylmercury, polychlorinated biphenyls, parasites, agricultural pesticides, microplastics, and toxic algal blooms. Then there's the fact that high levels of omega-3 have also been linked to prostate cancer.

So choosing healthy seafood isn't as simple as eating oysters only in months with the letter *r* in them, an adage that goes back at least to the 1500s from the advice only to eat oysters "that growes upon great ships bottomes, or in places not muddy; in those moneths that haue the letter R. in their names," which was mostly a precaution against eating raw seafood in the summer prior to the advent of refrigeration—or, as Anthony Bourdain advised in *Kitchen Confidential*, never ordering fish on a Monday unless you're eating at Le Bernardin, because most seafood vendors don't deliver on weekends.*

As nutrition professor and James Beard Award–winning author Marion Nestle writes, "To make an intelligent choice of fish at a supermarket, you have to know more than you could possibly imagine about nutrition, fish toxicology, and the life cycle and ecology of fish—what kind of fish it is, what it eats, where it was caught, and whether it was farmed or wild."

Yet even if we did know all this, it wouldn't make much of a difference, because fish fraud is also extremely rampant.

In 2008, two high school girls in Manhattan collected fish samples from restaurants and grocery stores for a school science project, preserving them in alcohol and sending them to a university lab for genetic fingerprinting, and found that half of the local restaurants and 60 percent of the grocery stores were selling mislabeled fish—including at least one endangered species.

Others who've run similar tests have come to similar conclusions. In 2012, researchers who collected 142 fish samples from New York restaurants and grocery stores found that 94 percent of the tuna, 79 percent of the snapper, and 20 percent of the salmon they ordered turned out to be other fish. In fact, seventeen of the eighteen fish sold as white tuna turned out to be escolar, also

---

* Note that Bourdain revised this guidance sixteen years later, explaining that although it's probably still not a great idea to order the mussels special at "the local fake Irish pub," on the whole, "Things have changed. Eat the damn fish."

known as oilfish or "ex-lax fish," a species that's banned in Japan and Italy (and that the FDA advises against importing) because it contains toxins and indigestible wax esters that can cause diarrhea, abdominal cramps, nausea, headache, and vomiting. Some fish sold as red snapper and halibut turned out to be tilefish, which is on the FDA's do-not-eat list for "women who are or might become pregnant, nursing mothers and young children," owing to its high mercury content.

And this isn't just limited to New York. In 2007, samples of fish labeled monkfish in Chicago turned out to be illegal and potentially deadly puffer fish, sending some customers to the hospital. And in 2016, an *Inside Edition* investigation of twenty-eight restaurants across the country found that 35 percent of sampled lobster dishes had substituted lobster with cheaper seafood. In the most egregious cases, one Florida restaurant's lobster rolls were made from a frozen mixture of lobster, whiting, and pollock (the last two being common ingredients in frozen fish sticks), and one restaurant in New York's Little Italy sold "lobster" ravioli that was filled only with cheese.

Meanwhile, a lot of restaurants, including Red Lobster, have gotten into hot water for replacing lobster ($24 a pound) with langostino ($4 a pound), a closer relative to hermit crab that's about two inches long and also known as pelagic crab or squat lobster.

"As a seafood expert, Red Lobster understands that the seasonality and availability of lobster can fluctuate, so our Lobster Bisque can contain meat from Maine lobster, langostino lobster, or, in some cases, a combination of both," explained a company spokesperson. "INSIDE EDITION's test was a matter of what we call 'the luck of the ladle' and both types of lobster provide the bisque with a rich, sweet taste that our guests love."

So once again, not much has changed in the last thousand or so years. In 1499, Henry VII had to issue a statute banning the sale of painted fish because fishmongers were painting and varnishing the gills of spoiled fish or brushing them with blood to make them look fresh. Other tactics at the time included blowing air into fish or stuffing them with fresh fish guts "as to make skinny, flabby fish look pump and fat"; fattening limp and watery lobsters by stuffing fresh haddock and wooden skewers through cracks in their tails; or using skewers to join pieces of broken lobsters and plugging the holes with wood.

Before that, in 1272, Edward I banned fishmongers from watering the fish on their slab more than once, a practice that preserved their appearance while adding costly water weight and accelerating spoilage. Corrupt vendors who were caught watering their fish were either fined or, after having their fish smelled by a jury of peers, sometimes put into stocks with their unscrupulously treated fish burned beneath them.

Today, of course, it's not just fish that are watered down to add weight and volume but meats, vegetables (both "fresh" and canned), honey, and fruit juice. In 2013, *Consumer Reports* found that, on average, nearly half of the advertised weight of the canned foods they examined came from the packing liquids (e.g., the tuna water, not the actual tuna). Meanwhile, consumer advocates in the United Kingdom have reported frozen chicken breasts containing as much as 40 percent added water.

Even the vitamins in our food aren't to be trusted. In addition to the vitamins and dietary supplements sold in grocery stores (taken by more than half of American adults to make up for a lack of nutrients in their diet), a lot of the foods in grocery stores contain added vitamins. Tropicana, for example, makes orange juice with added calcium and vitamin D, healthy heart orange juice with omega-3 (because what goes better with orange juice than tilapia, sardines, and anchovies?), vitamin C and zinc orange juice ("to help support a healthy immune system"), pineapple mango juice with probiotics, and apple cherry juice with fiber. Dannon makes probiotic yogurt and kids' cotton candy–flavored smoothies with added vitamin D, and a lot of breakfast cereals are fortified with vitamins and minerals.

Nestlé even has a helpful chart explaining how the vitamins in their cereals help release energy; contribute to healthy skin; help the nervous and immune systems work properly; reduce tiredness; and contribute to healthy blood, bones, and teeth—and in regard to Nesquik cereal, Nestlé writes, "We believe in kids' creativity. That's why NESQUIK Cereal helps nourish their mind with Vitamins B3, B5, B6 and Iron in those delicious chocolaty balls."

But some studies—conducted by people who do not sell vitamins or cereals for a living—suggest that the vitamins in those delicious chocolaty balls might actually be harmful.

For example, one study published in the *Journal of Clinical Oncology* found that men who supplemented their diet with high doses of vitamin B for ten years nearly doubled their risk of developing lung cancer. Another study found that women who supplemented their diet with vitamin B were 10 percent *more likely to die* during the study.

Other studies have found that large doses of vitamin B can cause nerve damage and liver disease and that too much calcium and vitamin D may increase the risk of heart disease.

Meanwhile, a 2014 analysis by the Environmental Working Group, "a non-profit, non-partisan organization dedicated to protecting human health and the environment," warned that the percentages of fortified vitamins listed on boxes of children's breakfast cereals were based on "woefully outdated" adult guidelines from 1968—and that a single serving of some cereals contained levels of vitamin A, zinc, or niacin that exceeded the tolerable upper intake levels for children set by the Institute of Medicine.

As for some of the supplements sold in supermarkets, DNA testing has shown that many contain *none* of the ingredients they claim to. A 2015 investigation by the attorney general of the state of New York found that only 21 percent of the store-brand herbal supplements tested contained DNA from the plants listed on their labels, including just 4 percent of store-brand Walmart supplements. Meanwhile, 35 percent of the supplements tested contained fillers and unlisted contaminants not identified on their label, including things like rice, beans, pine, and powdered houseplants. Other studies have found lead and arsenic in prenatal vitamins.

So either vitamins are good for us or they kill us or they're not even vitamins.

And the same is true for foods like olive oil, red snapper, and monkfish. (Fortunately, we're pretty certain they can't give us syphilis or be used to summon werewolves, so it's not as though we've learned *nothing* about food in the last few hundred years.)

Now, all of this may seem incredibly depressing; surely, it's not fun to realize that our favorite type of sushi might actually be oilfish and our gummy vitamins might eventually kill us. But if we've learned anything from history, it's that this adversity is nothing new. Certainly, it's tempting to picture our ancestors in perfect harmony with nature, but nature has always been trying to kill us—and every generation before us has faced culinary dangers of their own, whether from toxic roots, scarcity (e.g., crop failures, wartime supply issues), tainted meat and water, failed freezing experiments, or simply failing to pack proper fishing gear and having to resort to frying pans.

And, ultimately, it's these struggles that pushed them to adapt and persevere, thus paving the way for apple pie (and edible crust), vanilla ice cream and Rocky Road, and extra-chunky tomato sauce—not to mention smaller jaws, bigger brains, holiday traditions, and modern civilization. . . .

ACKNOWLEDGMENTS

Much like corn would not exist without human intervention, this book would not exist without the intervention of my agent, Dan Conaway, and editors, Daniel Halpern and Gabriella Doob.

Thank you also to Sean O'Donnell for talking me through the specifics of fly olfactory mechanics and meal preferences; to Gary K. Beauchamp for sharing his insight on the mechanics of human taste and food selection; to Scott Kleinman and Craig Callender for their help deciphering the literature and language of medieval cooking; to the library staff and faculty of the University of Richmond, the University of Michigan, the New York Public Library, and the Library of Congress for their help accessing materials before and during a pandemic; and to the long list of people who offered their invaluable support as sounding boards, critics, censors, therapists, or voices of reason, including but not limited to Morgann "Breakfast" Taylor, Heather Weintraub, Rachel Weiskittle, Jason King, Scott Little, Michael Chappell, Margaret Murray, Allen Gee, Karl Alcan, Everett Alcan, Waffles Weasley (my dog), and everyone I've ever had lunch or coffee with—especially those who paid.

NOTES

Epigraph

vii "History celebrates the battlefields": Jeffrey M. Pilcher, *The Oxford Handbook of Food History* (New York: Oxford University Press, 2012), 209.

vii "Of the many choices": B. W. Higman, *How Food Made History* (West Sussex: Wiley-Blackwell, 2012), 1.

Chapter 1: A History of Swallowing

1 "The pursuit of more": Reay Tannahill, *Food in History* (New York: Stein and Day, 1973), 7.

2 "Tell me what": Jean Anthelme Brillat-Savarin, *The Physiology of Taste; or, Meditations on Transcendental Gastronomy*, translated by M.F.K. Fisher (New York: Knopf, 2009), Apple Books ed.

2 "luxurious mouthfeel": Catherine Donnelly, ed., *The Oxford Companion to Cheese* (New York: Oxford University Press, 2016), 88.

2 its 1825 debut: Brillat-Savarin, *The Physiology of Taste; or, Meditations on Transcendental Gastronomy*.

2 "For proof one can cite": Ibid.

2 "Suggest to a charming": Ibid.

3 "I can remember": Ibid.

3 "although I carry": Brillat-Savarin, *The Physiology of Taste; or, Meditations on Transcendental Gastronomy*.

3 "A dinner which ends": Ibid.

3 "to forbid coffee": Ibid.

3 preferences for salt: Micah Leshem, "Salt Preference in Adolescence Is Predicted by Common Prenatal and Infantile Mineralofluid Loss," *Physiology and Behavior* 63, no. 4 (1998): 699–704.

4 exposure to flavors: L. Cooke and A. Fildes, "The Impact of Flavour Exposure in Utero and During Milk Feeding on Food Acceptance at Weaning and Beyond," *Appetite* 57 (2011): 808–11.

4 between 500 milliliters: Jack A. Pritchard, "Fetal Swallowing and Amniotic Fluid Volume," *Obstetrics and Gynecology* 28, no. 5 (1966): 606–10.

4 a full liter: Cooke and Fildes, "The Impact of Flavour Exposure in Utero and During Milk Feeding on Food Acceptance at Weaning and Beyond."

4 Researchers have detected: Jennifer S. Savage, Jennifer Orlet Fisher, and Leann L. Birch, "Parental Influence on Eating Behavior: Conception to Adolescence," *The Journal of Law, Medicine and Ethics* 35, no. 1 (2007): 22–34.

4 meanwhile, breast milk: Cooke and Fildes, "The Impact of Flavour Exposure in Utero and During Milk Feeding on Food Acceptance at Weaning and Beyond."

4 In one study: Julie A. Mennella, Coren P. Jagnow, and Gary K. Beauchamp, "Prenatal and Postnatal Flavor Learning by Human Infants," *Pediatrics* 107, no. 6 (2001): e88.

4 in another: Peter G. Hepper et al., "Long-Term Flavor Recognition in Humans with Prenatal Garlic Experience," *Developmental Psychobiology* 55, no. 5 (2013): 568–74.

4 adults who'd been fed: R. Haller et al., "The Influence of Early Experience with Vanillin on Food Preference Later in Life," *Chemical Senses* 24, no. 4 (1999): 465–67.

4 Children who were breastfed: Cooke and Fildes, "The Impact of Flavour Exposure in Utero and During Milk Feeding on Food Acceptance at Weaning and Beyond."

4 it was considered: Mennella et al., "Prenatal and Postnatal Flavor Learning by Human Infants."

5 An ancient Sanskrit text: *An English Translation of the Sushruta Samhita*, vol. 2, translated by Kaviraj Kunja Lal Bhishagratna (Calcutta, 1911).

5 a wet nurse: Ibid., 225–26.

5 "extremely pendulous": *An English Translation of the Sushruta Samhita*, 225–26.

5 "ye must be well": Rick Bowers, *Thomas Phaer and the Boke of Chyldren* (Tempe, Arizona: Arizona Center for Medieval and Renaissance Studies, 1999), 33.

5 Meanwhile, it was thought: Kelley L. Baumgartel, Larissa Sneeringer, and Susan M. Cohen, "From Royal Wet Nurses to Facebook: The Evolution of Breastmilk Sharing," *Breastfeeding Review* 24, no. 3 (2016): 25–32.

5 epigenetic inheritance: Mary Carolan-Olah, Maria Duarte-Gardea, and Julia Lechuga, "A Critical Review: Early Life Nutrition and Prenatal Programming for Adult Disease," *Journal of Clinical Nursing* 24, no. 23–24 (2015): 3716–29.

5 For example, fruit flies: Anita Öst et al., "Paternal Diet Defines Offspring Chromatin State and Intergenerational Obesity," *Cell* 159, no. 6 (2014): 1352–64.

5 mice that were fed: Peter Huypens et al., "Epigenetic Germline Inheritance of Diet-Induced Obesity and Insulin Resistance," *Nature Genetics* 48, no. 5 (2016): 497–99.

6 fetal exposure to poor nutrition: Carolan-Olah et al., "A Critical Review: Early Life Nutrition and Prenatal Programming for Adult Disease."

6 another study found: Yuriy Slyvka, Yizhu Zhang, and Felicia V. Nowak, "Epigenetic Effects of Paternal Diet on Offspring: Emphasis on Obesity," *Endocrine* 48, no. 1 (2015): 36–46.

6 roughly half of the population: Charles J. Wysocki and Gary K. Beauchamp, "Ability to Smell Androstenone Is Genetically Determined," *Pro-*

ceedings of the National Academy of Sciences of the United States of America 81, no. 15 (1984): 4899–902.

6 a smaller portion: Ibid.

6 People with a gene: Nicholas Eriksson et al., "A Genetic Variant Near Olfactory Receptor Genes Influences Cilantro Preference," *Flavour* 1 (2012): article 22.

6 also known as coriander: Alan Davidson, *The Oxford Companion to Food*, 3rd ed. (New York: Oxford University Press, 2014), 221.

6 "bug-infested bedclothes": Ibid.

6 the name *coriander*: Ibid.

6 aldehydes similar or identical: Harold McGee, "Cilantro Haters, It's Not Your Fault," *New York Times*, April 13, 2010.

6 including those of bedbugs: Dong-Hwan Choe et al., "Chemically Mediated Arrestment of the Bed Bug, *Cimex lectularius*, by Volatiles Associated with Exuviae of Conspecifics," *PLOS ONE*, July 19, 2016.

6 our sensitivity to bitter foods: Diane Catanzaro, Emily C. Chesbro, and Andrew J. Velkey, "Relationship Between Food Preferences and PROP Taster Status of College Students," *Appetite* 68 (2013): 124–31.

6 paper test strips: Ibid.

7 About half the population: Ibid.

7 Supertasters also tend: Ibid.

7 supertasters tend to be: Ibid.

7 it's no coincidence: Danielle Renee Reed and Antti Knaapila, "Genetics of Taste and Smell: Poisons and Pleasures," *Progress in Molecular Biology and Translational Science* 94 (2010): 213–40.

7 Meanwhile, a lot of plants: Jonathan Silvertown, *Dinner with Darwin: Food, Drink, and Evolution* (Chicago: University of Chicago Press, 2017), 61, 107.

7 The wild ancestors of pumpkins: Logan Kistler et al., "Gourds and Squashes (*Cucurbita* spp.) Adapted to Megafaunal Extinction and Ecological Anachronism Through Domestication," *Proceedings of the National Academy of Sciences of the United States of America* 112, no. 49 (2015): 15107–12.

7 and almonds: Susie Neilson, "How Almonds Went from Deadly to Delicious," National Public Radio, June 13, 2019, https://www.npr.org/sections /thesalt/2019/06/13/732160949/how-almonds-went-from-deadly-to -delicious.

7 breastfeeding can make it harder: Lee Goldman, *Too Much of a Good Thing: How Four Key Survival Traits Are Now Killing Us* (New York: Little, Brown, 2015), 26–27.

8 people would naturally stop: Brian Handwerk, "How Cheese, Wheat and Alcohol Shaped Human Evolution," *Smithsonian*, March 13, 2018, www .smithsonianmag.com/science-nature/how-cheese-wheat-and-alcohol -shaped-human-evolution-180968455.

8 our bodies developed: Stephen Le, *100 Million Years of Food: What Our Ancestors Ate and Why It Matters Today* (New York: Picador, 2016), 108.

8 The discovery of yogurt: Nissim Silanikove, "The Interrelationships Between Lactose Intolerance and the Modern Dairy Industry: Global Perspectives in Evolutional and Historical Backgrounds," *Nutrients* 7, no. 9 (2015): 7312–31.

8 roughly two-thirds: Handwerk, "How Cheese, Wheat and Alcohol Shaped Human Evolution."

8 Our genetic tolerance: Gary Paul Nabhan, *Why Some Like It Hot: Food, Genes, and Cultural Diversity* (Washington, DC: Shearwater Books, 2004), 28–29.

8 our ancestors' consumption: W.P.T. James et al., "Nutrition and Its Role in Human Evolution," *Journal of Internal Medicine* 285, no. 5 (2019): 543, https://onlinelibrary.wiley.com/doi/full/10.1111/joim.12878.

8 developed a tolerance: Alejandra Borunda, "Koalas Eat Toxic Leaves to Survive—Now Scientists Know How," *National Geographic*, July 2, 2018, www.nationalgeographic.com/animals/2018/07/scientists-sequenced -the-koala-genome-to-save-them.

8 highly toxic to other mammals: Rebecca N. Johnson et al., "Adaptation and Conservation Insights from the Koala Genome," *Nature Genetics* 50 (2018): 1102–11, https://www.nature.com/articles/s41588-018-0153-5.

8 our decision to start: Richard Wrangham, *Catching Fire: How Cooking Made Us Human* (New York: Basic Books, 2009), 83.

9 Cooking potatoes: Rachel N. Carmody and Richard W. Wrangham, "The Energetic Significance of Cooking," *Journal of Human Evolution* 57, no. 4 (2009), 379–91.

9 properly cooking lima beans: "Should I Worry About the Cyanide in Lima Beans?," OSU Extension Service, Oregon State University, https:// extension.oregonstate.edu/families-health/nutrition/should-i-worry -about-cyanide-lima-beans.

9 water-soluble nutrients tend: Hong-Wei Xiao et al., "Recent Developments and Trends in Thermal Blanching—A Comprehensive Review," *Information Processing in Agriculture* 4, no. 2 (2017): 101–27.

9 those that remain: Kristen J. Gremillion, *Ancestral Appetites: Food in Prehistory* (Cambridge, UK: Cambridge University Press, 2011), 26.

9 cooking makes foods softer: Rachel N. Carmody, Gil S. Weintraub, and Richard W. Wrangham, "Energetic Consequences of Thermal and Nonthermal Food Processing," *Proceedings of the National Academy of Sciences of the United States of America* 108, no. 48 (2011): 19199–203.

10 Two of our closest relatives: Nicola Temple, *Best Before: The Evolution and Future of Processed Food* (London: Bloomsbury Sigma, 2018), Kindle ed.

10 about 14 percent less: Katherine D. Zink and Daniel E. Lieberman, "Impact of Meat and Lower Palaeolithic Food Processing Techniques on Chewing in Humans," *Nature* 531, no. 7595 (2016): 500–03.

10 the redness of ripe: Rachel Herz, *Why You Eat What You Eat: The Science Behind Our Relationship with Food* (New York: Norton, 2017), Kindle ed.

11 just the name McDonald's: Thomas N. Robinson et al., "Effects of Fast Food Branding on Young Children's Taste Preferences," *Archives of Pediatrics and Adolescent Medicine* 161, no. 8 (2007): 792–97.

11 resulting in smaller jaws: Wrangham, *Catching Fire*, 40.

11 "Nutcracker Man": "*Paranthropus boisei*," Human Evolution Evidence, Smithsonian National Museum of Natural History, https://humanorigins .si.edu/evidence/human-fossils/species/paranthropus-boisei.

11 modern stomachs and colons: Wrangham, *Catching Fire*, 43.

11 human jaw sizes: Temple, *Best Before*.

11 The adoption of forks and knives: Bee Wilson, *Consider the Fork: A History of How We Cook and Eat* (New York: Basic Books, 2012), Kindle ed.

12 using roughly 20 percent: Wrangham, *Catching Fire*, 109.

12 "Our brains weigh": Peter S. Ungar, *Evolution's Bite: A Story of Teeth, Diet, and Human Origins* (Princeton, NJ: Princeton University Press, 2017), 160.

12 "by which hard": Charles Darwin, *The Descent of Man and Selection in Relation to Sex* (New York: Appleton, 1889), 49.

12 "probably the greatest": Ibid.

12 the shared development: Clive Gamble, J.A.J. Gowlett, and R.I.M. Dunbar, "The Social Brain and the Shape of the Palaeolithic," in *Lucy to Language: The Benchmark Papers*, edited by R.I.M. Dunbar, Clive Gamble, and J.A.J. Gowlett (Oxford, UK: Oxford University Press, 2014), 19–51.

12 children could be weaned: Wrangham, *Catching Fire*, 180.

13 This isn't to suggest: Gamble et al., "The Social Brain and the Shape of the Palaeolithic."

13 cooking also softened us: Wrangham, *Catching Fire*, 184.

13 natural and human selection: Reay Tannahill, *Food in History* (New York: Stein and Day, 1973), 31.

13 the Latin *com*: "Companion," *OED Online*, Oxford University Press, December 2020, www.oed.com/view/Entry/37402.

13 which our ancestors learned: Tannahill, *Food in History*, 31.

13 we started rounding: Mary Ellen Snodgrass, *Encyclopedia of Kitchen History* (New York: Fitzroy Dearborn, 2004), 553.

13 though much of Asia: Ibid., 211.

Chapter 2: Pie, Progress, and Plymouth Rock

15 "Take anything away": David Macrae, *The Americans at Home: Pen-and-Ink Sketches of American Men, Manners, and Institutions*, vol. 1 (Edinburgh: Edmonston and Douglas, 1870), 25.

15 "And we must": David Mamet, *Boston Marriage* (New York: Random House, 2002), 34.

16 Boston Tea Party: James Trager, *The Food Chronology: A Food Lover's Compendium of Events and Anecdotes, from Prehistory to the Present* (New York: Henry Holt, 1995), 172.

16 "indomitable perseverance": F. W. Searle, "Pie, Progress, and Ptomaine-Poisoning," *Journal of Medicine and Science* 4, no. 9 (1898): 353–55.

18 the first recipe: Samuel Pegge, *The Forme of Cury* (London: Society of Antiquaries, 1780), 119.

18 the apple itself originated: Bill Price, *Fifty Foods That Changed the Course of History* (New York: Firefly Books, 2014), 160.

18 "cleanse them well": *The Whole Duty of a Woman: Or, an Infallible Guide to the Fair Sex* (London: Reed, 1737), 235.

18 The trick with pigeon pie: Ibid., 508.

18 "Get a hare": Ibid., 509.

18 Thomas Coryat: Bee Wilson, *Consider the Fork: A History of How We Cook and Eat* (New York: Basic Books, 2012), Kindle ed; "Thomas Coryat, World Traveller, Discovers That Italians Use Forks," *Wired*, February 21, 2017.

19 only fork in America: Mary Ellen Snodgrass, *Encyclopedia of Kitchen History* (New York: Fitzroy Dearborn, 2004), 392.

19 called for keeping: Trudy Eden, *Cooking in America, 1590–1840* (Westport, CT: Greenwood Press, 2006), 24.

20 when the English did use: Maguelonne Toussaint-Samat, *A History of Food*, translated by Anthea Bell (Cambridge, UK: Blackwell, 1992), 634.

20 made with beef broth: Ina Lipkowitz, *Words to Eat By: Five Foods and the Culinary History of the English Language* (New York: Macmillan, 2011), 59.

20 during Lent, with cod's liver: Constant Antoine Serrure and Peter Scholier, *Keukenboek: Uitgegeven Naar een Handschrift der Vijftiende Eeuw* (Ghent: Annoot-Braeckman, 1872), https://lib.ugent.be/catalog/rug01:001393558, 5. (Translation by Christianne Muusers available at www.coquinaria.nl /kooktekst/Edelikespijse1.htm#1.16.)

20 Its name comes: Patricia Bunning Stevens, *Rare Bits: Unusual Origins of Popular Recipes* (Athens, OH: Ohio University Press, 1998), 254.

20 the word *humble* comes from: Ibid., 256.

20 "When European colonists": Sally Smith Booth, *Hung, Strung & Potted: A History of Eating in Colonial America* (New York: Potter, 1971), 1.

21 "starving times": James Trager, *The Food Chronology: A Food Lover's Compendium of Events and Anecdotes, from Prehistory to the Present* (New York: Henry Holt, 1995), 113.

21 "Though there be fish": John Smith, *The Travels of Captain John Smith*, vol. 1 (New York: Macmillan, 1907), 149.

21 "We attempted to catch": Ibid., 121–22.

22 people were eating better: Eden, *Cooking in America, 1590–1840*, xxv–xxvi.

22 "a little boye": John Smith, *The Complete Works of Captain John Smith*, vol. 1, edited by Philip L. Barbour (Chapel Hill: University of North Carolina Press, 2011), 342–43.

22 "the least boy": Francis Higginson, *New-Englands Plantation, with the Sea Journal and Other Writings* (Salem, MA: Essex Book and Print Club, 1908), 97.

22 Others describe lobsters: Waverly Root and Richard de Rochement, *Eating in America: A History* (New York: Ecco, 1981), 51.

22 most of Europe was living: John F. Mariani, *The Encyclopedia of American Food and Drink* (New York: Bloomsbury, 2013), 4.

22 "fat barbacu'd Venison": John Lawson, *A New Voyage to Carolina* (London, 1709), 18.

23 a single cockle: Ibid., 157–61.

23 Others describe great migrations: Booth, *Hung, Strung & Potted*, 96–97.

23 "as big as a child's": John Josselyn, *New-Englands Rarities Discovered* (Boston: American Antiquarian Society, 1860), 143–44.

23 feeding eight hungry men: Lawson, *A New Voyage to Carolina*, 149.

23 "fat, sweet and fleshy": Higginson, *New-Englands Plantation, with the Sea Journal and Other Writings*, 101.

23 "The Flesh of this Beast": Lawson, *A New Voyage to Carolina*, 116.

24 "great sexual prowess": Booth, *Hung, Strung & Potted*, 69.

24 Lawson describes drinking: Lawson, *A New Voyage to Carolina*, 116.

24 a writer in London: John L. Hess and Karen Hess, *The Taste of America* (New York: Viking, 1977), 28–29.

24 "Does he imagine": Ibid.

25 others, such as figs: Booth, *Hung, Strung & Potted*, 155.

25 The first apple seeds arrived: Mariani, *The Encyclopedia of American Food and Drink*, 38.

25 a landowner in Virginia: Mark McWilliams, *The Story Behind the Dish: Classic American Foods* (Santa Barbara, CA: Greenwood, 2012), 1.

25 parts of Ohio: Kenneth F. Kiple, *A Movable Feast: Ten Millennia of Food Globalization* (Cambridge, UK: Cambridge University Press, 2007), 195.

25 providing much of the supply: Gregory McNamee, *Movable Feasts: The History, Science, and Lore of Food* (New York: Praeger, 2007), 15.

26 seventy varieties: McWilliams, *The Story Behind the Dish*, 1.

26 thirty-six of those varieties: Mariani, *The Encyclopedia of American Food and Drink*, 38.

26 some *seventeen thousand* new varieties: Andrew F. Smith, ed., *The Oxford Encyclopedia of Food and Drink in America*, vol. 1 (New York: Oxford University Press, 2004), 45.

26 a currency for barter: Ibid.

26 consuming a few hundred gallons: Booth, *Hung, Strung & Potted*, 155.

26 many fruits were sugared: Ibid., 158.

26 McDonald's first dessert: "You Are Are the Apple to My Pie," McDonald's, July 4, 2016, https://news.mcdonalds.com/stories/about-our-food-details/you-are-apple-my-pie.

26 "The great beauty": R. K. Munkittrick, "Munkittrick Camps Out," *Los Angeles Herald*, September 18, 1891, 7.

27 one of the reasons: Bill Price, *Fifty Foods That Changed the Course of History* (New York: Firefly, 2014), 138.

27 "The pie is": Quoted in McWilliams, *The Story Behind the Dish*, 2.

27 wheat was initially scarce: Andrew F. Smith, *Eating History: 30 Turning Points in the Making of American Cuisine* (New York: Columbia University Press, 2009), 1.

28 *"a great American institution"*: "The Deflation of Pie," *The Nation*, November 22, 1922, 542.

28 "gems": Andrew F. Smith, ed., *The Oxford Encyclopedia of Food and Drink in America*, vol. 1 (New York: Oxford University Press, 2004), 130.

28 pie was so ubiquitous: Charles Dudley Warner, *Back-log Studies and My Summer in a Garden* (London: Ward Lock and Tyler, 1872), 24.

28 "This country was founded": "The Deflation of Pie."

28 "wage war upon the vices": "Founding Prospectus," *The Nation*, March 23, 2015, www.thenation.com/article/founding-prospectus.

28 "The present civil strife": "A Dyspeptic Republic," *The Lancet*, October 1, 1864, 388.

28 "the real social curse": George Augustus Sala, *My Diary in America in the Midst of War*, vol. 1 (London: Tinsley Brothers, 1865), 238.

29 "the Great Pie Belt": Quoted in "The Great Pie Belt," *Cambridge Tribune*, November 23, 1895.

29 "An indiscreet and perhaps malevolent": "The Pie Microbe," *New York Times*, July 23, 1884.

30 "the food of the heroic": "Pie," *New York Times*, May 3, 1902.

30 "What's the matter": "The National Emblem" [from the *Milwaukee Sentinel*], *Sacramento Daily Record-Union*, July 13, 1889, 8.

31 the Reagan administration finally settled: Joint Resolution to Designate the Rose as the National Flower Emblem., Publ. L. No. 99–449, 100 Stat. 1128, 1986.

31 goldenrod and arbutus: Richard J. Hayden, "National Flowers," *Bulletin of Popular Information, Arnold Arboretum, Harvard University* 6, no. 1 (1938): 4.

31 substantially taller than the British: Kiple, *A Movable Feast*, 197.

32 The majority of roses: Max Fisher, "There's a 1 in 12 Chance Your V-Day Flowers Were Cut by Child Laborers," *The Atlantic*, February 14, 2012.

32 having imported American apples: David Karp, "It's Crunch Time for the Venerable Pippin," *New York Times*, November 5, 2003, https://www .nytimes.com/2003/11/05/dining/it-s-crunch-time-for-the-venerable -pippin.html.

32 introduced the English: McNamee, *Movable Feasts*, 15.

32 "For my own part": Benjamin Franklin, *The Life of Benjamin Franklin*, vol. 3, edited by John Bigelow (Philadelphia: Lippincott, 1875), 252–53.

33 "chicken of Turkey": Dan Jurafsky, *The Language of Food: A Linguist Reads the Menu* (New York: Norton, 2014), 68.

33 "Do not suppose": Henry Ward Beecher, *Eyes and Ears* (Boston: Ticknor and Fields, 1862), 254.

33 "Sown by chance": Toussaint-Samat, *A History of Food*, 623.

Chapter 3: Breakfast of Champions

35 "It tastes like all": Sanitas Nut Food Company, *Sanitas Nut Preparations and Specialties* (Battle Creek, MI: Review and Herald Publishing Company, 1898).

35 "In this fast age": Ellen G. White, *The Ministry of Healing* (Mountain View, CA: Pacific Press Publishing Association, 1909), 325.

36 a morning staple: "Nielsen Podcast Insights, A Marketer's Guide to Podcasting, Q1 2018," Nielsen Company, March 20, 2018.

36 One of the reasons: Michael Park, "How to Buy Food: The Psychology of the Supermarket," *Bon Appétit*, October 30, 2014, www.bonappetit.com/test-kitchen/how-to/article/supermarket-psychology.

36 Trix over Fruity Pebbles: Aviva Musicus, Aner Tal, and Brian Wansink, "Eyes in the Aisles: Why Is Cap'n Crunch Looking Down at My Child?" *Environment and Behavior* 47, no. 7 (2015): 715–33.

36 egg consumption has dropped: Judith Jones Putnam and Jane E. Allshouse, *Food Consumption, Prices, and Expenditures, 1970–97*, Statistical Bulletin no. 965, Food and Rural Economics Division, Economic Research Service, U.S. Department of Agriculture, 1999, 18.

37 people tend to consume: Pleunie S. Hogenkamp et al., "Intake During Repeated Exposure to Low- and High-Energy-Dense Yogurts by Different Means of Consumption," *The American Journal of Clinical Nutrition* 91, no. 4 (2010): 841–47.

37 "unit bias": K. McCrickerd and C. G. Forde, "Sensory Influences on Food Intake Control: Moving Beyond Palatability," *Obesity Reviews* 17, no. 1 (2016): 18–29.

37 "cheerleader effect": Cindi May, "The Cheerleader Effect," *Scientific American*, December 3, 2013, www.scientificamerican.com/article/the-cheerleader-effect.

38 the Pavlovian response: Keri McCrickerd, Lucy Chambers, and Martin R. Yeomans, "Fluid or Fuel? The Context of Consuming a Beverage Is Important for Satiety," *PLOS ONE* 9, no. 6 (2014): e100406.

38 was 34 percent sugar: "Children's Cereals: Sugar by the Pound," Environmental Working Group, May 2014, 7.

38 55 percent sugar by weight: Ibid., 10.

38 updated the recipe: Natasha Blakely, "Honey Smacks will soon be back on the shelves after recall of Kellogg cereal," *USA Today*, October 23, 2018.

38 36-gram serving size: "Kellogg's. Honey Smacks. Cereal," Kellogg's Smart Label, May 5, 2020, http://smartlabel.kelloggs.com/Product/Index/00038000391033.

38 "depraved desire": John Harvey Kellogg, *Plain Facts for Old and Young* (Burlington, VT: Segner and Condit, 1881), 112.

39 decades after his death: Andrew F. Smith, *Food and Drink in American History: A Full Course Encyclopedia*, vol. 1 (Santa Barbara, CA: ABC-CLIO, 2013), 409.

39 "the rude state of nature": Sylvester Graham, *Lectures on the Science of Human Life* (New York: Fowler and Wells, 1869), 16.

39 "his body in the skins": Ibid.

39 a messenger of God: Gerald Carson, *Cornflake Crusade* (New York: Rinehart, 1957).

39 provoked an armed riot: Ibid.

39 accusing butchers of selling: Graham, *Lectures on the Science of Human Life*, 195.

39 using spoiled flour: Sylvester Graham, *A Treatise on Bread, and Bread-Making* (Boston: Light and Stearns, 1837), 44–45.

39 in his 1820 book: Fredrick Accum, *A Treatise on Adulterations of Food, and Culinary Poisons* (London: Mallett, 1820), 131–46.

40 flavoring wine with oak sawdust: Ibid., 96.

40 adding molten lead: Ibid., 110.

40 boiling various types of leaves: Ibid., 240.

40 recycling used tea leaves: Reay Tannahill, *Food in History* (New York: Stein and Day, 1973), 344.

40 "sham-coffee": Accum, *A Treatise on Adulterations of Food and Culinary Poisons*, 244.

40 powdered oyster shells: Ibid., 204.

40 fish skin or hartshorn shavings: Pamela Sambrook, *Country House Brewing in England, 1500–1900* (London: Hambledon Press, 1996), 105.

40 opium or nux vomica: Accum, *A Treatise on Adulterations of Food and Culinary Poisons*, 205.

40 also known as poison nut: "Nux vomica," Science Direct, www.sciencedirect.com/topics/medicine-and-dentistry/nux-vomica.

40 "The Industrial Revolution": Unabomber, "Industrial Society and Its Future," *Washington Post*, September 22, 1995, https://www.washingtonpost.com/wp-srv/national/longterm/unabomber/manifesto.text.htm.

41 Graham believed that: Graham, *Lectures on the Science of Human Life*, 252–53.

41 the evils of feather beds: Ibid., 626.

41 the horrors of masturbation: Sylvester Graham, *A Lecture to Young Men on Chastity*, 4th ed. (Boston: Light, 1838), 78–79.

41 Grahamites: Graham, *Lectures on the Science of Human Life*, 11.

41 "Sometimes this general": Graham, *A Lecture to Young Men on Chastity*, 120–21.

42 "If he attempts": Ibid., 122–23.

42 Graham's biggest impact: John F. Mariani, *The Encyclopedia of American Food and Drink* (New York: Bloomsbury, 1983), 232.

42 he believed white flour: Kenneth F. Kiple and Kriemhild Coneè Ornelas, eds., *The Cambridge World History of Food*, vol. 2 (Cambridge, UK: Cambridge University Press, 2000), 1489.

42 the bran and germ contain: "Whole Grains," The Nutrition Source, Harvard School of Public Health, www.hsph.harvard.edu/nutritionsource /what-should-you-eat/whole-grains/.

43 Called granula: Marty Gitlin and Topher Ellis, *The Great American Cereal Book* (New York: Abrams, 2012), 12–14.

43 Born in 1852: Mariani, *The Encyclopedia of American Food and Drink*, 120.

43 saw little need: Howard Markel, *The Kelloggs: The Battling Brothers of Battle Creek* (New York: Penguin Random House, 2017), Apple Books ed.

43 spent most of his childhood: Smith, *Food and Drink in American History*, vol. 1, 496.

43 "anything that was fun": Markel, *The Kelloggs*.

43 He was also plagued: Ibid.

43 "cycle of bleeding": Ibid.

44 In 1876: Ibid.

44 a humble two-story farmhouse: Ibid.

44 the luxurious Battle Creek Sanitarium: Ibid.

44 vibrotherapy: John Harvey Kellogg, *The Battle Creek Sanitarium: History, Organization, Methods* (Battle Creek, MI: Battle Creek Sanitarium, 1913).

44 more than fifty types: Markel, *The Kelloggs*.

44 at least one of which: Kellogg, *The Battle Creek Sanitarium*, 81.

44 "walk and trot around": Ibid., 99.

44 chopping wood in a loincloth: Ibid., 23, 99, 103, 136.

44 "to combine with": Ibid., 5.

45 Guests could have: Ibid., 44.

45 take an aerobics class: Markel, *The Kelloggs*, 2017.

45 receive Kellogg's thoughts: Kellogg, *Plain Facts for Old and Young*.

46 he mansplains such topics: John Harvey Kellogg, *Ladies' Guide in Health and Disease: Girlhood, Maidenhood, Wifehood, Motherhood* (Battle Creek, MI: Modern Medicine Publishing Company, 1898), v–xviii.

46 he was a strong advocate: Markel, *The Kelloggs*.

46 a chemical used: "Material Safety Data Sheet, Klean-Strip Naked Gun Spray Gun Paint Remover," Klean-Strip, April 17, 2014.

46 "covering the organs": Kellogg, *Plain Facts for Old and Young*, 383–84.

46 Jack the Ripper: "Who Was Jack the Ripper?," *National Geographic*, October 29, 2008; Markel, *The Kelloggs*.

46 "school-girls are": Kellogg, *Plain Facts for Old and Young*, 88–89.

47 kept a separate bedroom: Markel, *The Kelloggs.*

47 "it is difficult": Ibid.

47 Initially, the sanitarium's offerings: Ibid.

47 made, ideally: E. E. Kellogg, *Science in the Kitchen* (Battle Creek, MI: Health Publishing Company, 1892), 289.

47 which he eventually renamed: Smith, *Food and Drink in American History,* 161.

47 complaints of broken teeth: Markel, *The Kelloggs.*

47 Among his lesser-known creations: Sanitas Nut Food Company, *Sanitas Nut Preparations and Specialties.*

47 Nuttolene: Sanitas Nut Food Company, *Sanitas Nut Preparations and Specialties.*

47 Granose: Gitlin and Ellis, *The Great American Cereal Book,* 14–18.

47 Kellogg poured his first bowl: Markel, *The Kelloggs.*

48 followed by dozens more: Gitlin and Ellis, *The Great American Cereal Book.*

48 who allegedly stole: Jonathan Black, *Making the American Body: The Remarkable Saga of the Men and Women Whose Feats, Feuds, and Passions Shaped Fitness History* (Lincoln, NE: University of Nebraska Press, 2013), 8.

48 "scientific health food": Smith, *Food and Drink in American History,* vol. 1, 1351.

48 *Collier's* magazine: Smith, *Food and Drink in American History,* vol. 1, 1351–54.

48 "It am suttenly wunnerful": *The Delineator: A Magazine for Woman* 69, no. 1 (January 1907): 151.

48 "So-Hi the Chinese Boy": Gitlin and Ellis, *The Great American Cereal Book,* 163.

49 he ate oysters: Markel, *The Kelloggs.*

49 the chemical equivalent: John Harvey Kellogg, *The Health Question Box: Or, a Thousand and One Health Questions Answered* (Battle Creek, MI: Modern Medicine Publishing Company, 1920), 144.

49 little pay, little vacation time: Markel, *The Kelloggs.*

49 "as sweet as those": George Howe Colt, *Brothers: On His Brothers and Brothers in History* (New York: Simon & Schuster, 2012), 162.

49 to begin manufacturing: Markel, *The Kelloggs.*

49 the industry's first free prizes: Gitlin and Ellis, *The Great American Cereal Book,* 26.

49 endowed in 1979: Amy Trang, "Giving Back," Northwestern University Kellogg School of Management, December 21, 2010, www.kellogg .northwestern.edu/news_articles/2010/giving-back.aspx.

49 Will won the legal right: Markel, *The Kelloggs.*

49 now known for such creations: "Our Brands," Kellogg's, www.kelloggs .com/en_US/ourfoods.html.

50 nearly 90 percent: Marion Nestle, *What to Eat* (New York: Farrar, Straus and Giroux, 2010), Apple Books ed.

50 General Mills, which started out: Andrew F. Smith, ed., *The Oxford Encyclopedia of Food and Drink in America*, vol. 1 (New York: Oxford University Press, 2004), 80.

50 magically delicious cereals: "Cereal," General Mills, www.generalmillscf .com/products/category/cereal.

50 Quaker Oats, which began: Smith, *Food and Drink in American History*, vol. 1, 248.

50 is now owned by PepsiCo: "About Quaker," Quaker Oats Company, https://contact.pepsico.com/quaker/about-us.

50 has gone on to make: "Products," Quaker Oats Company, www.capn crunch.com.

50 Post, founded in 1895: Smith, *Food and Drink in American History*, vol. 1, 162.

50 now responsible: "Explore Our Cereals," Post Consumer Brands, https:// www.postconsumerbrands.com/explore-our-cereals/.

51 "A short list of aphrodisiacs": MacClancy, *Consuming Culture: Why You Eat What You Eat*, 77.

51 *olisbokollix*: Peter James and Nick Thorpe, *Ancient Inventions* (New York: Ballantine, 1994), 183.

51 baking loaves in the shape: MacClancy, *Consuming Culture*, 78–79.

52 "Those, therefore, who": Plato, *The Republic*, translated by Desmond Lee (New York: Penguin Classics, 2003), 327.

52 "an acceptance and appreciation": Beth Kempton, *Wabi Sabi: Japanese Wisdom for a Perfectly Imperfect Life* (New York: Harper Design, 2019), Kindle ed.

52 "Men who stuff themselves": Jean Anthelme Brillat-Savarin, *The Physiology of Taste; or, Meditations on Transcendental Gastronomy*, translated by M.F.K. Fisher (New York: Knopf, 2009), Apple Books ed.

52 "To whom a little": Quoted in William Wallace, *Epicureanism* (London, Society for Promoting Christian Knowledge, 1880), 48.

53 "I am thrilled": Quoted in Cyril Bailey, *Epicurus: The Extant Remains* (Oxford: Clarendon Press, 1926), 131.

53 "We ought to be": Quoted in Wallace, *Epicureanism*, 48–49.

Chapter 4: Children of the Corn

55 "And thus it is": Arthur C. Parker, "Iroquois Uses of Maize and Other Food Plants," *New York State Museum Bulletin* 144, no. 482 (1910): 15.

56 up until roughly: Kenneth F. Kiple and Kriemhild Coneè Ornelas, eds., *The Cambridge World History of Food*, vol. 1 (Cambridge, UK: Cambridge University Press, 2000), 100.

56 and neither was farming: Martin Elkort, *The Secret Life of Food: A Feast of Food and Drink History, Folklore, and Fact* (Los Angeles: Tarcher, 1991), 11.

56 foraging for things: Ken Albala, *Food: A Cultural Culinary History*, transcript book, The Great Courses, 2013, 20.

57 breed animals in dark: "Animals Used for Food," PETA, www.peta.org /issues/animals-used-for-food.

57 generally led to a decline: Albala, *Food*, 19.

58 farming returned only about: Ibid., 20.

58 Jack Rodney Harlan: Theodore Hymowitz, "Dedication: Jack R. Harlan Crop Evolutionist, Scholar," in *Plant Breeding Reviews*, vol. 8, edited by Jules Janick (Portland, OR: Timber Press, 1990), 1–6.

58 "the equivalent of more": Ibid.

58 "Instead of being": Felipe Fernández-Armesto, *Food: A History* (New York: Macmillan, 2001), 93.

59 the first instances of farming: Albala, *Food*, 33–34.

59 "people were impelled": B. W. Higman, *How Food Made History* (West Sussex, UK: Wiley-Blackwell, 2012), 9.

59 stockpiling them: Kristen J. Gremillion, *Ancestral Appetites: Food in Prehistory* (Cambridge, UK: Cambridge University Press, 2011), 45.

59 discovery of fermentation: Tom Standage, *A History of the World in Six Glasses* (New York: Bloomsbury, 2006), 14–15.

59 dug pits for food: Gremillion, *Ancestral Appetites*, 45.

60 rice in Asia: Gregory McNamee, *Movable Feasts: The History, Science, and Lore of Food* (New York: Praeger, 2007), 66.

60 *teosinte* bears almost no resemblance: Sherry A. Flint-Garcia, "Kernel Evolution: From Teosinte to Maize," in *Maize Kernel Development*, edited by Brian A. Larkins (Oxfordshire, UK: CABI, 2017), 1–15.

60 five to twelve *hundred*: Sergio O. Serna-Saldivar, ed., *Corn: Chemistry and Technology*, 3rd ed. (Duxford, UK: Elsevier, 2018), 150.

60 one-tenth the weight: Flint-Garcia, "Kernel Evolution."

60 there wasn't a central cob: Ibid.

60 Baby corn: "The Selective Science of Baby Corn," *All Things Considered*, NPR, April 8, 2006, www.npr.org/templates/story/story.php?storyId =5332519.

60 the first farmers popped: Flint-Garcia, "Kernel Evolution."

61 choosing only the seeds: Kiple and Ornelas, *The Cambridge World History of Food*, 101.

61 The French bulldog: Kat Eschner, "The Evolution of Petface," *Smithsonian*, January 31, 2018, www.smithsonianmag.com/science-nature/evolution -petface-180967987.

61 upward of 80 percent: Katy M. Evans and Vicki J. Adams, "Proportion of Litters of Purebred Dogs Born by Caesarean Section," *Journal of Small Animal Practice* 51, no. 2 (2010): 113–18.

61 interference with natural selection: William Feeney, "Natural Selection in Black and White: How Industrial Pollution Changed Moths," *The Con-*

versation, July 15, 2015; Helen Thompson, "Ten Species That Are Evolving Due to the Changing Climate," *Smithsonian*, October 24, 2014; Beth Marie Mole, "Swallows May be Evolving to Dodge Traffic," *Nature*, March 18, 2013; Cornelia Dean, "Research Ties Human Acts to Harmful Rates of Species Evolution," *New York Times*, January 12, 2009; John W. Doudna and Brent J. Danielson, "Rapid Morphological Change in the Masticatory Structures of an Important Ecosystem Service Provider," *PLOS ONE*, June 10, 2015.

62   the lack of a central cob: Flint-Garcia, "Kernel Evolution."

62   would naturally separate and fall: Andrew F. Smith, ed., *The Oxford Encyclopedia of Food and Drink in America*, vol. 1 (New York: Oxford University Press, 2004), 341–44.

62   The Iroquois planted corn: Marcia Eames-Sheavly, *The Three Sisters: Exploring an Iroquois Garden* (Ithaca, NY: Cornell University Press, 1993), 3.

62   that would convert: Robert Flynn and John Idowu, "Nitrogen Fixation by Legumes," Guide A-129, College of Agricultural, Consumer and Environmental Sciences, New Mexico State University, https://aces.nmsu.edu/pubs/_a/A129.

63   the squash would provide: Bill Price, *Fifty Foods That Changed the Course of History* (New York: Firefly, 2014), 51.

63   eating their own dogs: James Trager, *The Food Chronology: A Food Lover's Compendium of Events and Anecdotes, from Prehistory to the Present* (New York: Henry Holt, 1995), 113.

63   350,000-square-mile belt: Smith, *The Oxford Encyclopedia of Food and Drink in America*, 341–44.

63   we now have to inject: Margaret Visser, *Much Depends on Dinner: The Extraordinary History and Mythology, Allure and Obsessions, Perils and Taboos of an Ordinary Meal* (New York: Grove Press, 1986), 28.

63   "chemicals of interest": "Appendix A: Chemicals of Interest (COI) List," The Chemical Facility Anti-Terrorism Standards (CFATS) Chemicals of Interest List, Cybersecurity and Infrastructure Security Agency, 2019.

63   a key ingredient: "Anhydrous Ammonia Thefts and Releases Associated with Illicit Methamphetamine Production—16 States, January 2000–June 2004," *Morbidity and Mortality Weekly Report* 54, no. 14 (2005), 359–61.

63   spreading lab-created STDs: Katie Pratt, "UK Researchers One Step Closer to Corn Earworm Control," University of Kentucky College of Agriculture, Food and Environment, March 26, 2016, https://news.ca.uky.edu/article/uk-researchers-one-step-closer-corn-earworm-control.

63   seeding croplands: Serna-Saldivar, *Corn*, 12.

63   93 million acres of cropland: Brooke Barton and Sarah Elizabeth Clark, "Water & Climate Risks Facing U.S. Corn Production: How Companies & Investors Can Cultivate Sustainability," *Ceres*, 2014, 15.

63   spread across states: Ibid., 8.

63   consuming more fertilizer: Ibid., 45.

64 about 19 billion pounds: Ibid., 9.

64 roughly 400,000 gallons of water: Ibid., 34.

64 140 gallons of fuel: "Ethanol Fuel from Corn Faulted as 'Unsustainable Subsidized Food Burning' in Analysis by Cornell Scientist," *Cornell Chronicle*, August 6, 2001, https://news.cornell.edu/stories/2001/08/ethanol-corn-faulted-energy-waster-scientist-says.

64 pollute the groundwater: Barton and Clark, "Water & Climate Risks Facing U.S. Corn Production," 44.

64 primary source of calories: Serna-Saldivar, *Corn*, 436.

64 more than a third: Ibid., 19.

64 49.1 pounds per person: "Corn Sweeteners: Per Capita Availability Adjusted for Loss." "Loss-Adjusted Food Availability: Sugar and Sweeteners (Added)," US Department of Agriculture, January 5, 2021, https://www.ers.usda.gov/data-products/food-availability-per-capita-data-system.

64 cornstarch and corn flour: "A Tale of Two Corns," National Corn Growers Association, January 2018.

65 which rely on corn: Serna-Saldivar, *Corn*, 447.

65 a lot of beers: Ibid., 461.

65 nonfermented soy sauce: "Commercial Item Description, Soy Sauce," U.S. Department of Agriculture, April 28, 2006.

65 anything that contains: "Corn Allergy," American College of Allergy, Asthma and Immunology, March 8, 2019.

65 potential food allergens: Food Allergen Labeling and Consumer Protection Act of 2004, Pub. L. 108–282, Title II, 20 August 20, 2004, US Food and Drug Administration, www.fda.gov/food/food-allergens-and-gluten-free-guidance-documents-and-regulatory-information/food-allergen-labeling-and-consumer-protection-act-2004-falcpa.

65 consumes about three pounds: Visser, *Much Depends on Dinner*, 24.

65 the layer of food-grade wax: Sarah Zhang, "What Life Is Like When Corn Is off the Table," *The Atlantic*, January 18, 2019, www.theatlantic.com/science/archive/2019/01/what-its-like-be-allergic-corn/580594.

65 used to make them ripen quicker: Ibid.

65 corn-based dextrose: Ibid.

66 the coating that protected it: Martin Elkort, *The Secret Life of Food: A Feast of Food and Drink History, Folklore, and Fact* (Los Angeles: Tarcher, 1991), 146.

66 a slew of corn-based binders: Title 9, Animals and Animal Products, Chapter III, Food Safety and Inspection Service, Department of Agriculture, Subchapter E, Regulatory Requirements Under the Federal Meat Inspection Act and the Poultry Products Inspection Act, Part 424, Preparation and Processing Operations, Subpart C, Food Ingredients and Sources of Radiation.

66 when Taco Bell admitted: Eliza Barclay, "With Lawsuit Over, Taco Bell's Mystery Meat Is a Mystery No Longer," National Public Radio, April 19,

2011, www.npr.org/sections/health-shots/2011/04/22/135539926/with -lawsuit-over-taco-bells-mystery-meat-is-a-mystery-no-longer.

66 consumers filed a lawsuit: Michael Duvall and Bety Javidzad, "'Grass-Fed' Case Dismissed: Reasonable Consumers Would Not Expect Cows to Be Fed 'Only' Grass," JDSUPRA, April 2, 2019, www.jdsupra.com /legalnews/grass-fed-case-dismissed-reasonable-76511.

66 only around 10 percent: Elkort, *The Secret Life of Food*, 147.

66 it's also an industrial ingredient: "A Tale of Two Corns."

66 in the paper: Visser, *Much Depends on Dinner*, 23–24.

66 another few billion bushels: Barton and Clark, "Water & Climate Risks Facing U.S. Corn Production," 19.

66 roughly a third: Ibid.

66 The Energy Independence and Security Act: Energy Independence and Security Act of 2007, Alternative Fuels Data Center, US Department of Energy, December 19, 2007, https://afdc.energy.gov/laws/eisa.

67 Ethanol accounts for: "U.S. Bioenergy Statistics," US Department of Agriculture Economic Research Service, www.ers.usda.gov/data-products/us -bioenergy-statistics/us-bioenergy-statistics.

67 about 98 percent: "Monthly Grain Use for Ethanol Production," Renewable Fuels Association, https://ethanolrfa.org/statistics/feedstock-use-co -product-output.

67 approximately 10 percent: "How Much Ethanol Is in Gasoline, and How Does It Affect Fuel Economy?," US Energy Information Administration, May 14, 2019.

67 1.1 billion metric tons: "World Agricultural Production (Table 04: Corn Area, Yield, and Production)," US Department of Agriculture, February 2019, 18.

67 a primary food source: Serna-Saldivar, *Corn*, 436.

67 20 billion feed animals: "Global Livestock Counts: Counting Chickens," *The Economist*, July 27, 2011, www.economist.com/graphic-detail/2011 /07/27/counting-chickens.

67 more than $2.5 billion: "Ranked Sectors: Agribusiness," Open Secrets, www.opensecrets.org/federal-lobbying/ranked-sectors.

67 $5 billion in corn subsidies: "Corn Subsidies in the United States," Environmental Working Group Farm Subsidy Database, https://farm.ewg.org.

67 publicly emptying cans: "New Coke," *Encyclopaedia Britannica*, www .britannica.com/topic/New-Coke.

67 more than forty thousand complaints: David Treadwell, "New Formula Woes: Coke Furor May Be 'the Real Thing,'" *Los Angeles Times*, June 27, 1985.

67 Society for the Preservation of the Real Thing: "The Story of One of the Most Memorable Marketing Blunders Ever," Coca-Cola Company, www .coca-colacompany.com/news/the-story-of-one-of-the-most-memorable -marketing-blunders-ever.

68   up to 4,200 calls a day: Russel Sackett, "Thirsting for Days When the Fizz Was Familiar, Gay Mullins Crusades to Can the New Coke," *People*, June 24, 1985, https://people.com/archive/thirsting-for-days-when-the-fizz -was-familiar-gay-mullins-crusades-to-can-the-new-coke-vol-23-no-25.

68   back to its original formula: James B. Cobb, "What We Can Learn from Coca-Cola's Biggest Blunder," *Los Angeles Times*, July 10, 2015, https:// time.com/3950205/new-coke-history-america.

68   interrupted *General Hospital*: "Was the 'New Coke' Fiasco Just a Clever Marketing Ploy?," Snopes, May 2, 1999, www.snopes.com/fact-check /new-coke-fiasco.

68   "decision of historical significance": Jube Shiver, Jr., "'Classic' to Be Sold Along with Widely Resisted New Formula: Coca-Cola to Bring Back 'the Real Thing,'" *Los Angeles Times*, July 11, 1985.

68   the company had been: Pamela G. Hollie, "Advertising; Coke Held Not to Be Real Thing," *New York Times*, August 15, 1985, www.nytimes.com /1985/08/15/business/advertising-coke-held-not-to-be-real-thing.html.

68   it's deficient: Albala, *Food*, 293–94.

68   the human body can make: Tsutomu Fukuwatari and Katsumi Shibata, "Nutritional Aspect of Tryptophan Metabolism," *International Journal of Tryptophan Research* 6 (suppl. 1) (2013): 3–8.

68   neither corn, beans, nor squash: Jane Mt. Pleasant, "Food Yields and Nutrient Analyses of the Three Sisters: A Haudenosaunee Cropping System," *Ethnobiology Letters* 7, no. 1 (2016): 87–98.

68   nixtamalization: Simon Quellen Field, *Culinary Reactions: The Everyday Chemistry of Cooking* (Chicago: Chicago Review Press, 2012), 192.

68   from the Aztec *nextli*: Cynthia Clampitt, *Midwest Maize: How Corn Shaped the U.S. Heartland* (Champaign: University of Illinois Press, 2015), 7.

69   made corn kernels: Smith, *The Oxford Encyclopedia of Food and Drink in America*, vol. 1, 341–44.

69   released pectin: Paul Adams, "Transforming Corn," *Cook's Illustrated*, August 14, 2016, www.cooksillustrated.com/science/789-articles/feature /transforming-corn.

69   gave corn an earthier flavor: Ibid.

69   including much of: Kiple and Ornelas, *The Cambridge World History of Food*, vol. 1, 108.

69   so named in 1771: Trager, *The Food Chronology*, 160.

69   condition also causes: R.P.P.W.M. Maas and P.J.G.M. Voets, "The Vampire in Medical Perspective: Myth or Malady?," *QJM: An International Journal of Medicine* 107, no. 11 (2014): 945–46.

69   within a year of each other: Jeffrey S. Hampl and William S. Hampl III, "Pellagra and the Origin of a Myth: Evidence from European Literature and Folklore," *Journal of the Royal Society of Medicine* 90, no. 11 (1997): 636–39.

69   "Just as vampires": Ibid.

70 known as Casal's necklace: D. Segula et al., "Case Report—A Forgotten Dermatological Disease," *Malawi Medical Journal* 24, no. 1 (2012): 19–20.

70 the general vicinity of Transylvania: Katharina M. Wilson, "The History of the Word 'Vampire,'" *Journal of the History of Ideas* 46, no. 4 (1985): 577–83.

70 researchers also discovered: Mathilde L. Tissier et al., "Diets Derived from Maize Monoculture Cause Maternal Infanticides in the Endangered European Hamster Due to a Vitamin B3 Deficiency," *Proceedings of the Royal Society B: Biological Sciences* 284, no. 1847 (2017): 20162168.

70 developed black tongues: Jason Daley, "Diet Deficiency Can Lead to Cannibal Hamsters," *Smithsonian*, February 2, 2017, www.smithsonianmag.com/smart-news/corn-diet-turns-french-hamsters-cannibals-180961987.

71 it took scientists: Brian A. Larkins, ed., *Maize Kernel Development* (Oxfordshire: CABI, 2017), viii.

71 Joseph Goldberger: Daniel Akst, "The Forgotten Plague," *American Heritage* 51, no. 8 (2000), www.americanheritage.com/forgotten-plague.

71 sewage systems: Giulio Alessandrini and Alberto Sala, *Pellagra*, translated by E. M. Perdue (Kansas City: Burton, 1916), 318.

71 attempted to treat it: Akst, "The Forgotten Plague."

71 Goldberger had injected himself: Ibid.

71 "Meanwhile—a slow": *Real Life Comics*, Nedor Publishing Company, no. 12, July 1943.

Chapter 5: Honey Laundering

73 "Instead of dirt": "Jonathan Swift," *Oxford Essential Quotations*, 6th ed. (New York: Oxford University Press, 2018).

73 "*Haceos miel*": "W. Gurney Benham," *Cassell's Book of Quotations, Proverbs and Household Words* (London: Cassell, 1914), 738.

73 "He that would eat": Jennifer Speake, ed., *Oxford Dictionary of Proverbs*, 6th ed. (Oxford: Oxford University Press, 2015), 89.

73 "The honey is sweet": Benjamin Franklin, *Poor Richard's Almanack* (Waterloo: U.S.C. Publishing, 1914), 48.

74 exorcise evil spirits: Hilda M. Ransome, *The Sacred Bee in Ancient Times and Folklore* (New York: Dover, 2004), 36.

74 poured it onto walls: Bodog F. Beck, *Honey and Health* (New York: McBride, 1938), 201.

74 early Christians used it: Bee Wilson, *The Hive: The Story of the Honeybee and Us* (New York: Macmillan, 2014), Apple Books ed.

74 medieval Jews smeared it: Ivan G. Marcus, *Rituals of Childhood: Jewish Acculturation in Medieval Europe* (New Haven, CT: Yale University Press, 1996).

74 Chinese placed it: Beck, *Honey and Health*, 228.

74 in traditional Hindi weddings: Ibid., 224–25.

74 Hitler gave honey: Judith Sumner, *Plants Go to War: A Botanical History of World War II* (Jefferson, NC: McFarland, 2019), 127.

75 in ancient Germany: Beck, *Honey and Health*, 223.

75 honey can crystallize: "Honey Crystallization," Honey Hotline Fact Sheet, National Honey Board Food Technology, Product Research Program; "Composition of American Honeys," Technical Bulletin no. 1261, US Department of Agriculture, Agricultural Research Service, April 1962, 3, 11.

75 "is no sooner full": Ernest Weekley, *Words Ancient and Modern* (London: John Murray, 1965), 53.

75 *"Honie-moone"*: Ibid.

75 *"Hony-moon"*: Ibid.

76 *Il mele catta*: "Honey," *OED Online*, Oxford University Press, December 2020, www.oed.com/view/Entry/88159.

76 the practice goes back: Maggy Saldais, Tony Taylor, and Carmel Young, *Oxford Big Ideas History 7 Australian Curriculum* (South Melbourne: Oxford University Press, 2011), 128.

76 science of attracting: Personal interview with Sean O'Donnell, October 7, 2019.

76 Goldilocks concentrations: Hany K. M. Dweck et al., "The Olfactory Logic Behind Fruit Odor Preferences in Larval and Adult *Drosophila*," *Cell Reports* 23, no. 8 (2018): 2524–31.

77 possibly on the season: Rik Clymans et al., "Olfactory Preference of *Drosophila suzukii* Shifts Between Fruit and Fermentation Cues over the Season: Effects of Physiological Status," *Insects* 10, no. 7 (2019): 200.

77 the thirst and stress levels: Wolf Huetteroth and Scott Waddell, "Hungry Flies Tune to Vinegar," *Cell* 145, no. 1 (2011): 17–18.

77 you're probably best served: A. W. Morrill, "Experiments with House-Fly Baits and Poisons," *Journal of Economic Entomology* 7, no. 3 (1914): 268–74.

77 erythritol: Brooks Hays, "Popular Artificial Sweetener Also Works as Pesticide and Insect Birth Control," UPI, May 23, 2017.

77 beer outperformed: Morrill, "Experiments with House-Fly Baits and Poisons."

77 "the crack cocaine": Quoted in Erika Engelhaupt, "Flies Could Falsely Place Someone at a Crime Scene," *National Geographic*, February 22, 2016, www.nationalgeographic.com/science/phenomena/2016/02/22/flies-could-falsely-place-someone-at-a-crime-scene.

77 "white man's flies": Gilbert Waldbauer, *Fireflies, Honey, and Silk* (Berkeley: University of California Press, 2009), 140.

77 indigenous cultures were cutting: Harold McGee, *On Food and Cooking: The Science and Lore of the Kitchen* (New York: Scribner, 2004), 668.

77 people in the Middle East: Alan Davidson and Tom Jaine, *The Oxford Companion to Food*, 3rd ed. (New York: Oxford University Press, 2014), 787.

77 Romans were boiling: Darra Goldstein, *The Oxford Companion to Sugar and Sweets* (New York: Oxford University Press, 2015), 397.

78 today's legal limit: "Bottled Water Everywhere: Keeping It Safe," US Food and Drug Administration, April 1, 2019, www.fda.gov/consumers /consumer-updates/bottled-water-everywhere-keeping-it-safe.

78 lead intoxication: Milton A. Lessler, "Lead and Lead Poisoning from Antiquity to Modern Times," *The Ohio Journal of Science* 88, no. 3 (1988): 78–84; "Lead Toxicity: What Are Possible Health Effects from Lead Exposure?," Agency for Toxic Substances & Disease Registry, June 12, 2017.

78 Salem witch trials: Linnda R. Caporael, "Ergotism: The Satan Loosed in Salem?," *Science* 192, no. 4234 (1976): 21–26.

78 precursor of LSD: Dieter Hagenbach and Lucius Werthmüller, "Turn On, Tune In, Drop Out—and Accidentally Discover LSD," *Scientific American*, May 17, 2013, www.scientificamerican.com/article/lsd-finds -its-discoverer.

79 "Honey was so extraordinary": Wilson, *The Hive*.

79 "honey falls from the air": Aristotle, *Aristotle's History of Animals in Ten Books*, translated by Richard Cresswell (London: George Bell and Sons, 1887), 129.

79 "mostly at the rising": Quoted in Tickner Edwardes, *The Lore of the Honey-Bee* (New York: Dutton, 1911), 9.

79 enslaved insects: Christopher Lloyd, *What on Earth Evolved? . . . In Brief: 100 Species That Have Changed the World* (London: Bloomsbury, 2011).

80 bees merely transferred: Dovid Heber, "Do Bee Don't Bee: A Halachic Guide to Honey and Bee Derivatives," STAR-K Kosher Certification, Fall 2010, http://www.star-k.org/articles/kashrus-kurrents/624/do-bee -dont-bee.

80 scholars decided these: "Keeping Kosher: When Jewish Law Met Processed Food," Gastropod, July 25, 2016, https://gastropod.com/keeping -kosher-jewish-law-met-processed-food-transcript.

80 More than half: Martin Elkort, *The Secret Life of Food: A Feast of Food and Drink History, Folklore, and Fact* (Los Angeles: Tarcher, 1991), 197.

80 the FDA approved: "K053095-Derma Sciences API-MED Active Manuka Honey Absorbent Dressing," US Food and Drug Administration, July 12, 2007.

80 there's further evidence: James Austin Stewart, Owen Lane McGrane, and Ian S. Wedmore, "Wound Care in the Wilderness: Is There Evidence for Honey?," *Wilderness & Environmental Medicine* 25, no. 1 (2014): 103–10.

80 A 2004 study: Ibid.

80 outperforms leading cough medicines: Ibid.

80 kills antibiotic-resistant bacteria: Paulus H. S. Kwakman et al., "Medical-Grade Honey Kills Antibiotic-Resistant Bacteria In Vitro and Eradicates Skin Colonization," *Clinical Infectious Diseases* 46, no. 11 (2008): 1677–82.

81 honey is naturally acidic: Natasha Geiling, "The Science Behind Honey's Eternal Shelf Life," *Smithsonian*, August 22, 2013, www.smithsonianmag .com/science-nature/the-science-behind-honeys-eternal-shelf-life-121 8690.

81 This is why: Mickey Parish, "How Do Salt and Sugar Prevent Microbial Spoilage?," *Scientific American*, February 21, 2006, www.scientificamerican .com/article/how-do-salt-and-sugar-pre.

81 Honey also contains: Geiling, "The Science Behind Honey's Eternal Shelf Life."

81 primarily as a medical-grade: Cyril P. Bryan, trans., *Ancient Egyptian Medicine: The Papyrus Ebers* (Chicago: Ares, 1930), 23, 32, 73, 155.

81 penis water: Ibid., 18.

81 treating burns with crushed cake: Bryan, *Ancient Egyptian Medicine*, 33, 69, 102, 112.

81 no one else: Lucy M. Long, *Honey: A Global History* (London: Reaktion, 2017), 105–06.

81 Botulism spores thrive: "Botulism," World Health Organization, January 10, 2018, www.who.int/news-room/fact-sheets/detail/botulism.

82 There's an old story: Wilson, *The Hive*.

82 used honey as embalming fluid: Ibid.

82 Bronze Age burial sites: Paul Salopek, "Honey, I'm Dead," *National Geographic*, May 13, 2015, www.nationalgeographic.org/projects/out-of-eden -walk/articles/2015-05-honey-im-dead.

82 leaking out of coffins: Eva Crane, *The World History of Beekeeping and Honey Hunting* (New York: Routledge, 1999), 510.

82 but also into gall: Walter K. Kelly, trans., *The Poems of Catullus and Tibullus, and The Vigil of Venus* (London: George Bell and Sons, 1887), 82.

82 tameless and deceitful brat: Beck, *Honey and Health*, 212.

82 his habit of ruining marriages: Lucius Apuleius, *The Very Pleasant and Delectable Tale of Cupid and Psyche*, translated by Walter Pater (San Francisco: Taylor, Nash and Taylor), 1914.

83 "As Cupid was stealing": *Venus with Cupid the Honey Thief*, Metropolitan Museum of Art, www.metmuseum.org/art/collection/search/459077.

83 The inscription is based: "Theocritus," *Encyclopaedia Britannica*, www .britannica.com/biography/Theocritus.

83 tells the story: *Venus with Cupid the Honey Thief*.

83 beehives were used: Jeffrey A. Lockwood, *Six-Legged Soldiers: Using Insects as Weapons of War* (New York: Oxford University Press, 2009), 10.

83 Cavemen covered them: Ibid., 11.

83 Roman armies loaded them: Ibid., 24.

83 medieval Englishmen tossed them: Ibid., 22–23.

83 Mayans lobbed bee grenades: Ibid., 17.

83 ships' crews waged war: Ibid., 24.

83   from the Greek *bombos*: Ibid.

83   Ancient Persians and Native Americans: Ibid., 36–37.

84   "mad honeycomb": Abdulkadir Gunduz, Suleyman Turedi, and Hikmet Oksuz, "The Honey, the Poison, the Weapon," *Wilderness and Environmental Medicine* 22, no. 2 (2011): 182–84.

84   rigging jungle beehives: Lockwood, *Six-Legged Soldiers*, 231.

84   worth about $166 per pound: Vaughn Bryant, "Truth in Labeling: Testing Honey," *Bee Culture*, August 2014, 29.

84   prior to sacrifice: Long, *Honey*, 108; Raymond Constant Kerkhove, "Explaining Aztec Human Sacrifice" (master's thesis, University of Queensland, 1994).

84   "the land of milk and honey": Cyrus H. Gordon and Gary A. Rendsburg, *The Bible and the Ancient Near East*, 4th ed. (New York: Norton, 1997), 168.

84   the Buddha ate honeycomb: Long, *Honey*, 59.

84   the Norse god Odin: Beck, *Honey and Health*, 218.

85   "Wherever Christianity spread": Wilson, *The Hive*.

85   a churchly symbol: Ibid.

85   held by a single queen: Ibid.

85   "used by brothel-keepers": Wilson, *The Hive*.

85   both a lubricant: Jeremy MacClancy, *Consuming Culture: Why You Eat What You Eat* (New York: Holt, 1992), 80.

85   "There would be": Stephanie Strom, "A Bee Mogul Confronts the Crisis in His Field," *New York Times*, February 16, 2017, www.nytimes.com /2017/02/16/business/a-bee-mogul-confronts-the-crisis-in-his-field.html.

85   nearly three-quarters: Ibid.

85   California almonds alone depend: "Fact Sheet: The Economic Challenge Posed by Declining Pollinator Populations," The White House, June 20, 2014.

85   1.26 million acres: "2020 California Almond Objective Measurement Report," US Department of Agriculture National Agricultural Statistics Service, July 7, 2020.

86   farmers rent commercial hives: Heather Smith, "Bee Not Afraid: The Disappearance of the Honeybees Isn't the End of the World," Slate, July 13, 2007, https://slate.com/technology/2007/07/why-the-disappearance-of -the-honeybees-isn-t-the-end-of-the-world.html.

86   nearly eighteen hundred varieties: Frank C. Pellett, *American Honey Plants* (Hamilton, IL: *American Bee Journal*, 1920).

86   they're attracted to: Ibid.

86   Bees living near tourist attractions: Elkort, *The Secret Life of Food*, 198.

86   beekeepers in New York: Ian Frazier, "The Maraschino Mogul," *The New Yorker*, April 16, 2018, www.newyorker.com/magazine/2018/04/23/the -maraschino-moguls-secret-life.

86 In 1969, a graduate student: Meredith Elizabeth Hoag Lieux, "A Palyno-
logical Investigation of Louisiana Honeys" (PhD dissertation, Louisiana
State University and Agricultural and Mechanical College, 1969).

86 nearly 80 percent contained: Ibid., 74.

86 "seemed reluctant to admit": Ibid.

86 Some artisan beekeepers: Old Blue Raw Honey, www.oldbluenatural
resources.com.

87 helped the CIA search: Molly Kulpa, "The Buzz on Pollen: A Q&A with
Dr. Vaughn Bryant, One of the World's Prominent Palynologists," *Spirit
Magazine*, Texas A&M Foundation, Fall 2017, www.txamfoundation.com
/Fall-2017/Ask-Professor-X.aspx.

87 spent more than forty years: Vaughn Bryant, "Caveat Emptor: Let the
Buyer Beward," *Bee Culture*, April 24, 2017.

87 "consumers rarely get": Vaughn Bryant, "Truth in Labeling: Testing Honey,"
Bee Culture, August 2014, 29–32.

87 "Beekeepers and honey producers": Ibid.

87 "The federal laws": Bryant, "Caveat Emptor."

87 the current methods: Bryant, "Truth in Labeling."

87 Ever since the United States: Ben Schott, "Honey Laundering," *New
York Times*, June 16, 2010, https://schott.blogs.nytimes.com/2010/06/16
/honey-laundering.

88 loose federal regulations: Bryant, "Truth in Labeling."

88 remove unwanted materials: Bryant, "Caveat Emptor."

88 the United States gets: Personal interview with Jill Clark, October 11, 2019.

88 almost 100 million pounds: Bryant, "Caveat Emptor."

88 heavy metals such as lead: Andrew Schneider, "Asian Honey, Banned in
Europe, Is Flooding U.S. Grocery Shelves," Food Safety News, August 15,
2011, www.foodsafetynews.com/2011/08/honey-laundering.

88 potentially dangerous chemicals: Long, *Honey*, 135.

88 often contains traces: Schneider, "Asian Honey, Banned in Europe, Is
Flooding U.S. Grocery Shelves."

88 In 2011, inspectors found: Ibid.

88 some manufacturers take forgery: Ibid.

88 About 30 percent: Personal interview with Clark, October 11, 2019.

89 Some states: Bryant, "Caveat Emptor."

Chapter 6: The Vanilla of Society

91 "I've spent my life": "Howard Johnson, 75, Founder of the Restaurant Chain,
Dead," *New York Times*, June 21, 1972, www.nytimes.com/1972/06/21
/archives/howard-johnson-75-founder-ot-the-restaurant-chain-dead
-bought.html.

92 who call their lovers: Michael Oates and Larbi Oukada, *Entre Amis*, 6th
ed. (Boston: Cengage Learning, 2012), 283.

92 in which case *mon chou*: Barbara Ensrud, *The Pocket Guide to Wine and Cheese* (Dorset, UK: New Orchard Editions, 1981), 90.

92 etymology of *mon chou*: Oates and Oukada, *Entre Amis*, 238; Evelyne Bloch-Dano, *Vegetables: A Biography*, translated by Teresa Lavender Fagan (Chicago: University of Chicago Press, 2012), 51.

92 *la femme fraise*: Mary A. Knighton, "Down the Rabbit Hole: In Pursuit of Shōjo Alices, from Lewis Carroll to Kanai Mieko," *U.S.-Japan Women's Journal*, no. 40 (2011): 49–89.

92 *c'est la saison*: "Top Euphemisms for 'Period' by Language," Clue, March 10, 2016, https://helloclue.com/articles/culture/top-euphemisms -for-period-by-language.

92 taken as a compliment: "Vanille," *OED Online*, Oxford University Press, December 2020, www.oed.com/view/Entry/221378.

92 "Ah, you flavour": Lady Holland, *A Memoir of the Reverend Sydney Smith*, vol. 1 (London: Longman, Brown, Green, and Longmans, 1855), 262.

93 "I love you": "Cap o' Rushes," Jacqueline Simpson and Steve Roud, *A Dictionary of English Folklore* (Oxford: Oxford University Press, 2003).

93 the stereotype of sailors: "Salty," *OED Online*, Oxford University Press, December 2020, www.oed.com/view/Entry/170227.

93 because LGBTQ populations: "Vanilla," *OED Online*, Oxford University Press, December 2020, www.oed.com/view/Entry/221377.

93 world's most popular: Anne Cooper Funderburg, *Chocolate, Strawberry, and Vanilla: A History of American Ice Cream* (Bowling Green, OH: Bowling Green State University Press, 1995), 59.

93 second most expensive: Harold McGee, *On Food and Cooking: The Science and Lore of the Kitchen* (New York: Scribner, 2004), 430.

93 a kilo of which: "Mystery Solved: Biologists Explain the Genetic Origins of the Saffron Crocus," *Science Daily*, March 11, 2019.

94 vanilla is the only: Patricia Rain, *Vanilla: The Cultural History of the World's Most Popular Flavor and Fragrance* (New York: Penguin, 2004), 5.

94 more than 25,000 species: Ibid., 2.

94 It can take years: Ibid., 10.

94 which grow only: Ibid.

94 bloom only for a few hours: Ibid., 6.

94 their hermaphroditic sex parts: Ibid.

94 only one or two species: Ibid.

94 the melipona and euglossine bees: Ibid.

94 a 1 percent chance: Daphna Havkin-Frenkel and Faith C. Belanger, eds., *Handbook of Vanilla Science and Technology*, 2nd ed. (Hoboken: John Wiley and Sons, 2019), 15.

94 Nahuatl *ahuacatl*: Anju Saxena, ed., *Himalayan Languages Past and Present* (Berlin: De Gruyter, 2004), 364.

94 a Spanish diminutive: Tim Ecott, *Vanilla: Travels in Search of the Ice Cream Orchid* (New York: Grove Press, 2004), 23.

94 Greek *órxis*: Anju Saxena, ed., *Himalayan Languages Past and Present*.

95 It wasn't until 1841: Richard Bulliet et al., *The Earth and Its Peoples: A Global History*, 6th ed., vol. 2 (Stamford: Cengage Learning, 2015), 680.

95 a title now held: Javier De La Cruz Medina et al., "Vanilla: Post-harvest Operations," Food and Agriculture Organization of the United Nations, June 16, 2009, 3.

95 Because its flowers: Rain, *Vanilla*, 7.

95 another six to nine months: Ibid., 8.

95 they need to be cured: Ibid., 9.

95 six hundred dollars per kilo: Richard Gray, "Nine Surprising Things Worth More than This Shimmering Metal," BBC, May 31, 2018, www .bbc.com/worklife/article/20180530-nine-surprising-things-worth -more-than-this-shimmering-metal.

95 six hundred blossoms: Melody M. Bomgardner, "The Problem with Vanilla," *Scientific American*, September 14, 2016, www.scientificamerican .com/article/the-problem-with-vanilla.

95 contain only about about 2 percent: Ibid.

96 a few kilos of vanilla beans: Nancy Kacungira, "Fighting the Vanilla Thieves of Madagascar," BBC, August 16, 2018, www.bbc.co.uk/news/resources /idt-sh/madagascar_vanillla.

96 Some farmers harvest: Lovasoa Rabary and Hereward Holland, "Madagascar Vanilla Crop Quality Suffers as Thieves Spark Violence," Reuters, July 18, 2019.

96 more prone to disease: De La Cruz Medina, et al., "Vanilla: Post-harvest Operations."

96 seek vigilante justice: Finbarr O'Reilly, "Precious as Silver, Vanilla Brings Cash and Crime to Madagascar," *New York Times*, September 4, 2018, www.nytimes.com/interactive/2018/08/30/world/africa/madagascar -vanilla.html.

96 "tattoo" their beans: Ecott, *Vanilla*, 36.

96 up to 99 percent: Bomgardner, "The Problem with Vanilla."

96 derived from things: Iain Fraser, "Choosy Consumers Drive a Near 1,000% Spike in Vanilla Prices," The Conversation, February 27, 2017, https:// theconversation.com/choosy-consumers-drive-a-near-1-000-spike-in -vanilla-prices-72780.

96 chloroform: Simon Cotton, "Vanillin," Royal Society of Chemistry, February 29, 2008.

96 castoreum: C. Rose Kennedy, "The Flavor Rundown: Natural vs. Artificial Flavors," Science in the News, Harvard University, September 21, 2015, http://sitn.hms.harvard.edu/flash/2015/the-flavor-rundown-natural -vs-artificial-flavors.

96 In 2006, a Japanese scientist: Cotton, "Vanillin."

96 the FDA's definition: Kennedy, "The Flavor Rundown: Natural vs. Artificial Flavors."

96 applies only to visible contamination: Kimberly Kindy, "Consumers Are Buying Contaminated Meat, Doctors' Group Says in Lawsuit," *Washington Post*, April 17, 2019.

96 a 2015 study: Andrea Rock, "How Safe Is Your Ground Beef?," *Consumer Reports*, December 21, 2015, www.consumerreports.org/cro/food/how -safe-is-your-ground-beef.htm.

96 acceptable limits: "Food Defect Levels Handbook," US Food and Drug Administration, September 7, 2018.

97 odds are: "CFR—Code of Federal Regulations, Title 21," US Food and Drug Administration, April 1, 2019.

98 mix with wine or honey: Martin Elkort, *The Secret Life of Food: A Feast of Food and Drink History, Folklore, and Fact* (Los Angeles: Tarcher, 1991), 101–02; Maguelonne Toussaint-Samat, *A History of Food*, translated by Anthea Bell (Cambridge: Blackwell, 1992), 749.

98 comes from the Arabic *sharba*: "Sherbet," *OED Online*, Oxford University Press, December 2020, www.oed.com/view/Entry/177992.

98 *sharbat*, a drink made: "Hot Enough for You? Cool Off with a Brief History of Frozen Treats," National Public Radio, August 17, 2016, www .npr.org/sections/thesalt/2016/08/17/490386948/hot-enough-for-you -cool-off-with-a-brief-history-of-frozen-treats.

98 The Chinese made sherbet: Mary Ellen Snodgrass, *World Food: An Encyclopedia of History, Culture and Social Influence from Hunter Gatherers to the Age of Globalization* (Armonk, NY: Sharpe Reference, 2013).

98 the Mongols made ice cream: Ibid.

98 underground pits insulated: Margaret Visser, *Much Depends on Dinner: The Extraordinary History and Mythology, Allure and Obsessions, Perils and Taboos of an Ordinary Meal* (New York: Grove Press, 1986), 289.

98 "the Viennese are afraid": Ludwig van Beethoven, *Beethoven's Letters: A Critical Edition with Explanatory Notes by Dr. A. C. Kalischer*, translated with preface by J. S. Shedlock, vol. 1 (London: Dent, 1909), 10.

98 "P.S. The house I filled": George Washington, *The Papers of George Washington*, edited by W. W. Abbot, vol. 1, *1784–July 1784*, University Press of Virginia, 1992, 420–21.

99 "there was not": George Washington, *The Diaries of George Washington*, edited by Donald Jackson and Dorothy Twohig, vol. 4, *1784–June 1786*, University Press of Virginia, 1978, 148–49.

99 later spending: John F. Mariani, *The Encyclopedia of American Food and Drink* (New York: Bloomsbury, 2013), 264.

99 Francis Bacon: Visser, *Much Depends on Dinner*, 293–94.

99 "stale and rancid": Edgar Stanton Maclay, "The Social Side of Washington's Administration," *Daughters of the American Revolution Magazine* 52, no. 1 (1918): 209.

99 "Refined sugar was sold": Funderburg, *Chocolate, Strawberry, and Vanilla*, 4.

99 Thomas Jefferson's recipe: "Ice Cream," Thomas Jefferson's Monticello, www.monticello.org/site/research-and-collections/ice-cream.

101 "the average family": Funderburg, *Chocolate, Strawberry, and Vanilla*, 4.

101 many early American breweries: Ibid., 111. See also "Milk Products," *The Western Brewer and Journal of the Barley, Malt and Hop Trades* 54, no. 4 (1920): 127.

101 Pabst Blue Ribbon: Kat Eschner, "How Some Breweries Survived Prohibition," *Smithsonian*, April 7, 2017.

101 "The prohibition": "Ice-Cream Instead of Beer," *The National Advocate* 54, no. 12 (1919): 2.

102 ice cream consumption had grown: William H. Young and Nancy K. Young, *The Great Depression in America: A Cultural Encyclopedia*, vol. 2 (Westport, CT: Greenwood Press, 2007), 253.

102 mock apple pies: Julia C. Andrews, *Breakfast, Dinner, and Tea: Viewed Classically, Poetically, and Practically* (New York: Appleton, 1860), 174; Lisa Abraham, "Recipe: Ritz Mock Apple Pie—an Old Time Favorite," *Seattle Times*, June 23, 2009.

102 popularized by William Dreyer: "Dreyer's Grand Ice Cream," Oral History Center, Bancroft Library, University of California, www.lib.berkeley .edu/libraries/bancroft-library/oral-history-center/projects/dreyers.

102 owned by Unilever: Nathalie Jordi, "Don't Use the P Word: A Popsicle Showdown," *The Atlantic*, July 9, 2010, www.theatlantic.com/health /archive/2010/07/dont-use-the-p-word-a-popsicle-showdown/59412.

103 "the sick fucking Romans": John O'Bryan, *A History of Weapons: Crossbows, Caltrops, Catapults & Lots of Other Things That Can Seriously Mess You Up* (San Francisco: Chronicle Books, 2013), 73.

103 called *meurtrières*: Lise Hull, *Understanding the Castle Ruins of England and Wales: How to Interpret the History and Meaning of Masonry and Earthworks* (Jefferson, NC: McFarland, 2009), 52.

103 the Japanese were throwing: Heather Arndt Anderson, *Chillies: A Global History* (London: Reaktion, 2016), Apple Books ed.

103 converted fruit pits: Albert N. Merritt, *War Time Control of Distribution of Foods* (New York: Macmillan, 1920), 149.

103 Fat Salvage Committee: Adee Braun, "Turning Bacon into Bombs: The American Fat Salvage Committee," *The Atlantic*, April 18, 2014, www .theatlantic.com/health/archive/2014/04/reluctantly-turning-bacon-into -bombs-during-world-war-ii/360298.

104 "Don't throw away": "Out of the Frying Pan into the Firing Line," Walt Disney, 1942.

104 "For armies are": N. P. Milner, *Vegetius: Epitome of Military Science* (Liverpool, UK: Liverpool University Press, 2001), 67.

104 "fights from within": Ibid., 84.

105 all he needed: Tom Standage, *An Edible History of Humanity* (New York: Bloomsbury, 2009), Apple Books ed.

105 offered a twelve-thousand-franc reward: "Nicolas Appert," *Encyclopaedia Britannica*, www.britannica.com/biography/Nicolas-Appert.

105 It took fourteen years: Ibid.

105 *L'Art de conserver*: Ibid.

105 the French destroyed: Standage, *An Edible History of Humanity*.

105 tactical herbicides: Jeanne Mager Stellman and Steven D. Stellman, "Agent Orange During the Vietnam War: The Lingering Issue of Its Civilian and Military Health Impact," *American Journal of Public Health* 108, no. 6 (2018): 726–28.

105 Agent Orange: Ibid.

105 we actually employed: Committee to Review the Health Effects in Vietnam Veterans of Exposure to Herbicides, Board on the Health of Select Populations, Institute of Medicine, *Veterans and Agent Orange: Update 2012* (Ninth Biennial Update) (Washington, DC: National Academies Press, 2014).

105 "The crude contamination": Brian J. Lukey et al., eds., *Chemical Warfare Agents: Chemistry, Pharmacology, Toxicology, and Therapeutics*, 2nd ed. (Boca Raton, FL: CRC Press, 2008), 53.

106 The Assyrians poisoned: Ibid.

106 Confederate and Union soldiers: "Water Conflict Chronology," Pacific Institute, www.worldwater.org/conflict/list.

106 "A few dikes": "Text of Intelligence Report on Bombing of Dikes in North Vietnam Issued by State Department," *New York Times*, July 29, 1972, www.nytimes.com/1972/07/29/archives/text-of-intelligence-report-on -bombing-of-dikes-in-north-vietnam.html.

106 before Hoover became: "Herbert Hoover," The White House, www.white house.gov/about-the-white-house/presidents/herbert-hoover.

106 before the United States entered: "Years of Compassion, 1914–1923," Herbert Hoover Presidential Library and Museum, https://hoover.archives .gov/exhibits/years-compassion-1914-1923.

106 the entire nation of Belgium: George H. Nash, "An American Epic: Herbert Hoover and Belgian Relief in World War I," *Prologue* 21, no. 1 (1989), www.archives.gov/publications/prologue/1989/spring/hoover-belgium .html.

107 his own pirate nation: Seymour Morris, Jr., *Fit for the Presidency?: Winners, Losers, What-ifs, and Also-rans* (Lincoln: University of Nebraska Press, 2017), 183.

107 delivering, in total: William Clinton Mullendore, *History of the United States Food Administration, 1917–1919* (Stanford, CA: Stanford University Press, 1941), 39.

107 Hoover himself volunteered: "Sow the Seeds of Victory! Posters from the Food Administration During World War I," National Archives, www .archives.gov/education/lessons/sow-seeds.

107 "of the nature": Mullendore, *History of the United States Food Administration, 1917–1919*, 52.

107 "spirit of self-denial": Ibid., 53.

107 "food will win the war": "Sow the Seeds of Victory! Posters from the Food Administration During World War I."

108 Within months he'd built: Mullendore, *History of the United States Food Administration, 1917–1919*, 87.

108 Restaurants and public eateries: Ibid., 97.

108 urging consumers to consume less: Ibid., 89.

108 an estimated $19,417,600: Ibid., 89–90.

108 Even the White House: "Sow the Seeds of Victory! Posters from the Food Administration During World War I."

108 18 million tons: Jeff Lyon, "The Misunderstood President," *Chicago Tribune*, April 29, 1985.

108 "If English medical men": *The Ice Cream Review* 1, no. 10 (1918): 2.

108 "Reports from nearly": Ibid.

109 "In this country": Ibid.

109 it wouldn't be patented: Jefferson M. Moak, "The Frozen Sucker War: Good Humor v. Popsicle," *Prologue* 37, no. 1 (2005), www.archives.gov /publications/prologue/2005/spring/popsicle-1.html.

109 depended on toxic gases: Sam Kean, "Einstein's Little-Known Passion Project? A Refrigerator," *Wired*, July 23, 2017, www.wired.com/story /einsteins-little-known-passion-project-a-refrigerator.

109 introduced in the 1930s: Ibid.

109 the United States was still: Mullendore, *History of the United States Food Administration, 1917–1919*, 169.

109 before the war had imported: Ibid., 167.

110 "Ice cream is no longer": "New Sugar Regulations," United States Food Administration, *Food Conservation Notes*, no. 15, July 6, 1918.

110 Howard Johnson: Anthony Mitchell Sammarco, *A History of Howard Johnson's: How a Massachusetts Soda Fountain Became an American Icon* (Charleston, SC: History Press, 2013).

110 purchased a dilapidated drugstore: "Howard Johnson, 75, Founder of the Restaurant Chain, Dead."

110 an ice cream recipe: Ibid.

110 The recipe, which called: "Howard D. Johnson," Rosenberg International Franchise Center, Peter T. Paul College of Business and Economics, University of New Hampshire, https://www.unh.edu/rosenbergcenter /howard-d-johnson.

111 it was the largest: "The Last Howard Johnson's Restaurant Is for Sale: The Demise of a Once-Great Food Chain," *The Economist*, February 16, 2017, www.economist.com/united-states/2017/02/16/the-last-howard -johnsons-restaurant-is-for-sale.

111   debut of the Eskimo Pie: Moak, "The Frozen Sucker War: Good Humor v. Popsicle."

111   originally called the "Epsicle": Ibid.

111   who inserted lollipop sticks: "Good Humor Ice Cream Truck," Smithsonian Institution, June 21, 2011, www.si.edu/newsdesk/snapshot/good-humor -ice-cream-truck.

111   bells initially borrowed: "100 Years of Good Humor," Good Humor, www .goodhumor.com/us/en/our-history.html.

111   "You are at all times": "NMAH-AC0451–0000012," Gold Bond–Good Humor Collection, National Museum of American History, Archives Center.

111   around 1916, a Polish immigrant: Peter Smith, "The Stunt That Launched Nathan's Famous Stand on Coney Island," Smithsonian, July 3, 2012, www.smithsonianmag.com/arts-culture/the-stunt-that-launched-nathans -famous-stand-on-coney-island-312344.

111   paying college students: David Gerard Hogan, Selling 'em by the Sack: White Castle and the Creation of American Food (New York: New York University Press, 1997), 17.

112   "Let me advise you": S. S. Schoff and B. S. Caswell, The People's Own Book of Recipes (Kenosha, WI: Schoff and Winegar, 1867), 189.

112   had part of their fleet: Ron Grossman, "Flashback: Good Humor Delighted Generations with Its Curbside Delivery of Ice Cream Bars—and Not Even the Mob Could Stop It," Chicago Tribune, August 2, 2019.

112   "Ellis Island Authorities Gently Lead": "Ice Cream as Americanization Agent," The Soda Fountain 20, no. 7 (1921): 81.

112   "It augurs well": Ibid.

113   which accounted for roughly: Mariani, The Encyclopedia of American Food and Drink, 518.

113   endorsing carrots on sticks: Jill Reilly, "In My Day, All We Got for Easter Was a Carrot on a Stick: Newsreel Reveals What Children Got Instead of Chocolate Eggs in WW2," Daily Mail, April 2, 2012, www.dailymail .co.uk/news/article-2123981/In-day-got-Easter-carrot-stick-World-War -Two-showreel-reveals-children-swapped-ice-cream-carrots.html.

113   mock fudge: Lee Edwards Benning, The Cook's Tales: Origins of Famous Foods and Recipes (Old Saybrook: Globe Pequot, 1992), 119.

113   building pop-up ice cream factories: Funderburg, Chocolate, Strawberry, and Vanilla, 143.

114   breaking into the freezer: Ibid., 142.

114   US bomber crews used to make: McGee, On Food and Cooking, 43.

114   soldiers on the ground: "Transcript of an Oral History Interview with Richard T. Meland, Communications, Anti-Aircraft Artillery, Army, World War II," Wisconsin Veterans Museum Research Center, 1995, 14.

114   the most decorated member: "Gen. Chesty Puller Dies; Most Decorated Marine," New York Times, October 12, 1971, www.nytimes.com/1971

/10/12/archives/cert-chesty-puller-diesi-most-decoralted-marine-com missioned-at-20.html.

114 called it a "sissy food": Betty Cuniberti, "Celebrating 40 Years of 31 Flavors," *Los Angeles Times*, December 11, 1985.

114 during which he was photographed: Meyer Liebowitz, "Fidel Castro Eating Ice Cream," April 2, 1959, Getty Images, www.gettyimages.com/detail /news-photo/cuban-president-fidel-castro-eats-an-ice-cream-cone-as -he-news-photo/2967514.

114 "ice cream cathedral": Myles Karp, "The History of Cuba's Ongoing Obsession with Ice Cream," Vice, May 10, 2018, www.vice.com/en_us/article /mbkje8/history-of-ice-cream-cuba-fidel-castro-ubre-blanca-coppelia.

114 (after the French ballet *Coppélia*): Jason Motlagh, "The Future of Cuba's Socialist Ice-Cream Cathedral," *The Guardian*, April 14, 2015, www .theguardian.com/world/2015/apr/14/future-of-coppelia-cuba-socialist -ice-cream-cathedral.

115 "[finish] off a good-sized lunch": Gabriel García Márquez, "A Personal Portrait of Fidel," in Fidel Castro, *Fidel: My Early Years*, edited by Deborah Shnookal and Pedro Álvarez Tabío (Melbourne: Ocean Press, 2005), 13.

115 the CIA tried to assassinate: Anthony Boadle, "Closest CIA Bid to Kill Castro Was Poisoned Drink," Reuters, July 5, 2007, www.reuters.com /article/us-cuba-cia/closest-cia-bid-to-kill-castro-was-poisoned-drink -idUSN0427935120070705.

115 when Castro got into a fight: Guillermo Cabrena Infante, *Mea Cuba* (New York: Farrar, Straus and Giroux, 1994), 324.

115 a breed of miniature cows: Peter Fritsch and Jose De Cordoba, "Castro Hopes to Clone a Famous Milk Cow," *Wall Street Journal*, May 21, 2002, www.wsj.com/articles/SB1021927734453270880.

115 Ubre Blanca: Karp, "The History of Cuba's Ongoing Obsession with Ice Cream."

115 241 pounds of milk: Fritsch and De Cordoba, "Castro Hopes to Clone a Famous Milk Cow."

115 "our great champion": Fidel Castro, "Fidel Castro Addresses Medical Students," Havana Domestic Television Service, March 12, 1982, Castro Speech Data Base, Latin American Network Information Center, http:// lanic.utexas.edu/project/castro/db/1982/19820314.html.

115 eulogized her with military honors: Karp, "The History of Cuba's Ongoing Obsession with Ice Cream."

115 Cotoni and Swiss dairy farmers: Samantha Clark, "Santa Cruz County Supervisors Support Cotoni-Coast Dairies as Name for Proposed National Monument," *Santa Cruz Sentinel*, June 23, 2015, www.santacruzsentinel .com/2015/06/23/santa-cruz-county-supervisors-support-cotoni-coast -dairies-as-name-for-proposed-national-monument.

116 "No G.I. who passed": Lee Kennett, *G.I.: The American Soldier in World War II* (Norman: University of Oklahoma Press, 1997), 197.

116 maggot-infested rice: Sue Shephard, "A Slice of the Moon," in *Food and the*

Memory: Proceedings of the Oxford Symposium on Food and Cookery 2000, edited by Harlan Walker (Devon, UK: Prospect, 2001), 226–29.

116 "as obtainable": Quoted in ibid., 225.

116 "Somebody listening in": Ibid., 223.

116 pictures of food: Ibid., 235.

116 "perhaps it was just": Quoted in Jan Thompson, "Prisoners of the Rising Sun: Food Memories of American POWs in the Far East During World War II," in *Food and the Memory: Proceedings of the Oxford Symposium on Food and Cookery 2000*, edited by Harlan Walker (Devon, UK: Prospect, 2001), 274, 280.

116 "Belly empty": Quoted in Shephard, "A Slice of the Moon," 235.

116 "During the forty-three months": Quoted in Thompson, "Prisoners of the Rising Sun," 278–79.

117 "Few tried to recall": Shephard, "A Slice of the Moon," 233.

117 "There are today": Visser, *Much Depends on Dinner*, 315–16.

118 Researchers testing: Peter Walla et al., "Food-Evoked Changes in Humans: Startle Response Modulation and Event-Related Brain Potentials (ERPs)," *Journal of Psychophysiology* 24, no. 1 (2010): 25–32.

119 human milk is significantly sweeter: Mark Kurlansky, *Milk!: A 10,000-Year Food Fracas* (New York: Bloomsbury, 2018).

119 contains more fat: Harold H. Williams, "Differences Between Cow's and Human Milk," *The Journal of the American Medical Association* 175, no. 2 (1961): 104–07.

119 calming and pain reduction effects: Mahnaz Jebreili et al., "Comparison of Breastmilk Odor and Vanilla Odor on Mitigating Premature Infants' Response to Pain During and After Venipuncture," *Breastfeeding Medicine* 10, no. 7 (2015): 362–65.

119 "spent significantly more time": Julie A. Mennella and Gary K. Beauchamp, "The Human Infants' Response to Vanilla Flavors in Mother's Milk and Formula," *Infant Behavior and Development* 19, no. 1 (1996): 13–19.

119 "what all prisoners of war": Russell Braddon, *The Naked Island* (New York: Doubleday, 1953), 159.

Chapter 7: The Ghosts of Cockaigne Past

121 "It has been": Clement A. Miles, *Christmas in Ritual and Tradition, Christian and Pagan* (Detroit: Gale, 1968), 17.

121 "A couple of flitches": William Cobbett, *Cottage Economy* (London, 1823).

123 before the winter frost: Madeline Shanahan, *Christmas Food and Feasting* (Lanham, MD: Rowman & Littlefield, 2019), 36.

123 the old German and Anglo-Saxon names: R. S. Ferguson, "Culvershouses," *The Archaeological Journal*, June 1887, 106.

123 "labours of the months": "Labours of the Months: December," Victoria and Albert Museum, http://collections.vam.ac.uk/item/O7617/labours-of-the-months-december-panel-unknown.

123 Latin calendar descriptions: Piero Camporesi, *The Magic Harvest: Food, Folklore and Society*, translated by Joan Krakover Hall (Malden, MA: Blackwell, 1998), 43.

123 having had time: Shanahan, *Christmas Food and Feasting*, 36.

123 freshly fermented: Ibid., 10.

124 And to ensure: Joan P. Alcock, "The Festival of Christmas," in *Oxford Symposium on Food and Cookery 1990*, edited by Harlan Walker (Devon, UK: Prospect, 1990), 27.

124 This is also where: Ibid.

124 "a kind of safety valve": Ken Albala and Trudy Eden, *Food and Faith in Christian Culture* (New York: Columbia University Press, 2011), 16.

124 from the Latin roots: Anais N. Spitzer, *Derrida, Myth and the Impossibility of Philosophy* (London: Continuum, 2011), 107.

124 observed around the time: Frederick B. Jonassen, "Lucian's *Saturnalia*, the Land of Cockaigne, and the Mummers' Plays," *Folklore* 101, no. 1 (1990): 58–68.

124 Saturnalia sought to re-create: Ibid.

124 it was a time of the year: E. O. James, *Seasonal Feasts and Festivals* (New York: Barnes & Noble, 1961), 176.

125 of the grape harvest: Victor Shea and William Whitla, eds., *Victorian Literature: An Anthology* (West Sussex, UK: John Wiley and Sons, 2015), 749.

125 wine, intoxication, ritual madness, ecstasy: "Dionysus," in *The Oxford Classical Dictionary*, 3rd rev. ed., edited by Simon Hornblower and Antony Spawforth (Oxford University Press, 2005).

125 raw flesh torn: Ibid.

125 sacrificial humans: William Smith, *Dictionary of Greek and Roman Antiquities* (Boston: Little, Brown, 1859), 413.

125 it was considered bad manners: Ibid., 411.

125 also because they involved: Ibid., 410–14.

125 some scholars have suggested: A.J.M. Wedderburn, *Baptism and Resurrection: Studies in Pauline Theology Against Its Graeco-Roman Background* (Tübingen, Germany: Mohr Siebeck, 1987), 323.

126 lighting yule logs: Clement A. Miles, *Christmas Customs and Traditions: Their History and Significance* (New York: Dover, 1976), 244–45.

126 a Teutonic or Norse festival: Alcock, "The Festival of Christmas," 27.

126 a Saxon rite of sacrifice: W. F. Dawson, *Christmas: Its Origins and Associations* (Detroit: Gale, 1968), 15.

126 *hwéol*: Miles, *Christmas Customs and Traditions*, 171–72.

126 *iol*, or *iul*: Dawson, *Christmas*, 15.

126 it was eventually adopted: "Yule," in Jacqueline Simpson and Steve Roud, *A Dictionary of English Folklore* (Oxford: Oxford University Press, 2003).

126 There is also a theory: "Jolly," *OED Online*, Oxford University Press, December 2020, www.oed.com/view/Entry/101618.

126 "No singular one": Shanahan, *Christmas Food and Feasting*, 10.

126 celebrate the birth: Alcock, "The Festival of Christmas," 27.

127 "Christian symbolism": Miles, *Christmas in Ritual and Tradition, Christian and Pagan*, 183.

127 "Because they are wont": Ibid., 179.

128 "The medieval year resembled: Bridget Ann Henisch, *Fast and Feast: Food in Medieval Society* (University Park: Pennsylvania State University Press, 1976), 28.

128 demonstrations of power: Ibid., 10–11.

128 would have been heavily salted: Massimo Montanari, *Medieval Tastes: Food, Cooking and the Table*, translated by Beth Archer Brombert (New York: Columbia University Press, 2012), 155–56.

128 "The end of the year": Reay Tannahill, *Food in History* (New York: Stein and Day, 1973), 209.

129 like bread: Montanari, *Medieval Tastes*, 58.

129 there are accounts: E. J. Kahn, Jr., *The Staffs of Life* (Boston: Little, Brown, 1984), 169.

129 given the "upper crust": Mary Ellen Snodgrass, *Encyclopedia of Kitchen History* (New York: Fitzroy Dearborn, 2004), 68.

129 "The medieval 'course'": Madeleine Pelner Cosman, *Fabulous Feasts: Medieval Cookery and Ceremony* (New York: George Braziller, 1976), 20.

129 The coronation banquet: Ibid.

129 the funeral collation: Ibid., 24.

130 an umble pie: Alex Johnson and Vincent Franklin, *Menus That Made History* (New York: Hachette, 2019).

130 meant to resemble: Ibid.

130 "superb insignia": Cosman, *Fabulous Feasts*, 45.

130 "indicators of ostentatious waste": Ibid.

130 Pepper was said: Marjorie Shaffer, *Pepper: A History of the World's Most Influential Spice* (New York: St. Martin's Press, 2013), 6–7.

130 *cinnamologus*: W. Geoffrey Arnott, *Birds in the Ancient World from A to Z* (New York: Routledge, 2007), 97–98.

130 powered by courage alone: Andrew Dalby, *Dangerous Tastes: The Story of Spices* (University of California Press, 2000), 38.

130 grew in lakes: Ibid., 37.

131 whenever spices became affordable: Ken Albala, *Food: A Cultural Culinary History*, The Great Courses, transcript book, 2013, 371–72.

131 crushed pearls and rose water: Ibid., 282.

131 "This means, of course": William Edward Mead, *The English Medieval Feast* (New York: Houghton Mifflin, 1931), 58.

131 "oysters in gravy bastard": Ibid., 55.

131 "dyschefull of snowe": Albala, *Food*, 388–89.

131 having wine or rose water: Katherine C. Little and Nicola McDonald, eds., *Thinking Medieval Romance* (Oxford: Oxford University Press, 2018), 13.

132 blood for brown or black: Cosman, *Fabulous Feasts*, 61–63.

132 the Easter egg: "A Hunt for Medieval Easter Eggs," *Medieval Manuscripts Blog*, British Library, April 14, 2017, https://blogs.bl.uk/digitised manuscripts/2017/04/a-hunt-for-medieval-easter-eggs.html.

132 *coqz heaumex*: Terrence, Scully, ed., *The Viandier of Taillevent: An Edition of All Extant Manuscripts* (Ottawa: University of Ottawa Press, 1988), 300.

132 *cignes revestuz*: Ibid., 303.

132 stuffing a ball of cloth: Richard Warner, *Antiquitates Culinariae, or, Curious Tracts Relating to the Culinary Affairs of the Old English* (London, 1791), xxiii.

132 "Take an olde cok": Ibid., 66.

133 "one last pagan fling": Emmanuel Le Roy Ladurie, *Carnival in Romans*, translated by Mary Feeney (New York: George Braziller, 1979), 307–08.

133 the need to use: Henisch, *Fast and Feast*, 38.

133 a mock swordfight: Ken Albala, *Food in Early Modern Europe* (Westport, CT: Greenwood Press, 2003), 196.

133 Sometimes Lent would be: Samuel Kinser, *Rabelais's Carnival* (Berkeley: University of California Press, 1990), 48.

133 Carnival would wear: Terence Scully, *The Art of Cookery in the Middle Ages* (Woodbridge, UK: Boydell Press, 1995), 63.

134 reenactments of Adam and Eve: Herman Pleij, *Dreaming of Cockaigne: Medieval Fantasies of the Perfect Life*, yranslated by Diane Webb (New York: Columbia University Press, 2001), 7.

134 "designed to make": Ibid., 6.

134 Middle Low German *kokenje*: "Cockaigne," *The Oxford Dictionary of Phrase and Fable*, 2nd ed., edited by Elizabeth Knowles (Oxford University Press, 2005).

134 the Dutch similarly had: Pleij, *Dreaming of Cockaigne*, 77.

134 *leuzig*: "Lazy," *OED Online*, Oxford University Press, December 2020, www.oed.com/view/Entry/106558.

134 *likken*: "Lick," *OED Online*, Oxford University Press, December 2020, www.oed.com/view/Entry/108002.

134 the Germans had: Hans Hinrichs, *The Glutton's Paradise* (Mount Vernon, NY: Peter Pauper Press, 1955).

134 *schlaff*: Anatoly Liberman, *An Analytic Dictionary of the English Etymology: An Introduction* (Minneapolis: University of Minnesota Press, 2008), 114.

135 "By the Middle Ages": Pleij, *Dreaming of Cockaigne*, 3.

135 rain the occasional pie: Ibid., 34.

135 snow a dusting: Ibid., 42.

135   The streets were paved: Ibid., 35

135   the rivers flowed: Ibid., 34, 41.

135   Houses were made: Ibid., 40.

135   their beams were made: Ibid., 34, 40.

135   their rooftops were tiled: Ibid.

135   perfectly stewed and sprinkled: "The Land of Cockaygne," MS Harley 913, ff. 3r-6v, British Library, London.

135   a pig would run up: Jonassen, "Lucian's 'Saturnalia,' the Land of Cockaigne, and the Mummers' Plays."

135   a grilled fish might jump: Pleij, *Dreaming of Cockaigne*, 3.

135   "shit nothing but sweet figs": Ibid., 41.

135   poached eggs: Hinrichs, *The Glutton's Paradise*, 7.

135   "the encumbrance": Pleij, *Dreaming of Cockaigne*, 39.

135   "Loose women": Ibid., 43.

136   In fact, Schlaraffenland: Hinrichs, *The Glutton's Paradise*, 21–27.

136   "sexual and economic predator[s]": Carla Freccero, "A Race of Wolves," in *Animots: Postanimality in French Thought*, edited by Matthew Senior, David L. Clark, and Carla Freccero, Yale French Studies, no. 127 (New Haven, CT: Yale University Press, 2015), 121.

136   a fountain of youth: Hinrichs, *The Glutton's Paradise*, 23.

136   you were paid: Pleij, *Dreaming of Cockaigne*, 43–44.

136   you had to swim: Ben Parsons, "Fantasy and Fallacy in the Old French Cocaingne," *Viator* 46, no. 3 (2015): 173–93.

136   "There is nothing": Pleij, *Dreaming of Cockaigne*, 43–44.

Chapter 8: The Choices of a New Generation

139   *"Pour avoir assez"*: Bee Wilson, *First Bite: How We Learn to Eat* (New York: Perseus, 2015), 105.

139   "Choose life": *Trainspotting*, directed by Danny Boyle, based on the novel by Irvine Welsh, Miramax, 1996.

140   delay the annual slaughter: Alexander Tille, *Yule and Christmas: Their Place in the Germanic Year* (Glasgow, Robert MacLehose and Company, 1899), 68–70.

141   "Average Americans and Europeans": Gregg Easterbrook, *The Progress Paradox: How Life Gets Better While People Feel Worse* (New York: Random House, 2003), 80–81.

141   More than 36 percent: Cheryl D. Fryar et al., "Fast Food Consumption Among Adults in the United States, 2013–2016," NCHS Data Brief no. 322, October 2018.

141   increasing to 80 percent monthly: Adam Chandler, "What McDonald's Does Right," *The Atlantic*, June 25, 2019, www.theatlantic.com/ideas/archive/2019/06/how-fast-food-can-unite-america/592441.

141   "No other institution": Ibid.

141 customize drive-through menus: Amelia Levin, "Tech Ushers In a Drive-Thru Renaissance," *QSR*, October 2019, www.qsrmagazine.com/drive -thru/tech-ushers-drive-thru-renaissance.

142 testing the use: Camilla Hodgson, "Fast-Food Chains Consider Trying License Plate Recognition in Drive-Throughs," *Los Angeles Times*, July 11, 2019, www.latimes.com/business/la-fi-license-plate-recognition-drive -through-restaurant-20190711-story.html.

142 The initial success: "Our History," McDonald's, www.mcdonalds.com/us /en-us/about-us/our-history.html.

142 just three items: Andrew F. Smith, *Eating History* (New York: Columbia University Press, 2009), Kindle ed.

142 you weren't allowed: Ken Albala, *Food: A Cultural Culinary History*, The Great Courses, transcript book, 2013, 616.

142 reducing the wait time: Smith, *Eating History*, 221–22.

142 "A McDonald's outlet,": Jeremy MacClancy, *Consuming Culture: Why You Eat What You Eat* (New York: Holt, 1992), 189.

143 to reduce splatter: Richard Evershed and Nicola Temple, *Sorting the Beef from the Bull* (London: Bloomsbury Sigma, 2016), Kindle ed.

143 the same chemical: Preethi S. Raj, "Re-review of the Safety Assessment of Dimethicone, Methicone, and Substituted-Methicone Polymers," Cosmetic Ingredient Review Memorandum, November 15, 2019.

143 breast implants: Evershed and Temple, *Sorting the Beef from the Bull*.

143 The real watershed moment: Sophie Egan, *Devoured: From Chicken Wings to Kale Smoothies—How What We Eat Defines Who We Are* (New York: HarperCollins, 2016), Apple Books ed.

144 "Hold the pickles": Olivia B. Waxman, "Here's What $80 Worth of Extra Pickles on a Whopper Looks Like," *Time*, February 26, 2016, https://time .com/4238762/burger-king-whopper-80-pickles.

144 2005 "Fantasy Ranch" commercial: "Burger King: Fantasy Ranch," AdAge, February 24, 2005, https://adage.com/creativity/work/fantasy-ranch /9247.

145 "nagging wives": Carrie Packwood Freeman and Debra Merskin, "Having It His Way: The Construction of Masculinity in Fast-Food TV Advertising," in *Food for Thought: Essays on Eating and Culture*, edited by Lawrence C. Rubin (Jefferson, NC: McFarland, 2008), 286.

146 "It's ok": "Be Your Way at Burger King Restaurants," Burger King, May 20, 2014, https://company.bk.com/news-press/be-your-way-burger-king® -restaurants.

146 "221,184 different ways": Ibid.

146 that also brags about: John L. Hess, "A Sizzling Battle in the Burger Business," *New York Times*, March 13, 1977, www.nytimes.com/1977/03/13 /archives/a-sizzling-battle-in-the-burger-business-sizzling-battle-in-th e.html.

146 McDonald's once owned 90 percent: Haley Peterson, "The Ridiculous

Reason McDonald's Sold Chipotle and Missed Out on Billions of Dollars," Business Insider, May 22, 2015.

147   "It's as though": Elizabeth Farrelly, *Blubberland: The Dangers of Happiness* (Cambridge, MA: MIT Press, 2008), 100–01.

147   Starbucks, for example: Egan, *Devoured.*

147   is made of sugar, water: "Naturally Flavored Vanilla Syrup," Starbucks at Home, https://athome.starbucks.com/product/naturally-flavored-vanilla -syrup.

147   sea salt topping: "Salted Caramel Hot Chocolate," Starbucks, www.star bucks.com/menu/product/762/hot?parent=%2Fdrinks%2Fhot-drinks %2Fhot-chocolates.

148   "If a person orders": Heejung Kim and Hazel Rose Markus, "Deviance or Uniqueness, Harmony or Conformity? A Cultural Analysis," *Journal of Personality and Social Psychology* 77, no. 4 (1999): 785.

148   $100 billion per year: Solvie Karlstrom and Christine Dell'Amore, "Why Tap Water Is Better than Bottled Water," *National Geographic*, March 13, 2010, www.nationalgeographic.com/news/2010/3/why-tap-water-is-better.

148   more than 4 billion pounds: "Tap Water vs. Bottled Water," Food and Water Watch, www.foodandwaterwatch.org/about/live-healthy/tap-water -vs-bottled-water.

148   a fraction of the cost: Karlstrom and Dell'Amore, "Why Tap Water Is Better Than Bottled Water."

148   no less safe or clean: Ibid.

148   into water systems: "National Primary Drinking Water Regulations," United States Environmental Protection Agency, February 14, 2020, www.epa.gov/ground-water-and-drinking-water/national-primary -drinking-water-regulations; Edward T. Furlong et al., "Nationwide Reconnaissance of Contaminants of Emerging Concern in Source and Treated Drinking Waters of the United States: Pharmaceuticals," *Science of the Total Environment*, no. 579 (2017): 1629–42; "Drugs in the Water," Harvard Health Publishing, June 2011, www.health.harvard.edu/news letter_article/drugs-in-the-water.

148   bottled from the very same source: "Tap Water vs. Bottled Water," Food and Water Watch.

149   "is an example": Paul Bloom, *How Pleasure Works: The New Science of Why We Like What We Like* (New York: Norton, 2010), 43.

149   Before the first self-service: "Food and Beverage Retailing in 19th and Early 20th Century America," Janice B. Longone Culinary Archive, William L. Clements Library, University of Michigan.

149   By the 1940s: Smith, *Eating History*, 180.

149   We can now choose: "Oreo," Snack Works, www.snackworks.com.

150   "stuf" inside Oreos: Olivia Tarantino, "What Really Is the White Stuff in the Center of an Oreo?" Eat This, Not That!, March 28, 2017, www.eat this.com/oreo-filling; "2 Flavors of Oreos Recalled over Undeclared Milk

Allergen," Fox News, October 31, 2016, www.foxnews.com/health/2 -flavors-of-oreos-recalled-over-undeclared-milk-allergen.

150 This isn't counting: Josh Hafner, "Oreo Launches New Hot Chicken Wing and Wasabi Flavors, but They May Not Be Easy to Find," *USA Today*, August 28, 2018.

150 Halloween Whoppers: Hayley Peterson, "Burger King Is Bringing One of Its Most Bizarre Burgers to the US," Business Insider, September 25, 2015, www.businessinsider.com/burger-king-is-selling-burgers-with-black -buns-2015-9.

150 hot pink Fruity Pebbles: "National Cereal Day Magic Fruity Pebbles Cereal," Post Consumer Brands, http://natlcerealday.wpengine.com /?products=magic-fruity-pebbles-cereal.

151 heading to grocery stores soon: David Johnson and Siobhan O'Connor, "These Charts Show Every Genetically Modified Food People Already Eat in the U.S.," *Time*, April 30, 2015, https://time.com/3840073/gmo -food-charts; Sophia Chen, "Genetically Modified Animals Will Be on Your Plate in No Time," *Wired*, July 6, 2015, www.wired.com/2015 /07/eating-genetically-modified-animals; "Modified Cows to Produce 'Human' Milk," *Fast Company*, March 23, 2011, www.fastcompany.com /1742119/genetically-modified-cows-produce-human-milk.

151 "It's no longer enough": Sophie Egan, *Devoured*.

151 Starbucks' Unicorn Frappuccino: "Starbucks Weaves Its Magic with New Color and Flavor Changing Unicorn Frappuccino," Starbucks' Stories & News, April 18, 2017.

151 KFC's Double Down: "KFC's 'Double Down' to Go Nationwide," UPI, April 9, 2010, www.upi.com/Odd_News/2010/04/09/KFCs-Double -Down-to-go-nationwide/77741270842514/.

151 Chicken and Donut sandwiches: "KFC Is Rolling Out Its Viral Fried-Chicken-and-Doughnut Sandwich Nationwide," Business Insider, February 20, 2020, www.businessinsider.com/kfc-chicken-and-donuts-sand wich-basket-launches-nationwide-2020-2.

151 Heinz's limited-edition: "Heinz Made a Ketchup Bottle Adorned with Ed Sheeran's Tattoo," AdAge, August 14, 2019, https://adage.com/creativity /work/heinz-ed-sheeran-tattoo-ketchup/2191451.

151 Burger King's Flamin' Hot: "Do You Dare? BURGER KING® Restaurants and the CHEETOS® Brand Introduce Flamin' Hot® Mac n' Cheetos™," Business Wire, November 29, 2017, www.businesswire.com /news/home/20171129005248/en/Do-You-Dare-BURGER-KING® -Restaurants-and-the-CHEETOS®-Brand-Introduce-Flamin'-Hot® -Mac-n'-Cheetos™.

151 had to hire fifteen thousand: Ashley Lutz, "How Taco Bell's Lead Innovator Created the Most Successful Menu Item of All Time," Business Insider, February 26, 2014, www.businessinsider.com/taco-bell-doritos - locos-taco-story-2014–2.

152 Malcolm Gladwell gave: Malcolm Gladwell, "Choice, Happiness and Spa-

ghetti Sauce," TED2004, www.ted.com/talks/malcolm_gladwell_choice
_happiness_and_spaghetti_sauce.

152 "that sounds like": Ibid.

153 Prego alone now offers: "Sauces," Prego, www.prego.com/sauces.

153 "embracing the diversity": Gladwell, "Choice, Happiness and Spaghetti
Sauce."

154 "In evolutionary terms": Farrelly, *Blubberland: The Dangers of Happiness*, 14.

154 "To whom a little": William Wallace, *Epicureanism* (London: Society for
Promoting Christian Knowledge, 1880), 48.

154 adding food options: Sheena Iyengar, *The Art of Choosing* (New York: Hachette, 2010), 190.

154 "The more choice": Ibid., 204.

155 "When people have": Barry Schwartz, *The Paradox of Choice: Why More Is
Less* (New York: HarperCollins, 2004), 2.

155 Iyengar drew her conclusions: Iyengar, *The Art of Choosing*, 184–86.

155 "supplier of jams": Ibid., 184.

156 "the relative merits": Ibid., 186.

156 "When the options": Ibid., 204–05.

157 "prose and recipes": Molly O'Neill, "Food Porn," *Columbia Journalism
Review*, September–October 2003, 39.

157 Today, *food porn*: Anne E. McBride, "Food Porn," *Gastronomica* 10, no. 1
(2010): 38–46.

157 lipstick to redden berries: Angelina Chapin, "WD-40 and Microwaved
Tampons: Secrets of Food Photography Revealed," *The Guardian*, January 4, 2016, www.theguardian.com/lifeandstyle/2016/jan/04/food-stylist
-photography-tricks-advertising.

157 eyeliner to paint in grill marks: Shaunacy Ferro, "How Fake Is Food Styling?," *Fast Company*, September 9, 2014, www.fastcompany.com/3034644
/how-fake-is-food-styling.

158 personal lubricants: Delores Custer, *Food Styling: The Art of Preparing Food
for the Camera* (Hoboken, NJ: John Wiley and Sons, 2010), 130.

158 vegetable shortening: Chapin, "WD-40 and Microwaved Tampons: Secrets of Food Photography Revealed."

158 shaving cream: Michael Zhang, "Tricks Food Photographers Use to
Make Food Look Delicious." Petapixel, November 20, 2018, https://peta
pixel.com/2018/11/30/tricks-food-photographers-use-to-make-food
-look-delicious.

158 Scotchgard: Perri O. Blumberg, "16 Secrets a Food Stylist Won't Tell
You," *Reader's Digest*, November 18, 2019, www.rd.com/food/fun/food
-stylist-secrets/.

158 might actually be: Zhang, "Tricks Food Photographers Use to Make Food
Look Delicious."

158 lit cigarettes: Chapin, "WD-40 and Microwaved Tampons: Secrets of Food Photography Revealed."

158 wet, microwaved tampons: Ibid.

158 they're not pretty enough: Suzanne Goldenberg, "Half of All US Food Produce Is Thrown Away, New Research Suggests," *The Guardian*, July 13, 2016, www.theguardian.com/environment/2016/jul/13/us-food -waste-ugly-fruit-vegetables-perfect.

158 "abnormal physical characteristics": Elysha Enos, "Ugly Fruit and Vegetables Can Now Be Sold in Quebec," CBC, July 26, 2016, www.cbc.ca /news/canada/montreal/ugly-fruit-vegetables-quebec-produce-1.3695059.

158 American farmers report: Dana Gunders, "Wasted: How America Is Losing Up to 40 Percent of Its Food from Farm to Fork to Landfill," issue paper IP:12–06-B, Natural Resources Defense Council, August 2012, 8.

158 are often sprayed: P. V. Mahajan et al., "Postharvest Treatments of Fresh Produce," *Philosophical Transactions of the Royal Society A* 372, no. 2017 (2014).

158 spraying too much water: C. Claiborne Ray, "Keeping Greens Green," *New York Times*, November 14, 2011, www.nytimes.com/2011/11/15 /science/does-spraying-greens-with-water-keep-them-fresh.html.

158 in the 1990s: Peter Applebome, "Mist in Grocery's Produce Section Is Linked to Legionnaires' Disease," *New York Times*, January 11, 1990, www.nytimes.com/1990/01/11/us/mist-in-grocery-s-produce-section-is -linked-to-legionnaires-disease.html.

158 the real purpose: Jake Rossen, "The Real Reason Grocery Stores Spray Water on Their Produce," Mental Floss, May 22, 2019, www.mentalfloss.com /article/583777/real-reason-grocery-stores-spray-water-on-their-produce.

159 Seventy percent of the French fries: Paul C. Bethke et al., "History and Origin of Russet Burbank (Netted Gem) a Sport of Burbank," *American Journal of Potato Research* 91, no. 6 (2014): 594–609.

159 McDonald's, the largest buyer: Albala, *Food*, 619–20.

159 wants their fries: Charles R. Brown, "Russet Burbank: No Ordinary Potato," *Hortscience* 50, no. 2 (2015): 157–60.

159 "retention of good fry quality": Ibid.

159 "Down to World War I": B. W. Higman, *How Food Made History* (West Sussex, UK: Wiley-Blackwell, 2012), 71–72.

159 "Store-bought tomatoes": Rachel Herz, *Why You Eat What You Eat: The Science Behind Our Relationship with Food* (New York: Norton, 2017), Kindle ed.

160 "are bulldozed": Martin Teitel, *Rain Forest in Your Kitchen* (Washington, DC: Island Press, 1992), 62.

160 McDonald's is also: *Food, Inc.*, directed by Robert Kenner, Magnolia Pictures, 2008.

160 yet 94 percent: "Do You Know This About Holstein Cattle?," Holstein Association USA, www.holsteinusa.com.

160 bred for its industrial uniformity: "Holstein Breed Characteristics," Holstein Association USA, www.holsteinusa.com/holstein_breed/breed history.html.

160 "To think that": Michael Symons, *A History of Cooks and Cooking* (Champaign: University of Illinois Press, 2000), 339.

161 "We always knew": Farrelly, *Blubberland*, 154.

Chapter 9: Forbidden Berries (or Appetite for Distraction)

163 "Healthy, sane humans": Jason G. Goldman, "On Capsaicin: Why Do We Love to Eat Hot Peppers?," *Scientific American*, November 30, 2011.

164 botanically they're fruits: Maricel E. Presilla, *Peppers of the Americas* (Berkeley, CA: Ten Speed Press, 2017), 13.

164 Sanskrit *pippali*: John F. Mariani, *The Encyclopedia of American Food and Drink* (New York: Bloomsbury, 2013), 388.

164 called capsaicinoids: Shane T. McDonald, David A. Bolliet, and John E. Hayes, eds., Chemesthesis: Chemical Touch in Food and Eating (West Sussex: Wiley Blackwell, 2016), 32–33.

165 also eliminates: Presilla, *Peppers of the Americas*, 18.

165 nearly 400 percent better odds: Evan C. Fricke et al., "When Condition Trumps Location: Seed Consumption by Fruit-Eating Birds Removes Pathogens and Predator Attractants," *Ecology Letters* 16, no. 8 (2013): 1031–36.

165 can sense capsaicin: Jeff Potter, *Cooking for Geeks: Real Science, Great Cooks, and Good Food*, 2nd ed. (Sebastopol, CA: O'Reilly Media, 2015), 59.

165 the human threshold: Ibid.

165 our trigeminal or chemical sense: McDonald et al., *Chemesthesis*, 268.

165 the same pain sensor: Michaeleen Doucleff, "Sriracha Chemistry: How Hot Sauces Perk Up Your Food and Your Mood," NPR, February 24, 2014, www.npr.org/sections/thesalt/2014/02/24/281978831/sriracha -chemistry-how-hot-sauces-perk-up-your-food-and-your-mood.

165 trigger a series: McDonald et al., *Chemesthesis*, 268.

166 "The traditional view": Personal interview with Gary K. Beauchamp, September 17, 2019.

166 "Anyone who has": Jean Anthelme Brillat-Savarin, *The Physiology of Taste; or, Meditations on Transcendental Gastronomy*, translated by M.F.K. Fisher (New York: Knopf, 2009).

166 Capsaicin is an effective: Joshua J. Tewksbury et al., "Evolutionary Ecology of Pungency in Wild Chilies," *Proceedings of the National Academy of Sciences of the United States of America* 105, no. 33 (2008): 11808–11.

166 no match for elephants: Matthew Mutinda et al., "Detusking Fence-Breaker Elephants as an Approach in Human-Elephant Conflict Mitigation," *PLOS ONE* 9, no. 3 (2014): e91749.

166 some farmers in Africa: Shreya Dasgupta, "How to Scare Off the Biggest Pest in the World," BBC, www.bbc.com/earth/story/20141204-five -ways-to-scare-off-elephants.

166 burn bricks: Rachael Bale, "How Chili Condoms and Firecrackers Can Help Save Elephants," *National Geographic*, June 23, 2016, www.national geographic.com/news/2016/06/elephant-conflict-deterrent-chili-condoms -firecrackers.

167 Ranchers smear capsaicin: Rebecca Rupp, "Peppers: Can You Take the Heat?," *National Geographic*, November 3, 2014, www.nationalgeographic .com/culture/article/hot-hotter-hottest.

167 manufacturers have put it: Alexandra W. Logue, *The Psychology of Eating and Drinking*, 4th ed. (New York: Taylor and Francis, 2015), 266.

167 some carmakers have started: Bob Weber, "Squirrels Love the New Chevy Traverse, But There's a Way to Stop Them," *Chicago Tribune*, January 3, 2019, www.chicagotribune.com/autos/sc-auto-motormouth-0102-story .html.

167 keep mussels from attaching: Maj-Britt Angarano et al., "Exploration of Structure-Antifouling Relationships of Capsaicin-like Compounds That Inhibit Zebra Mussel (Dreissena Polymorpha) Macrofouling," *Biofouling* 23, no. 5 (2007): 295–305.

167 natives of the San Blas Islands: Jean Andrews, *Peppers: The Domesticated Capsicums* (Austin: University of Texas Press, 1990), 79.

167 numerous attempts: José I. Castro, "Historical Knowledge of Sharks: Ancient Science, Earliest American Encounters, and American Science, Fisheries, and Utilization," *Marine Fisheries Review* 75, no. 4 (2013): 1–26.

167 help of Julia Child: "Julia Child: Cooking Up Spy Ops for OSS," Central Intelligence Agency, March 30, 2020, https://www.cia.gov/stories/story /julia-child-cooking-up-spy-ops-for-oss/.

167 In the 1960s: Stuart Casey-Maslen and Sean Connolly, *Police Use of Force Under International Law* (Cambridge, UK: Cambridge University Press, 2017), 161.

168 to their breasts: Paul Bloom, *How Pleasure Works: The New Science of Why We Like What We Like* (New York: Norton, 2010), 28.

168 or to children's thumbs: Andrews, *Peppers*, 78.

168 in the 1980s: Ari L. Goldman, "Youths Stealing Subway Tokens by Sucking on Turnstile Slots," *New York Times*, February 7, 1983, www.nytimes .com/1983/02/07/nyregion/youths-stealing-subway-tokens-by-sucking -on-turnstile-slots.html.

168 about thirty hours: "History of the General Hourly Minimum Wage in New York State," New York State Department of Labor, https://labor.ny .gov/stats/minimum_wage.shtm.

168 Repeated attempts to induce: Paul Rozin, Leslie Gruss, and Geoffrey Berk, "Reversal of Innate Aversions: Attempts to Induce a Preference for Chili Peppers in Rats," *Journal of Comparative and Physiological Psychology* 93, no. 6 (1979): 1001–14.

168 "One cannot fail": Ibid.

169 space peppers: C. M. Wade, "China Grows Green Peppers from Outer Space," UPI, December 25, 2000.

169 if we count a greenhouse: "Record Harvest and Instructive Challenges," EDEN-ISS, September 13, 2018, https://eden-iss.net/index.php/2018/09 /13/record-harvest-and-instructive-challenges.

169 roughly a third: Goldman, "On Capsaicin."

169 six thousand years after: Brendan Borrell, "What's So Hot About Chili Peppers?," *Smithsonian*, April 2009, www.smithsonianmag.com/science -nature/whats-so-hot-about-chili-peppers-116907465.

169 up to four hundred times: Chris Malloy, "Flavor Tripping on the Pepper So Spicy It'll Give You Visions of the Cosmos," *Saveur*, September 15, 2017, www.saveur.com/carolina-reaper-hottest-chile-pepper.

169 They revered chilies: Ken Albala, *Food: A Cultural Culinary History*, The Great Courses, transcript book, 2013, 297.

169 used them medicinally: Heather Arndt Anderson, *Chillies: A Global History* (London: Reaktion, 2016), Apple Books ed.

169 rubbing chilies on the genitals: Albala, *Food*, 297.

170 holding their children over piles: Rupp, "Peppers."

170 Other Aztec punishments: "Disciplining Children—Codex Mendoza [Painting]," Children & Youth in History, Item 277, http://chnm.gmu .edu/cyh/items/show/277.

170 "The majority of adults": Paul Rozin and Deborah Schiller, "The Nature and Acquisition of a Preference for Chili Pepper by Humans," *Motivation and Emotion* 4, no. 1 (1980): 77–101.

170 the latter of which: Earl Carstens et al., "It Hurts So Good: Oral Irritation by Spices and Carbonated Drinks and the Underlying Neural Mechanisms," *Food Quality and Preference* 13, no. 7 (2002): 431–43.

170 chilies also happen: Logue, *The Psychology of Eating and Drinking*, 268.

170 spicy foods tend to be: Anderson, *Chillies*.

170 they found that the number: Jennifer Billing and Paul W. Sherman, "Antimicrobial Functions of Spices: Why Some Like It Hot," *The Quarterly Review of Biology* 73, no. 1 (1998): 3–49.

171 inhibiting around 67 percent: Ibid.

171 compared to 80 percent: Logue, *The Psychology of Eating and Drinking*, 268.

171 Surprisingly, sour acids: Billing and Sherman, "Antimicrobial Functions of Spices."

171 has a cooling effect: McDonald et al., *Chemesthesis*, 228.

171 *akutuq*: Zona Spray Starks, "What Is Eskimo Ice Cream?," *Smithsonian*, July 25, 2016, www.smithsonianmag.com/travel/eskimo-ice-cream-atlas -of-eating-native-cuisine-food-eats-smithsonian-journeys-travel-quarterly -180959431.

171 described by Anthony Bourdain: "10 Questions for Anthony Bourdain," *Time*, October 31, 2007, http://content.time.com/time/magazine/article /0,9171,1680149,00.html.

171 another low-tech way: John D. Speth, "Putrid Meat and Fish in the Eurasian

Middle and Upper Paleolithic: Are We Missing a Key Part of Neanderthal and Modern Human Diet?," *PaleoAnthropology*, 2017, 44–72.

172 It could also be: Morten L. Kringelbach and Kent C. Berridge, *Pleasures of the Brain* (Oxford: Oxford University Press, 2009), 325–27.

172 feel-good chemicals: Bloom, *How Pleasure Works*, 51–52.

172 "Only hot water": John Launer, "The Itch," *QJM: An International Journal of Medicine* 97, no. 6 (2004): 383–84.

172 a common ingredient: Rachel Herz, *Why You Eat What You Eat: The Science Behind Our Relationship with Food* (New York: Norton, 2017), Kindle ed.

172 the Aztecs used chilies: Anderson, *Chillies: A Global History*.

172 "*Quæ fuit durum*": W. Gurney Benham, Cassell's Book of Quotations, rev. ed. (London: Cassell, 1914), 645.

172 "The evolutionary advantages": Terry Burnham and Jay Phelan, *Mean Genes: From Sex to Money to Food: Taming Our Primal Instincts* (New York: Perseus, 2000), 116.

173 research shows a correlation: Laurent Bègue, "Some Like It Hot: Testosterone Predicts Laboratory Eating Behavior of Spicy Food," *Physiology and Behavior* 139 (2015): 375–77.

173 personality constructs associated: Nadia K. Byrnes and John E. Hayes, "Personality Factors Predict Spicy Food Liking and Intake," *Food Quality and Preference* 28, no. 1 (2013): 213–21.

173 Back in Aztec times: Elizabeth Morán, *Sacred Consumption: Food and Ritual in Aztec Art and Culture* (University of Texas Press, 2016), 26.

173 "Mardudjara aboriginal boys": Chip Brown, "Making a Man," *National Geographic Magazine* 231, no. 1 (2017): 75–103.

173 the intercollegiate goldfish-swallowing competitions: Laura Clark, "The Great Goldfish Swallowing Craze of 1939 Never Really Ended," *Smithsonian*, February 27, 2015, www.smithsonianmag.com/smart-news/great -goldfish-swallowing-craze-1939-180954429.

174 "the seeking of varied": Marvin Zuckerman, *Behavioral Expressions and Biosocial Bases of Sensation Seeking* (Cambridge, UK: Cambridge University Press, 1994), 27.

174 This would explain: Talia Mindich, "In Space, 'Take Your Protein Pills' and Get Your Sriracha On," PBS, May 21, 2014, www.pbs.org/newshour /science/astronauts-crave-tabasco.

174 boredom likely plays: "Even Astronauts Get the Blues: Or Why Boredom Drives Us Nuts," NPR, March 15, 2016, https://www.npr.org/transcripts /470416797.

174 canned biscuits: Charles Perry, "MREs: Meals Really Edible?," *Los Angeles Times*, July 1, 1998.

174 Many soldiers found Spam: Carolyn Wyman, *SPAM: A Biography* (New York: Harcourt, Brace, 1999), 23.

174 rations included things: Andrew F. Smith, *The Oxford Companion to American Food and Drink* (Oxford: Oxford University Press, 2007), 141.

174 Today's MREs: "MRE 39 (2019)," Defense Logistics Agency, www.dla
.mil/TroopSupport/Subsistence/Operationalrations/mre.aspx.

175 It's also why Tabasco sauce: Caitlin Kearney, "Tabasco and the War Against
Bland Military Meals," National Museum of American History Behring
Center, April 30, 2015, https://americanhistory.si.edu/blog/tabasco-and
-war-against-bland-military-meals.

175 jalapeño ketchup: Julian E. Barnes, "Army Orders Up MREs with Kick
in the Pesto," *Chicago Tribune*, June 16, 2006, www.chicagotribune.com
/news/ct-xpm-2006-06-16-0606160092-story.html.

175 *benign masochism*: Kendra Pierre-Louis, "Mayonnaise Is Disgusting, and
Science Agrees," *Popular Science*, October 31, 2017, www.popsci.com
/mayonnaise-disgust.

175 "initially negative experiences": Paul Rozin et al., "Glad to be Sad, and
Other Examples of Benign Masochism," *Judgment and Decision Making*
8, no. 4 (2013): 439–47.

175 "Some teenage girls": Bloom, *How Pleasure Works*, xi.

175 "It's not that we like": Ibid., 51.

176 "We watch movies": Burnham and Phelan, *Mean Genes*, 84.

176 "descended from the humans": Ibid., 88.

Chapter 10: Attack of the Killer Tomatoes

177 "There are known knowns": "Donald Rumsfeld," *Oxford Essential Quotations*, 5th ed. (Oxford: Oxford University Press, 2017).

178 three hundred years after: Andrew F. Smith, *The Tomato in America: Early
History, Culture, and Cookery* (Champaign, University of Illinois Press,
2001), 17.

178 it took the US Supreme Court: *Nix v. Hedden*, 149 U.S. 304, 1893.

179 this argument was contested: Smith, *The Tomato in America*, 151.

179 "are, like potatoes": *Nix v. Hedden*, 149 U.S. 304, 1893.

179 "without cheese is": Jean Anthelme Brillat-Savarin, *The Physiology of Taste;
or, Meditations on Transcendental Gastronomy*, translated by M.F.K. Fisher
(New York: Knopf, 2009).

179 tomato dessert recipes: Smith, *The Tomato in America*, 187–88.

179 tomatoes weren't poisonous: Matt Blitz, "How Witches and Expensive
Dishes Stopped People from Eating Tomatoes," *Food and Wine*, July 31, 2017,
https://www.foodandwine.com/lifestyle/how-witches-and-expensive
-dishes-stopped-people-eating-tomatoes.

179 *Solanum lycopersicum*: "Lycopersicum," *Johnson's Gardener's Dictionary*, edited
by C. H. Wright and D. Dewar (London: George Bell & Sons, 1894), 582.

179 *Wolfspfirsich*: Rolf H. J. Schlegel, *History of Plant Breeding* (Boca Raton, FL:
CRC Press, 2018), Kindle ed.

179 tomato crops infested: Smith, *The Tomato in America*, 58.

179 causing them to leach: Ibid., 59.

180 "sour trash": Ibid., 41–42.

180 they were once thought: E. J. Kahn, Jr., *The Staffs of Life* (Boston: Little, Brown, 1984), 111.

180 bearing a resemblance to: Tom Standage, *An Edible History of Humanity* (New York: Bloomsbury, 2009), Apple Books ed.

180 "the Devil's apples": Kahn, *The Staffs of Life*, 109.

180 caused mothers to bear children: Ibid., 111.

180 growing potato plants: Ibid., 110.

180 wearing potato flowers: Ibid., 113.

180 widespread famine and crop failures: Standage, *An Edible History of Humanity*.

180 "were threatened with forty lashes": Ibid.

180 Friedrich Wilhelm I threatened: Kahn, *The Staffs of Life*, 90.

180 Antoine-Augustin Parmentier took: Standage, *An Edible History of Humanity*.

180 per capita annual consumption: "Loss-Adjusted Food Availability—Vegetables," Food Availability (Per Capita) Data System, US Department of Agriculture Economic Research Service, September 23, 2020.

181 led largely by French fries: "Potatoes and Tomatoes Are the Most Commonly Consumed Vegetables," US Department of Agriculture Economic Research Service, August 28, 2019.

181 the consumption of onions: Ibid.

181 is only about nine pounds: "Loss-Adjusted Food Availability—Vegetables."

181 consumption of corn: "Loss-Adjusted Food Availability—Grains," "Loss-Adjusted Food Availability—Sugar and sweeteners (added)," Food Availability (Per Capita) Data System, US Department of Agriculture Economic Research Service, January 5, 2021.

181 "death by fruit": Bee Wilson, *First Bite: How We Learn to Eat* (New York: Basic Books, 2015), Kindle ed.

181 a 1569 ban: Kate Colquhoun, *Taste: The Story of Britain through Its Cooking* (New York: Bloomsbury, 2007), 107.

181 it was common practice: Terence Scully, *The Art of Cookery in the Middle Ages* (Woodbridge, UK: Boydell Press, 1995), 20.

181 they were rebranded: G. Bruce Knecht, *Hooked: Pirates, Poaching, and the Perfect Fish* (Emmaus, PA: Rodale, 2006), 9.

181 they're neither technically a bass: Ibid.

181 many come from waters: "Patagonian toothfish (*Dissostichus eleginoides*)," Food and Agriculture Organization of the United Nations, www.fao.org /3/y5261e/y5261e09.htm.

181 579 metric tons in 1979: "Global Capture Production for Species (Tonnes)" graph, "Species Fact Sheets: *Dissostichus eleginoides* (Smitt, 1898)," Food and Agriculture Organization of the United Nations, FAO FishStat.

181 when they were known: Paul Greenberg, "The Catch," *New York Times*,

October 23, 2005, www.nytimes.com/2005/10/23/magazine/the-catch
.html.

182 more than 44,000 tons in 1995: "Global Capture Production for Species
(Tonnes)."

182 The same thing happened: Jennifer L. Jacquet and Daniel Pauly, "Trade
Secrets: Renaming and Mislabeling of Seafood," *Marine Policy* 32, no. 3
(2008): 309–18.

182 "whore's eggs": Christa Weil, "More than One Way to Crack an Urchin" in
*Eggs in Cookery: Proceedings of the Oxford Symposium on Food and Cookery
2006*, edited by Richard Hosking (Devon, UK: Prospect, 2007), 266.

182 "Today's seafood is often": David A. Fahrenthold, "Unpopular, Unfamiliar Fish Species Suffer From Become Seafood," *Washington Post*, July 31,
2009.

182 "spaghetti plantations": "Is This the Best April Fool's Ever?," BBC News,
March 31, 2014.

182 where they could buy: "On This Day: 1 April 1957: BBC Fools the Nation,"
BBC News.

182 In the 1980s: Elizabeth Green, "Why Do Americans Stink at Math?,"
New York Times Magazine, July 23, 2014, https://www.nytimes.com
/2014/07/27/magazine/why-do-americans-stink-at-math.html.

182 lawmakers in West Virginia: Nathan Takitch, "DHHR: Results Inconclusive in Raw Milk Investigation," WSAZ NewsChannel 3, March 8, 2016.

183 among them: "Raw (Unpasteurized) Milk," Centers for Disease Control
and Prevention, www.cdc.gov/features/rawmilk/index.html.

183 Scott Cadle: Eric Eyre and David Gutman, "Agency Investigates Lawmaker Who Distributed Raw Milk to Celebrate Bill Passage," *Charleston
Gazette-Mail*, March 8, 2016.

183 "It didn't have": Jonathan Mattise, "Lawmakers Celebrate Raw Milk,
Deny Being Sickened by It," Associated Press, March 9, 2016.

183 "It ain't because": Eyre and Gutman, "Agency Investigates Lawmaker
Who Distributed Raw Milk to Celebrate Bill Passage."

183 he flushed the remainder: Eric Eyre, "Results of Raw Milk Inquiry at WV
Capitol Inconclusive, DHHR Says."

183 a twenty-page pamphlet: "Nutrition and Your Health: Dietary Guidelines
for Americans," US Department of Agriculture, February 1980.

183 Their 2015 guidelines: *2015–2020 Dietary Guidelines for Americans*, US Department of Agriculture, January 7, 2016.

183 "The U.S. has joined": "New Dietary Guidelines Remove Daily Limit on
Cholesterol and Include Eggs in Recommended Eating Patterns," press
release, American Egg Board, January 7, 2016.

183 "makes more than enough": *2015–2020 Dietary Guidelines for Americans*,
U.S. Department of Agriculture, 32.

184 Appendix 3, Table A3-1: Ibid., 79–82.

184 Appendix 2, Table A2-1: Ibid., 77–78.

184 Appendix 4, Table A4-1: Ibid., 83–85.

184 One large egg, for example: Ibid., 19.

184 an egg has to weigh: "Specifications for Shell Eggs: A 'How to' Guide for Food Service Suppliers and Volume Food Buyers," US Department of Agriculture, November 10, 2017, 4.

184 4 ounces of pork: *2015–2020 Dietary Guidelines for Americans*, U.S. Department of Agriculture, 19.

184 still about 300 milligrams: Ibid., 32.

184 they're simultaneously charged: Marion Nestle, *What to Eat* (New York: Farrar, Straus and Giroux, 2010), Apple Books ed.

185 The USDA is responsible: "Exhibit 3-1: FDA/USDA Jurisdiction," *Investigations Operations Manual 2021*, US Food and Drug Administration, 2021.

185 while the FDA is responsible: Ibid.

185 fish other than catfish: "FDA Transfers Siluriformes Fish Inspection to USDA," US Food and Drug Administration, constituent update, May 2, 2016.

185 The division of eggs: "Exhibit 3-1: FDA/USDA Jurisdiction."

185 roughly 78 percent: "Fact Sheet: FDA at a Glance," US Food and Drug Administration, November 2020.

185 the FDA oversees: Ibid.

186 the use of medicinal maggots: Bob Carlson, "Crawling Through the Millennia: Maggots and Leeches Come Full Circle," *Biotechnology Healthcare* 3, no. 1 (2006): 14–17.

186 go more than five years: *The Role and Performance of FDA in Ensuring Food Safety* (Washington, DC: US Government Printing Office, 2012), 67.

186 a much larger percentage: Neal D. Fortin, *Food Regulation: Law, Science, Policy, and Practice* (Hoboken, NJ: Wiley, 2011).

186 "48 million people": "Burden of Foodborne Illness: Overview," Centers for Disease Control and Prevention, November 5, 2018.

186 "so opaque or confusing": Barbara Presley Noble, "All About/Product Labeling; After Years of Deregulation, a New Push to Inform the Public," *New York Times*, October 27, 1991, www.nytimes.com/1991/10/27 /business/all-about-product-labeling-after-years-deregulation-new -push-inform-public.html.

186 research tends to negate this: F. De Alzaa, C. Guillaume, and L. Ravetti, "Evaluation of Chemical and Physical Changes in Different Commercial Oils During Heating," *Acta Scientific Nutritional Health* 2, no. 6 (2018): 2–11.

186 an ability to lower: "Olive Oil 101: Health and Nutrition," California Olive Oil Council, www.cooc.com/health-nutrition.

187 analysts estimate: Larry Olmsted, *Real Food/Fake Food* (Chapel Hill, NC: Algonquin Books of Chapel Hill, 2016), 91.

187 "virtually every investigation": Ibid.

187 Fredrick Accum warned: Fredrick Accum, *A Treatise on Adulterations of Food and Culinary Poisons* (London: Mallett, 1820), 334–35.

187 an estimated ten thousand: Spencer D. Segalla, *Empire and Catastrophe: Decolonization and Environmental Disaster in North Africa and Mediterranean France Since 1954* (Lincoln: University of Nebraska Press, 2020), 78.

187 turned out to be machine oil: Richard Lorant, "Mass Poisoning in Spain Still Steeped in Mystery," *Los Angeles Times*, June 16, 1991.

187 faking its graded virginity: Rodney J. Mailer and Stefan Gafner, "Adulteration of Olive (*Olea europaea*) Oil," *Botanical Adulterants Prevention Bulletin*, Botanical Adulterants Prevention Program, October 2020.

187 there's a lot of methylmercury: Nestle, *What to Eat*.

187 high levels of omega-3: Peter Wehrwein, "High Intake of Omega-3 Fats Linked to Increased Prostate Cancer Risk," *Harvard Health Blog*, Harvard Medical School, August 1, 2013.

187 "that growes upon": Henry Butts, *Dyets Dry Dinner* (London: Creede, 1599).

188 which was mostly a precaution: Joanna Klein, "Oysters, Despite What You've Heard, Are Always in Season," *New York Times*, May 5, 2017, www.nytimes.com/2017/05/05/science/oysters-summer-safe-r-months.html.

188 as Anthony Bourdain advised: Anthony Bourdain, *Kitchen Confidential: Adventures in the Culinary Underbelly* (New York: Bloomsbury, 2000), 64–65.

188 Bourdain revised: "Anthony Bourdain Tells Us It's OK to Eat Fish on Mondays Now—Here's Why," Business Insider, October 31, 2016.

188 "To make an intelligent choice": Nestle, *What to Eat*.

188 two high school girls: John Schwartz, "A Fish Story with a DNA Hook," *New York Times*, August 22, 2008, A1.

188 collected 142 fish samples: Kimberly Warner, Walker Timme, and Beth Lowell, "Widespread Seafood Fraud Found in New York City," Oceana, December 2012.

189 "ex-lax fish": Olmsted, *Real Food/Fake Food*, 48.

189 contains toxins: *Fish and Fishery Products: Hazards and Controls Guidance*, 4th ed., Department of Health and Human Services, Public Health Service, Food and Drug Administration, Center for Food Safety and Applied Nutrition, Office of Food Safety, March 2020, 6–2.

189 "women who are": Warner et al., "Widespread Seafood Fraud Found in New York City."

189 In 2007, samples: "Tetrodotoxin," *Bad Bug Book: Handbook of Foodborne Pathogenic Microorganisms and Natural Toxins*, US Food and Drug Administration, 2012.

189 an *Inside Edition* investigation: "A Third of Tested Restaurant Lobster Dishes Actually Contain Cheaper Seafood, Investigation Shows," *Inside Edition*, February 8, 2016, www.insideedition.com/headlines/14518-a

-third-of-tested-restaurant-lobster-dishes-actually-contain-cheaper-sea food-investigation-shows.

189 Meanwhile, a lot of restaurants: "Lobstermen Seeing Red over Langostinos," NPR, October 27, 2006, www.npr.org/transcripts/6394216.

189 "As a seafood expert": "A Third of Tested Restaurant Lobster Dishes Actually Contain Cheaper Seafood, Investigation Shows."

190 In 1499, King Henry VII: J. Lawrence-Hamilton, "Fish Frauds," *The Lancet* 2, November 16, 1889, 1024–25.

190 "as to make skinny": Ibid.

190 stuffing fresh haddock: Ibid.

190 plugging the holes: George Smeeton, *Doings in London; Or, Day and Night Scenes of the Frauds, Frolics, Manners, and Depravities, of the Metropolis* (Southwark, UK: Smeeton, 1828), 141.

190 in 1272, Edward I: J. Lawrence-Hamilton, "Ice Spoils Fish," *The Lancet* 2, September 21, 1889, 614–16.

190 Corrupt vendors who were caught: J. Lawrence-Hamilton, "'Fish' and 'Fish' Inspection," *Public Health, the Journal of the Incorporated Society of Medical Officers of Health*, 6, no. 1 (1893): 20–21.

190 nearly half of the advertised weight: "Have Some Oranges with That Liquid," *Consumer Reports*, February 2013, www.consumerreports.org/cro /magazine/2013/02/have-some-oranges-with-that-liquid/index.htm.

190 frozen chicken breasts: Felicity Lawrence, "Supermarkets Selling Chicken That Is Nearly a Fifth Water," *The Guardian*, December 6, 2013, www .theguardian.com/world/2013/dec/06/supermarket-frozen-chicken-breasts -water.

190 taken by more than half: "Poll Finds 86% of Americans Take Vitamins or Supplements Yet Only 21% Have a Confirmed Nutritional Deficiency," American Osteopathic Association, January 16, 2019.

190 orange juice with added calcium: "Tropicana Pure Premium® Calcium + Vitamin D (No Pulp)," Tropicana, www.tropicana.com/products/pure -premium/no-pulp-calcium-vitamin-d.

190 healthy heart orange juice: "Tropicana Pure Premium® Healthy Heart," Tropicana, www.tropicana.com/products/pure-premium/healthy-heart.

191 vitamin C and zinc orange juice: "Tropicana Pure Premium® Vitamin C + Zinc (No Pulp)," Tropicana, https://www.tropicana.com/products /trop50/vitamin-c-zinc-no-pulp-trop50.

191 pineapple mango juice with probiotics: "Tropicana Essentials® Pineapple Mango Probiotics," Tropicana, www.tropicana.com/products/tropicana -essentials/pineapple-mango-tep.

191 apple cherry juice with fiber: "Tropicana Essentials® Apple Cherry Fiber," Tropicana, www.tropicana.com/products/tropicana-essentials/apple-cherry -fiber.

191 Dannon makes probiotic yogurt: "Probiotic Yogurt," Activia, www.activia .us.com/probiotic-yogurt.

191   cotton candy–flavored smoothies: "Cotton Candy Smoothie," Dannon Company, http://danimals.com/kids-yogurt-and-smoothies/kids-smoothies /cotton-candy.

191   Nestlé even has: "Fortification: It's All About Defenses!," Nestlé, www .nestle-cereals.com/me/en/ingredients/our-cereal-ingredients/fortified -cereals.

191   "We believe": "Nestlé Nesquik: Nourishing Possibility," Nestlé, www .nestle-cereals.com/global/en/nesquikr.

191   one study published: Theodore M. Brasky, Emily White, and Chi-Ling Chen, "Long-Term, Supplemental, One-Carbon Metabolism-Related Vitamin B Use in Relation to Lung Cancer Risk in the Vitamins and Lifestyle (VITAL) Cohort," *Journal of Clinical Oncology* 35, no. 30 (2017): 3440–48.

191   Another study found: Alice Park, "Vitamins and Supplements Linked to Higher Risk of Death," *Time*, October 11, 2011, https://healthland.time .com/2011/10/11/vitamins-and-supplements-linked-to-higher-risk-of -death-in-older-women.

191   large doses of vitamin B: Shawn Bishop, "Take Vitamin Supplements with Caution: Some May Actually Cause Harm," Mayo Clinic, January 4, 2013, https://newsnetwork.mayoclinic.org/discussion/take-vitamin-supple ments-with-caution-some-may-actually-cause-harm.

191   too much calcium and vitamin D: "The Truth About Heart Vitamins and Supplements," Johns Hopkins Medicine, www.hopkinsmedicine.org /health/wellness-and-prevention/the-truth-about-heart-vitamins-and -supplements.

191   a 2014 analysis: "How Much Is Too Much? Excess Vitamins and Minerals in Food Can Harm Kids' Health," Environmental Working Group, June 2014, www.ewg.org/research/how-much-is-too-much.

191   "a non-profit, non-partisan organization": "About Us," Environmental Working Group, www.ewg.org/about-us.

192   "woefully outdated": "How Much Is Too Much? Excess Vitamins and Minerals in Food Can Harm Kids' Health," 3.

192   A 2015 investigation: "A.G. Schneiderman Asks Major Retailers to Halt Sales of Certain Herbal Supplements as DNA Tests Fail to Detect Plant Materials Listed on Majority of Products Tested," New York State Office of the Attorney General, February 3, 2015, https://ag.ny.gov/press -release/2015/ag-schneiderman-asks-major-retailers-halt-sales-certain -herbal-supplements-dna.

192   Other studies have found: Gerry Schwalfenberg, Ilia Rodushkin, and Stephen J. Genuis, "Heavy Metal Contamination of Prenatal Vitamins," *Toxicology Reports* 5 (2018): 390–95.

INDEX